D1627037

On Reading Ruskin

Marcel Proust

On Reading Ruskin

Prefaces to *La Bible d'Amiens*
and *Sésame et les Lys*
with Selections from the
Notes to the Translated Texts

Translated and Edited by
Jean Autret, William Burford, and Phillip J. Wolfe

With an Introduction by
Richard Macksey

Yale University Press
New Haven and London

Published with the assistance of the Frederick W. Hilles Publication
Fund of Yale University.

Designed by Susan P. Fillion and set in Garamond No. 3 type by
Keystone Typesetting Company. Printed in the United States of
America by Vail-Ballou Press, Binghamton, New York.

Library of Congress Cataloging-in-Publication Data

Proust, Marcel, 1871–1922.
On reading Ruskin.
Bibliography: p.
1. Ruskin, John, 1819–1900—Aesthetics. 2. Ruskin, John,
1819–1900. Bible of Amiens. 3. Ruskin, John, 1819–
1900. Sesame and lilies. 4. Proust, Marcel, 1871–1922—
Aesthetics. 5. Proust, Marcel, 1871–1922—Translations,
English. 6. Aesthetics. 7. Cathédrale d'Amiens. I. Title.
PR5267.A35P76   1987   824'.8   86–22467
ISBN 0–300–03513–6

The paper in this book meets the guidelines for permanence and
durability of the Committee on Production Guidelines for Book
Longevity of the Council on Library Resources.

10   9   8   7   6   5   4   3   2   1

Contents

Note by the
Editors-Translators

Marcel Proust's preface to his translation of *The Bible of Amiens,* by John Ruskin, appears here in English for the first time. His preface to his translation of *Sesame and Lilies* was first published in English on the occasion of the Proust centennial (as *On Reading,* New York: Macmillan Publishing Company, 1971). As presented here, the prefaces, with their notes and with selected notes to the translated texts, mark a crucial stage in Proust's development, showing how deeply Proust was influenced by his momentous encounter with Ruskin. From his running dialogue with the English writer some of the most important ideas integrated into Proust's aesthetic doctrine emerge. These ideas deal particularly with the nature of inspiration, the role and mission of the artist, his duties toward himself, and his submission to the work of art he bears within him, to the revelation of which he must sacrifice everything. Thanks in large part to the teaching of Ruskin, Proust came to believe in his own talent and found the willpower to dedicate himself to an original work of his own. He got beyond Ruskin, asserting himself finally against the older writer's influence, in order to start his own work. Had he simply remained a worshiper of Ruskin all his life, we would never have had *A la recherche du temps perdu*. Nevertheless, Ruskin was a kind of beginning.

The translations for which Proust wrote these prefaces were his first exercises of discipline, and when he undertook them he faced an arduous task, for he was not fluent in English, nor was he yet fully attuned to Ruskin's way of writing. In consequence, his rendering was at times awkward and lacking in clarity, though generally accurate. In our own translations, while clarity as well as accuracy has been a goal, we have also aimed at the other sort of fidelity which Proust himself suggests when he describes his pleasure in reading seventeenth-century French literature: we have sought to preserve something of the flavor of Proustian French rather than to turn Proust into a contemporary American or English writer.

We have included in the book illustrations reproduced from the plates of the Library Edition of *The Bible of Amiens* (cited below) as an aid to the reader in following Proust's descriptions and commentaries. Following the notes to each preface, we have provided, under the heading "Selected Notes," the most important of Proust's annotations to the translated texts.

For Proust's prefaces and the selected notes, we have used:

La Bible d'Amiens, traduction, notes et préface par Marcel Proust (Paris: Mercure de France, 1910), cinquième édition.

Sésame et les lys, "Des Trésors des rois," "Des Jardins des reines," traduction, notes et préface par Marcel Proust (Paris: Mercure de France, s.d.), septième édition.

For Ruskin, our source is:

The Complete Works of John Ruskin, edited by E. T. Cook and Alexander Wedderburn, Library Edition, 39 volumes (London: George Allen; New York: Longmans, Green, and Co., 1903–12), cited as *CW*. Volume 33 contains *The Bible of Amiens*; volume 18 contains *Sesame and Lilies*.

We have used this edition for the English text of all passages that Proust quotes in his translation, rather than retranslating Proust's French (except when Proust diverges from or omits portions of

Ruskin's original text). Citations refer first to chapter and section and then to volume and page in the *Complete Works*. The illustrations following page 96 are taken from volume 33.

Jean Autret
William Burford
Phillip J. Wolfe

Introduction

by Richard Macksey

. . . je m'apercevais que le livre essentiel, le seul livre vrai, un grand écrivain n'a pas, dans le sens courant, à l'inventer, puisqu'il existe déjà en chacun de nous, mais à le traduire. Le devoir et la tâche d'un écrivain sont ceux d'un traducteur.
Marcel Proust, *ARTP,* III, 890 (III, 926)

. . . un livre est un grand cimetière où sur la plupart des tombes on ne peut plus lire les noms effacés.
Marcel Proust, *ARTP,* III, 903 (III, 940)

Toward the end of the vast novel that was to occupy and consume the mature years of his life, Proust has his narrator—who has quite literally just stumbled on the "resurrection" of his "lost time"—remark that the "essential book," the one that each of us carries within, is for the great writer not a matter of invention but of translation. He concludes that "the duty and task of the writer are those of a translator." For all the tone of assurance in these late pages, it has been a search, like that of Augustine, long deferred and recurrently deflected: "Sero te amavi, pulchritudo tam antiqua et tam nova, sero te amavi! et ecce intus eras et ego foris, et ibi te

xiii

quaerebam" (*Confessions,* X, 27). But that which the narrator had sought "outside himself" and ultimately found within, "the only true book," has neither the ground nor the presence of Augustine's beauty; the text of this "only true book" is itself a challenge to a new *recherche* of decipherment and translation. Both the reading of a partially effaced text and its translation into a new and public text are for Proust supremely problematic activities. The shadows of death and erasure are seldom far away. Thus, only a few pages after the triumphal announcement of the writer's duty and task, where the vocation of the book is recovered, the narrator is moved to observe that "a book is a great cemetery where on the majority of the tombs we can no longer read the effaced names."[1]

Early and late, then, often in highly suspect language, the moral itinerary of Marcel's career is marked out—from the "journées de lecture" at Combray to his final vocation—by these problematic encounters with literature and its translation. The acts of reading and translation are at once exemplary experiences central to the artist's highest calling and powerful seductions. Overtly and covertly they implicate much of the metaphorics of Proust's fiction—the dialectics of container and contained, the dynamics of desire and possession, the optics of vision and blindness. In the ethical sphere (and throughout his artistic career Proust was a stern if paradoxical moralist), the double vocation to the tasks of reading and translation establishes a tense opposition between the unifying powers of memory and the imagination and the corresponding, substitutive errors

1. The two Proustian texts discussed in this paragraph also serve as epigraph. They appear in *Le Temps retrouvé* in the section of "La Matinée chez la princesse de Guermantes" in the long excursus on the "lesson" of the three centripetal "moments" that confirm the narrator's vocation. He has been discussing the difficulty of deciphering the "interior book" (and, paradoxically, the "vanity of literary theories"). The edition of *A la recherche du temps perdu* cited here and throughout the Introduction is the text established by Pierre Clarac and André Ferre in three volumes (Paris: Editions de la Pléiade, 1954), hereafter cited as *ARTP* (III, 890 and III, 903).

of "fetishism" and "idolatry." That these opposing terms are, in fact, each integrally embedded in his doctrine of signs has been repeatedly argued by recent commentators on Proust's semiotic and rhetoric.

From a certain perspective, the vector of Proust's works as figured in the two epigraphs from *Le Temps retrouvé* only emerged when the author himself was within the shadow of his own death. Yet in his case, supremely among modern writers, all of the fugitive works, all of the indecisions and passions of a tardy "career," all of the ceaseless revisions contribute to a single palimpsest that can be deciphered only in the fullness of time—that "grimoire compliqué et fleuri," the manuscript of the novel in which he sought to read his life. His almost six years of apprenticeship to John Ruskin—as disciple, pilgrim, critic, and translator—thus become one more vital layer often nearly effaced but still persisting in the archaeology of the novel. The persistence of Ruskin can best be gauged by the reader who comes from an immersion in the novel itself to the essays and notes collected for the first time in this volume.

Proust's apprenticeship to Ruskin, from the end of 1899 through the completion of his translation of *Sesame and Lilies* (published in the spring of 1906) was a period haunted by the younger author's doubts of his vocation and punctuated by death: of Ruskin at the beginning of 1900, of Proust's father in November 1903, and of his mother in September 1905. But it was also a period when Proust learned a discipline, when he comprehended a vision, and when he sensed fully the terrible risks that attended authorship. These were lessons that, like the shadow of Ruskin, persisted in his mature work.

The overt references to Ruskin in *A la recherche du temps perdu* are few and deceptively casual: Swann circling in despair around the torment of the Maison Dorée and, like the fabulous beasts described by Ruskin in the "Desolation of Nineveh" depicted on the West Porch of Amiens, "ébranlant pierre à pierre tout son passé" (*ARTP*, I, 372); an allusion evoked by the church at Balbec (*ARTP*, I, 648–

49); the egregious Bloch making a condescending reference to "les *Stones of Venaïce* de Lord John Ruskin" (*ARTP,* I, 738); "Of Queens' Gardens" and the mistaken Madeleine evoked when Marcel, Saint-Loup, and "Rachel quand du Seigneur" are among the angelic flowering trees of quite another garden (*ARTP,* II, 160–61); passing reference to the work that the narrator had undertaken on Ruskin (*ARTP,* III, 645); and Jupien's labored joke that alludes to the copy of the translation that Marcel had sent to Charlus (*ARTP,* III, 833).

Immensely more important are the covert references to Ruskin that constitute an important pattern in the fabric of the novel: the deeper debts in the painting and architecture so often seen through Ruskin's eyes, in the conception of the emblematic artists Elstir and Bergotte, in the discussion of Giotto and allegory, in the ever-present temptation of "idolatry" that haunted both authors, and in the evocation of Venice, whose humblest stones ultimately supply one of the final triggers to the restoration through involuntary memory.

But most important of all in terms of Ruskin's final legacy to Proust are the emblems of the Gothic cathedral and the book of memory that inform the narrator's perilous vocation and the novel's ultimate closure. In a footnote to the text of his translation of *Sesame and Lilies* (pp. 145–46 below), Proust describes the retrospective design in a key sentence of Ruskin's; the "plan secret" could well stand as a gloss for its translator's own compositional strategy:

> Je vois que, dans la note placée à la fin de la conférence, j'ai cru pouvoir noter jusqu'à 7 thèmes dans la dernière phrase. En réalité Ruskin y range l'une à côté de l'autre, mêle, fait manoeuvrer et resplendir ensemble toutes les principales idées—ou images—qui ont apparu avec quelque désordre au long de sa conférence. C'est son procédé. Il passe d'une idée à l'autre sans aucun ordre apparent. Mais en réalité la fantaisie qui le mène suit des affinités profondes qui lui imposent malgré lui une logique supérieure. Si bien qu'à la fin il se trouve avoir obéi à une sorte de plan secret qui, dévoilé à la fin,

impose rétrospectivement à l'ensemble une sorte d'ordre et le fait apercevoir magnifiquement étagé jusqu'à cette apothéose finale.[2]

This comes close to what Proust later has to say about his "composition en rosace" and the "secret" that he confesses in his first letter to Jacques Rivière, the reader who had intuited his design (February 1914).

Yet the lesson of Ruskin could not be fully absorbed until his pupil had passed through all the successive stages of infatuation, discipleship, and disillusion. The trajectory of Proust's "affair" with the Sage of Coniston—from his first mention of Ruskin in a letter to his mother (September 1899) to publication of *Sésame et les lys* and its deconstructive Preface, "Sur la lecture," in 1906—describes a pattern that will become familiar as he charts the course of so many passions in his novel. Proust had, in fact, already signaled his break with Ruskin as unqualified master in the "Post-Scriptum" that he attached to the otherwise adulatory Preface to the earlier translation of *The Bible of Amiens* (1904). In "Sur la lecture," however, Proust finds his own voice in the first-person of memory, the evocation of Illiers, and the "journées de lecture" that form the overture to that essay. He then proceeds to his discussion of the power and limitations of reading. On the last threshold of his Ruskinian labors, Proust writes of the liminal character of all reading: "La lecture est au seuil de la vie spirituelle; elle peut nous y introduire: elle ne la constitue pas."[3] He takes issue with Ruskin (and Descartes) that

2. *Sésame et les lys* (Paris: Mercure de France, 1906), pp. 62–63*n,* hereafter cited as *SL.* The texts of Proust's two volumes of translation are of considerable rarity, the OCLC catalogue listing only four copies in American research libraries. (There are but twelve copies listed of all impressions of the *Bible d'Amiens* translation.)

3. *SL,* p. 35. Republished in *Contre Sainte-Beuve, précédés de "Pastiches et mélanges" et suivi de "Essais et articles",* ed. Pierre Clarac and Yves Sandre (Paris: Editions de la Pléiade, 1971), p. 178; this edition, which I employ for quotations from the Proust prefaces, is hereafter cited as *CSB.* The French texts are used in the Introduction to give the reader some sense of Proust's own style, but the second page entry refers to the English translation in this volume.

reading can ever be "une conversation avec des hommes beaucoup plus sages et plus intéressants que ceux que nous pouvons avoir l'occasion de connaître autour de nous." Reading, however miraculous its powers to engage our imagination (and Proust alludes to his early seduction by *Le Capitaine Fracasse* that was later to figure in the novel), is ultimately too partial an experience to satisfy all the needs of the reader: the author is comprehended, but the reader is stimulated to compose his own text: "Et c'est là, en effet, un des grands et merveilleux caractères des beaux livres (et qui nous fera comprendre le rôle à la fois essentiel et limité que la lecture peut jouer dans notre vie spirituelle) que pour l'auteur ils pourraient s'appeler 'Conclusions' et pour le lecteur 'Incitations' " (*CSB*, p. 176; p. 114 below). Reading thus comprehended can be an incitement to a different sort of translation, the duty and task of inscribing his own text; and this was the portal to the next stage of the novelist's palimpsest, the interval of pastiches, of *Contre Sainte-Beuve,* of false starts and indirections that preceded the confirmation of the *Recherche* itself.

Proust's initial engagement with Ruskin began innocently enough as holiday reading. While vacationing at Evian-les-Bains in September 1899, the twenty-eight-year-old Proust writes to his mother, asking her to send him his copy of Robert de La Sizeranne's *Ruskin et la religion de la beauté,* published two years earlier.[4] This is

4. *Correspondance de Marcel Proust,* ed. Philip Kolb (Paris: Plon, 1976), II, 348. Robert de La Sizeranne's book was published by Hachette in 1897; portions of it had appeared serially in the *Revue des deux mondes* from December 1895 to April 1897. Proust seems to have read it soon after its appearance, since Douglas Ainslie, an English friend of Robert de Billy, records conversations at the Café Weber during 1897 on the respective merits of Ruskin and Walter Pater in which Proust was a partisan of the former. See *Correspondance,* II, 220–22. That Proust had at least some secondhand knowledge of Ruskin dating from an even earlier period seems likely. His professor of philosophy at the Ecole Libre des Science Politiques, Paul Desjardins, published brief translations from Ruskin in his journal, the *Bulletin de l'Union pour l'Action Morale,* every year from 1893 through 1903 (save for 1894 and 1901). Robert de Montesquiou, whose portrait had been painted by Whistler, gave Proust an elaborately bound copy of *Le Gentil Art de se faire des*

the first reference in the Proust correspondence to the English author who was to engage his imagination and his energies over the next six years. It began with the casualness of a love affair, gradually supplanting Proust's earlier infatuations with George Eliot, Flaubert, and Emerson. Although there was little evidence at this stage in his development of the great clinician of human love whose analyses would eventually find their place in a tradition that includes Racine and Stendhal, Proust's literary affair with Ruskin could stand as a paradigm for the trajectory of all those amorous case histories chronicled later in his synoptic novel. And like the fictional affairs analyzed there, this relationship achieved its ultimate meaning as an "incitement" to reading, a reading not of a master's texts but rather of that "inner book" composed of past moments, places, and events embedded in the architectural program of memory.

A week after the first letter, on October 2, Madame Proust receives a renewed plea from her son for La Sizeranne's "presentation" of Ruskin, that he may "voir les montagnes avec les yeux de ce grand homme."[5] Thus Ruskin, who found "the world of Literature

_____

ennemis and opinions of the Ruskin-Whistler trial. In later letters Proust argued that one of Whistler's *mots* at the trial was in fact pure Ruskin. (Proust never quite mastered the painter's name, always referring to him in the correspondence as "Wisthler.") Jean Autret in *L'Influence de Ruskin sur la vie, les idées et l'oeuvre de Marcel Proust* (Genève: Droz, 1955), pp. 16–17, advances an earlier date, following Robert Vigneron, for the first appearance of Ruskin in Proust's correspondence: "En décembre 1897, Proust écrit à Pierre Lavallée: 'Si tu vas à la bibliothèque, aie la gentillesse de regarder si vous possédez *The Queen of {the} Air* par Ruskin et mets-moi un mot chez mon concierge.'" The *carte-lettre* to his friend from the Condorcet, now a librarian at the Ecole des Beaux-Arts, has, however, been positively dated by Philip Kolb in *Correspondance*, II, 375–76, as "jeudi soir 30 novembre 1899"; the note bears a postmark of the following morning: "PARIS DEPART N/1 DEC 99." Thus, this reference, rather than anticipating all others, dates from the period of intense Ruskin studies in late 1899, when Proust was moving from reliance on La Sizeranne to an exploration of the original English texts.

5. *Correspondance*, II, 357. Later in the month of October Proust wrote his mother asking her to translate for him some passages from *The Seven Lamps of Architecture*. *Correspondance*, II, 365. Proust's attitude toward La Sizeranne (1866–

more or less divided into Thinkers and Seers," is first invoked by Proust as an instrumentality of sight. This is the Ruskin who concluded in *Modern Painters* that "the greatest thing a human soul ever does in this world is to *see* something, and to tell what it *saw* in a plain way. . . . To see clearly is poetry, prophecy, and religion—all in one."[6] And Robert de La Sizeranne, who was to be Proust's Galeotto at this stage in the affair, chooses to begin his study of Ruskin, in a chapter entitled "La Contemplation," with the recreation of a moment in the summer of 1833 when the fourteen-year-old Ruskin arrived with his parents and cousin at the gates of Schaffhausen, about to discover for himself the Alps.[7] He quotes the aged Ruskin of more than fifty years later, engaged in a final heroic effort to "bind and blend" the lost moments and occluded sights of a lifetime into a book of recollection, *Praeterita*:

> Thus in perfect health of life and fire of heart, not wanting to be anything but the boy I was, not wanting to have anything more than I had; knowing of sorrow only so much as to make life serious to me, not enough to slacken in the least its sinews; and with so much of science mixed with feeling as to make the

---

1932) as a guide to Ruskin was obviously not without its ambivalences; in an unpublished letter written many years later (January 31, 1917) he remarks, "Il y a chez Ruskin trop de génie obscurci et captif au milieu de théories caduques, pour qu'un ruskinien non encore complètement initié doive lire autre chose que des *Pages choisies,* ce qui pour Ruskin, pourrait s'appeler plutôt des pages délivrées. J'avais fait un recueil de ces pages, mais je l'ai détruit à la prière, ou plutôt sur l'injonction— car c'est plutôt sa manière—de M. de la Sizeranne qui a··ait fait lui-même un recueil de ce genre non encore publié alors et ne voulait pas se laisser 'damer le pion.' Je me suis fait un cas de conscience, ruskinien si vous voulez, d'obéir à quelqu'un que je ne tiens nullement pour un maître, mais qui, en ce qui concerne Ruskin tout au moins, était pour moi un ancien avec qui je tenais à garder les distances, les distances qui sans aucune fausse humilité de ma part, sont très grandes. Ayant le chemin libre, alors, il a fait paraître un recueil chez Hachette." To Jacques Hébertot.

    6. *The Complete Works of John Ruskin,* ed. E. T. Cook and Alexander Wedderburn, Library Edition, 39 vols. (London: George Allen; New York: Longmans, Green, and Co., 1903–12), V, 333; hereafter cited as *CW*.

    7. *Ruskin et la religion de la beauté* (Paris: Hachette, 1897), pp. 11–23.

sight of the Alps not only the revelation of the beauty of the earth, but the opening of the first page of its volume,—I went down that evening from the garden-terrace of Schaffhausen with my destiny fixed in all that was to be sacred and useful. To that terrace, and the shore of the Lake of Geneva, my heart and faith return to this day, in every impluse that is yet nobly alive in them, and every thought that has in it help or peace.[8]

Ruskin recognizes, from the gathering silence of his last years, that this precocious first vision of the Alps was already refracted through authors who had transformed man's relations with the landscape— Rousseau and Wordsworth; and he adds in the manuscript that the same day on which he recorded his memory of the garden-terrace of Schaffhausen he had been reading Ernest Chesneau's account of the boyhood of Géricault, which in its sunless deprivation contrasted so markedly with the natural and human vistas of his own earliest years.

Proust came down from his vision of the mountains, from his brief stay at the Splendide Hôtel d'Evian, far from a confirmed traveler of the Ruskin variety. His subsequent "pilgrimages" (concentrated in the years 1900–02) were few and usually anxious, though nearly all of them were in some way marked by his encounter with Ruskin. Instead, he came down from the Alps to return to Paris, to Maman, to a characteristic bout of asthma, and then to busy weeks at the Bibliothèque Nationale studying the texts of Ruskin then available in French. Soon he was turning to the librarian of the Ecole des Beaux-Arts for editions of Ruskin in English

8. *CW*, XXXV, 116. For a life finally oppressed by clouds, consider the first sight of the Alps: "There was no thought in any of us for a moment of their being clouds. They were clear as crystal, sharp on the pure horizon sky, and already tinged with rose by the sinking sun. Infinitely beyond all that we had ever thought or dreamed,—the seen walls of the lost Eden could not have been more beautiful to us; nor more awful, round heaven, the walls of sacred Death." Ibid., p. 115. For Ruskin's contemporary response, see "The Alps! the Alps! it is no cloud." *CW*, II, 367. (Compare Marcel's first attempts at literary creation after seeing the spires of Martinville from Dr. Percepied's carriage. *ARTP*, I, 180–82.)

as well.[9] He was also corresponding with Reynaldo Hahn's Manchester cousin, Marie Nordlinger, who was to be his guide to Ruskin's grammar, seeking additional books and translations. By February 1900, when he is asking her for fragments of letters and passages from the works dealing with the cathedrals of France ("excepté celle d'Amiens"), he quickly adds that she need not bother with references to *The Seven Lamps of Architecture, the Bible of Amiens, Val d'Arno, Lectures on Architecture and Painting,* and *Praeterita,* since he already knows these books "par coeur."[10] Ruskin was already beginning to circulate in Proust's veins; the younger writer had by this stage moved beyond La Sizeranne as his cicerone and had consciously conceived his vocation as translator and critic of the Sage of Coniston. In addition to Marie Nordlinger, he now enlisted other friends to help with his Ruskin studies, notably the "fidèle et compréhensif" François d'Oncieu, to whom he had earlier lent his copy of La Sizeranne.

On January 20, 1900, after a decade of silence, John Ruskin died at Brantwood. Proust, as he records in a letter to Marie Nordlinger, was immediately moved to write an obituary, which appeared over the signature "M. P." a week later in *La Chronique des arts et de la curiosité,* a supplement to the *Gazette des beaux-arts.*[11] He introduced this brief notice with the lugubrious observation that, with Nietzsche mad, with Tolstoy and Ibsen at the end of their careers, the death of Ruskin marked a turning point: Europe was losing, one

9. By late November he had progressed to seeking out Ruskin titles in English, writing to Pierre Lavallée, the librarian at the Beaux-Arts, for a copy of *The Queen of the Air,* "Mets-moi un mot chez mon concierge (je ne m'éveille guère avant 2 heures)". *Correspondance,* II, 375.

10. Ibid., p. 387. The correspondence with Marie Nordlinger from the autumn of 1899 through 1905 affords a continuing record of Proust's struggles as a reader and translator of Ruskin. He was delighted to discover that she came from Rusholme, the Manchester suburb where Ruskin had delivered the two lectures of *Sesame and Lilies,* which became Proust's second volume of translations. He apparently secured her annotated copy of *The Queen of the Air.* Ibid., p. 385.

11. "John Ruskin," *CSB,* pp. 69–141; pp. 29–49 below. For the letter to Marie Nordlinger, see *Correspondance,* II, 384–85.

after the other, its great "directeurs de conscience." He also seized the opportunity to announce that the *Gazette des beaux-arts* would publish in its next number a more extended impression of Ruskin's achievement. This critical project, which appeared in the April and August numbers of the journal under the title "Sur Ruskin," was later reworked into the preface to Proust's translation of *The Bible of Amiens* (pp. 48–61 and 61–77, constituting the third section of the Preface). This early evaluation of Ruskin was further qualified by the "P.-S." that he added to the 1904 translation (pp. 78–95; pp. 49–61 below), the point at which he finally raised the question of Ruskin's "idolatry." These three texts taken together were again published by Proust as the third part of "En mémoire des églises assassinées" in *Pastiches et mélanges* of 1919 (pp. 148–97).[12]

Even before the appearance of the essays in the *Gazette des beaux-arts*, Proust had found a new vehicle for his Ruskinian passions. He had met, probably through Léon Daudet, Gaston Calmette, who had recently assumed the editorship of *Le Figaro*. This was a literary relationship that was to extend over the years, forming for Proust (as for the narrator of his novel) a considerable beachhead in Parisian

12. *CSB*, pp. 69–141. The component elements of this palimpsest are discussed below. The earliest parts of the *Gazette des beaux-arts* essay may date from an unfinished (or at least unpublished) article commissioned by Louis Ganderax for the *Revue de Paris* at the earliest stage of Proust's acquaintance with Ruskin. In a letter to Jean-Louis Vaudoyer (*Correspondance générale* [Paris, 1933], IV, 42–46) written in March 1912, Proust offers an amusing account of the fate of this first venture at Ruskin criticism: "L'étude sur Ruskin a failli paraître parce que Ruskin ayant fini par vieillir et mourir dans l'intervalle, le manuscrit détestable comme littérature se trouvait admirable comme actualité. Tel autre critique se récusa. Le directeur-ami étant pris en ce dilemme de laisser sa Revue sans nécrologie de ce grand homme ou de faire paraître ce qui a été ensuite ma préface à la *Bible d'Amiens*, préféra encore le premier désastre. Et la raison que, pour tous ces écrits, il me donna uniformément, tristement, affectueusement, de ses refus, était 'qu'il n'avait pas assez de temps à lui pour les *refaire* et les *écrire*'" (pp. 44–45). As Bernard de Fallois has observed, however, "l'oeuvre inédite de Proust n'existe pas." Everything was recuperated, redacted, or rescued for some later use. But however much of the first section of the *GBA* article may descend from the Ganderax commission, the author had carefully reworked it to reflect the death of Ruskin.

letters. "Pèlerinages ruskiniens en France" appeared in *Le Figaro* of February 13, 1900.[13] It is a pendant piece to the original obituary notice, but it marks an important turn in Proust's relations to Ruskin. Moving from the library to the places that informed Ruskin's imagination, Proust quotes him as confessing, "There have been, in sum, three centres of my life's thought: Rouen, Geneva, and Pisa. All that I did at Venice was bye-work. . . . But Rouen, Geneva, and Pisa have been the tutresses of all that I know, and were mistresses of all that I did, from the first moments that I entered their gates" (*Praeterita, CW,* XXXV, 156). Proust concentrates his attention on the first of these "thought-centres" and proposes to Ruskin's French friends not a pilgrimage to his grave at Coniston but to Rouen and the other cathedral cities of France that "gardent son âme." The pilgrim is urged to visit and read the "Stones" of the great medieval monuments that are the pretext and inspiration of so many pages of Ruskin, including, as Proust remarks, pages of those books that Ruskin did not have time to write, the projected volumes on the cathedrals of Rouen (*The Springs of Eure*) and Chartres (*Domrémy*) that were to succeed *The Bible of Amiens*. For Ruskin, one structure and architectural program reads another (thus Proust echoes his judgment of Abbeville "qui est comme la préface et l'interprétation de Rouen"), but all are woven into the texture of the author's thought, determining what Proust elsewhere calls "l'optique de Ruskin."

Proust himself literally undertook the role of pilgrim at this stage in his apprenticeship. Having reread on the day of Ruskin's death a passage in the fifth chapter of *The Seven Lamps of Architecture* that describes one of the more than three hundred small beasts and grotesques populating the intervals of the reliefs and outer pedestals of the North Portal of Rouen, Proust journeyed with Madeleine and

13. *CSB,* pp. 441–44. This text is to be distinguished from what was to become the central panel of "En mémoire des églises assassinées" in *Pastiches et mélanges* (*CSB,* pp. 69–105): "Journées de pèlerinage." Proust, with characteristic scrupulosity, bothered a number of friends in order to determine what had become of Shelley's heart.

Léon Yeatman to the cathedral in order to get this tiny figure that had captured Ruskin's imagination "right," much as Bergotte in *A la recherche* makes his final pilgrimage to Vermeer's *View of Delft* in order to comprehend the "petit pan de mur jaune" (*ARTP,* III, 187–88). This tiny, brooding figure, emblem for Ruskin in its individuality of the "noble vitality" of Gothic art, is but a detail of a portal commonly known as that of the "Booksellers" (cf. *ARTP,* III, 116); yet, following his pilgrimage with the Yeatmans (some time after January 20 and before the appearance of the article in *Le Figaro*), Proust chose it as the graphic emblem with which to conclude the second of his essays in the *Gazette des beaux-arts.* Significantly, this little grotesque with the wrinkled cheek, discovered among a wealth of detail by his friend Madeleine Yeatman, is facing the tympanum of the "portail des Libraires" where the Resurrection of the Dead is enacted; and it elicits from Proust the following observation, one that anticipates his comments on Bergotte, Elstir, and Vinteuil:

L'artiste mort depuis des siècles a laissé là, entre des milliers d'autres, cette petite personne qui meurt un peu chaque jour, et qui était morte depuis bien longtemps, perdue au milieu de la foule des autres, à jamais. Mais il l'avait mise là. Un jour, un homme pour qui il n'y a pas de mort, pour qui il n'y a pas d'infini matériel, pas d'oubli, un homme qui, jetant loin de lui ce néant qui nous opprime pour aller à des buts qui dominent sa vie, si nombreux qu'il ne pourra pas tous les atteindre alors que nous paraissons en manquer, cet homme est venu, et, dans ces vagues de pierre où chaque écume dentelée paraissait ressembler aux autres, voyant là toutes les lois de la vie, toutes les pensées de l'âme, les nommant de leur nom, il dit: "Voyez, c'est ceci, c'est cela." Tel qu'au jour du Jugement, qui non loin de là est figuré, il fait entendre en ses paroles comme la trompette de l'archange et il dit: "Ceux qui ont vécu vivront, la matière n'est rien." . . . Et la petite figure inoffensive et monstrueuse aura ressuscité, contre toute espérance, de cette mort qui semble plus totale que les autres, qui est la disparition au sein de l'infini du nombre et sous le nivellement des

ressemblances, mais d'où le génie a tôt fait de nous tirer
aussi. . . . J'ai été touché en la retrouvant là, rien ne meurt
donc de ce qui a vécu, pas plus la pensée du sculpteur que la
pensée de Ruskin. [*CSB*, pp. 125–26; pp. 45–46 below]

The artist and the critic are united, across the centuries, in an act of
attention; the integrity of the anonymous craftsman and the clarity
of the confirming vision survive the insults of time and the "leveling" of similarity through that act which was to become for Proust a
model of the reader's task. As with another passionate pilgrim, the
survival of the artistic expression depends upon the double function
of the intensity of "felt life" and the collaborating eye of the critic. It
is worth remarking that the passage from Ruskin that motivated the
pilgrimage to Rouen appears as a bridge between chapters entitled
"The Lamp of Life" and "The Lamp of Memory."

In addition to suggesting the role of critic as pilgrim, the *Figaro*
essay also announces Proust's assumption of the role of critic as
translator. Here he alludes to the project that was not completely
realized until four years later, with the publication of the complete
introduction to and translation of *The Bible of Amiens*. Meanwhile,
the translation begun, Proust's "pèlerinages ruskiniens" extended
by April of 1900 across the Alps to Venice, where accompanied by
his mother he met Reynaldo Hahn, Hahn's mother, and her niece,
Marie Nordlinger, to explore the monuments memorialized by
Ruskin. With *The Stones of Venice* and *Saint Mark's Rest* as his guides
to the city, he could continue the work on the Amiens translation
with Marie as his guide to the mysteries of a new language. This
Venetian pilgrimage, with an excursion in Ruskin's footsteps to
Padua for Giotto's frescoes in the Arena Chapel and Mantegna's in
Eremitani, would be translated, many years later, into Marcel's
thwarted Italian dreams (themselves a tissue of phrases drawn from
Ruskin)[14] in *Swann* and—much later in the narrative—the actual

14. *ARTP*, pp. 389–93. This passage on the evocative—and deceptive—
power of names is one of the great set pieces of the third part of *Swann*, "Nom de
pays: le nom." The Italian trip that provokes this *rêverie*, a synesthetic anthology of

voyage to Venice and Padua in *La Fugitive*. Outside his fictions Proust returned to Venice but once, in October of the same year, this time without his mother—a much more mysterious and perhaps somber visit.

The brief essay in *Le Figaro* concludes with one final prophetic note: summing up the range of Ruskin's concerns and gifts, his renunciation of his fortune and dedication of his talents, Proust likens him to the figure of Charity in Giotto's cycle of the Virtues and Vices at the Arena Chapel. While this rather surprising image evokes memories of Ruskin's own discussions of Giotto's allegorical figures (especially in *Fors Clavigera*), it anticipates the familiar passage in *Swann* where Giotto's Charity (translated into the humble *fille de cuisine* of Combray) introduces a complex sequence of meditations on the reading of allegory and the allegory of reading.[15] Marcel is at first mystified by the chasm between the *name* "Caritas" and the *reality* of the humble, energetic figure with which it is associated—whether in the fresco or in the pregnant servant girl whom Swann had dubbed "la Charité de Giotto." He concludes, however, that this is but an instance of the general case, of the gulf between the "idea" and the precise material of observation resolved only by the greatest artists (like the anonymous sculptor of the Rouen portal):

> Mais plus tard j'ai compris que l'étrangeté saisissante, la beauté spéciale de ces fresques tenait à la grande place que le

---

images drawn from Ruskin's texts, is unrealized but leaves an indelible mark: "Ces images irréelles, fixes, toujours pareilles, remplissant mes nuits et mes jours, différencièrent cette époque de ma vie de celles qui l'avaient précédée . . . comme dans un opéra un motif mélodique introduit une nouveauté qu'on ne pourrait pas soupçonner si on ne faisait que lire le livret." Ibid., p. 390.

15. Compare Paul de Man, *Allegories of Reading* (New Haven and London: Yale University Press, 1979), pp. 57–76. De Man's radical reading of the Giotto passage and the ensuing scene of reading as inescapably founded on error and a "deferral" of meaning is oddly enough based on a minor misreading of Ruskin interpreting the Charity allegory. (Ruskin actually gives *three* successive readings of the figure's emblematic gesture.) The quotation from Ruskin is itself not quoted exactly (p. 75).

symbole y occupait, et que le fait qu'il fût représenté, non comme un symbole puisque la pensée symbolisée n'était pas exprimée, mais comme réel, comme effectivement subi ou matériellement manié, donnait à la signification de l'oeuvre quelque chose de plus littéral et de plus précis, à son enseignement quelque chose de plus concret et de plus frappant. . . . Il fallait que ces Vertus et ces Vices de Padoue eussent en eux bien de la réalité puisqu'ils m'apparaissaient comme aussi vivants que la servante enceinte, et qu'elle-même ne me semblait pas moins allégorique. [*ARTP*, I, 82]

This respect for the preciseness of vision and for "real things, actually felt or materially handled" in the service of artistic truth is the first lesson that Proust learned from John Ruskin. He appropriated from one side of Ruskin's program the insistence on the priority of observed impressions, of the "literal" and the "concrete." This theory of aesthetic perception in which the artist's act of seeing takes precedence over any received "ideas" or "symbols" or the exactitude of scientific "description" clearly descends from Ruskin's analysis of Turner's perceptual "impressionism." Thus, in *The Harbours of England,* he writes in terms that Proust was later to translate to Elstir: "He always painted, not the place itself, but his impression of it, and this on steady principle; leaving to inferior artists the task of topographical detail; and he was right in this principle . . . when the impression was a genuine one" (*Turner, CW,* XIII, 51). But this lesson in "seeing" was supplemented for Proust, as for Ruskin, by the artist's burden of "reading," of discovering through the clarified reality of the creation the "allegorical" dimension of the quotidian actuality. We learn to "read" the sprawling world around us through the resolving optic of the artist's personal vision. "La Charité de Giotto" is transfigured by the architecture of the novel in which she plays a small but significant role. (It is not irrelevant that the passage cited above, where the frescoes of the Arena Chapel and the *fille de cuisine* are imbricated, forms the prelude to one of Proust's most complex—and paradoxical—discussions of the act of reading.)

Meanwhile, through the spring and summer of 1900 Proust had

published those articles, already prefigured in the obituary and the *Figaro* piece, that were to establish his claims as a serious critic of Ruskin. Dedicated to Léon Daudet, "Ruskin à Notre-Dame d'Amiens" had appeared at the beginning of April in the pages of the *Mercure de France*, which later provided the imprint for his two volumes of Ruskin translations. This essay, redacted as the second part of the Preface to *La Bible d'Amiens* and subsequently published as the second section of "En mémoire des églises assassinées: II. Journées de pèlerinage" in *Pastiches et mélanges* (*CSB*, pp. 69ff.), extends Proust's notion of the spatial work of art as a book and its converse. Proust insists on the necessity in reading Ruskin, as in "reading" an architectural program, of being able to juxtapose related texts and compositional elements. In a note, he underlines the initial task of the critic as an aide to this juxtaposition: "Au fond, aider le lecteur à être impressionné par ces traits singuliers, placer sous ses yeux des traits similaires qui lui permettent de les tenir pour les traits essentiels du génie d'un écrivain devrait être la première partie de la tâche de tout critique" (*CSB*, p. 76*n*; p. 6 below). The image of the work of art as a book and the achieved book as a temporal multiplicity of panels resolved into a unity of vision will persist long beyond Proust's apprenticeship to Ruskin and finally resonate in the concluding pages of *Le Temps retrouvé*.

But addressing what Ruskin styles "the Bible of Amiens," the sculptural program of the West Portal, Proust remarks that we are asked to read a very specific book: "Le porche d'Amiens n'est pas seulement, dans le sens vague où l'aurait pris Victor Hugo, un livre de pierre, une Bible de pierre: c'est 'La Bible' en pierre" (*CSB*, pp. 88–89; p. 19 below). After a brief flight into a visual evocation of the western facade of Amiens seen for the first time (and at successive hours à la Monet's experiment at Rouen), Proust returns to the Ruskinian image of the cathedral as text, the first Text of the Western imagination and the first text of the critic's own childhood:

> Mais une cathédrale n'est pas seulement une beauté à sentir. Si même ce n'est plus pour vous un enseignement à suivre, c'est

du moins encore un livre à comprendre. Le portail d'une cathédrale gothique, et plus particulièrement d'Amiens, la cathédrale gothique par excellence [an allusion to Emile Mâle], c'est la Bible. Avant de vous l'expliquer je voudrais, à l'aide d'une citation de Ruskin vous faire comprendre que, quelles que soient vos croyances, la Bible est quelque chose de réel, d'actuel, et que nous avons à trouver en elle autre chose que la saveur de son archaïsme et le divertissement de notre curiosité. [*CSB,* p. 89; p. 20 below]

Proust then ranges over extended quotations from the third chapter of *The Bible of Amiens* ("The Lion Tamer") where Ruskin presents Jerome as the translator who initiated European literature, his work of translation being the "library of Europe" wherein " 'The Book of Books' took the abiding form of which all the future art of the Western nations was to be an hourly enlarging interpretation" (*CW,* XXXIII, 109–10). The quotations include Ruskin on the Psalms as the sum of personal and social wisdom, on the range of historical and didactic writing encompassed in the Bible, but most significantly for Proust's own quest there is Ruskin on the role of the Bible as a first Book in his own affective life, as the speculum by which he first approached other cultures and, in fact, the experience of reading itself:

I am no despiser of profane literature. . . . But it was from the Bible that I learned the symbols of Homer, and the faith of Horace: the duty enforced upon me in early youth of reading every word of the gospels and prophecies as if written by the hand of God, gave me the habit of awed attention which afterwards made many passages of the profane writers, frivolous to an irreligious reader, deeply grave to me. [*CW,* XXXIII, 118–19; cf. *Praeterita,* i, 46; *CW,* XXXV, 39–41]

Any casual reader of the Library Edition of Ruskin is immediately struck by the constant orchestration of the author's prose to a continuo of Biblical quotation and subterranean allusion (all faithfully recorded in the footnotes). The sound of the Bible and the evocative weight of the texts, learned in childhood, supply the distinctive tone as well as the moral directions of Ruskin's prose; they also give some clue to what Proust was later to sense as "idolatry." Each present text is, for Ruskin and Proust, a palimpsest of remembered texts.

The way in which the Biblical figures—prophets, kings, and apostles—animate the sculptural work of Amiens, the way in which the moral dimensions of the embodied narratives organize the structural relations of the building, seem to have suggested to Proust the power of the architectural image that was to supply a recurrent metaphor for his work as a novelist. In a letter to Jean de Gaigneron of 1919 he confesses to a presiding ambition in his composition, one that became much more overt in the metaphorics of the concluding volume:

> Et, quand vous me parlez des cathédrales, je ne peux pas ne pas être ému d'une intuition qui vous permet de deviner ce que je n'ai jamais dit à personne et que j'écris ici pour la première fois: c'est que j'avais voulu donner à chaque partie de mon livre le titre: *Porche, Vitraux de l'abside*, etc., pour répondre d'avance à la critique stupide qu'on me fait de manquer de construction dans des livres où je vous montrerai que le seul mérite est dans la solidité des moindres parties. J'ai renoncé tout de suite à ces titres d'architecture parce que je les trouvais trop prétentieux, mais je suis touché que vous les retrouviez par une sorte de divination de l'intelligence. [16]

The sculptural program of the cathedral supplies a key to the composition; the architectural elements physically provide for its structural integrity. Through the design of the builder the opposed piers of the gothic arch were enlisted so as to sustain the great mass of the towering edifice. And just as in the cathedral moral directions were embodied in space, so the extremes and the aspiration toward

---

16. Quoted by André Maurois in *A la recherche de Marcel Proust* (Paris: Hachette, 1949), p. 175. In this and other exfoliations of Proust's cathedral image it is interesting to compare his remarks on fictional composition with Ruskin's distinction between architecture and building in the first chapter of *The Seven Lamps of Architecture*.

unity of Proust's life work are suggested in his system of structural oppositions—the two "ways," the two "moments," the two methods (of metaphor and memory), the two "truths" (*générales* and *essentielles*), the two experiences (of disillusion and vision)—that form the piers of his fictional building.

For Proust as for Ruskin originality was a quality of "vision," a way of seeing the world whole and unique. The novelist saw his task as that of enclosing his world in a new structure, which, like the great cathedrals or the humbler parish church of Saint-Hilaire, would include in its unity "un espace à quatre dimensions—la quatrième étant celle du Temps" (*ARTP*, I, 61). The vocabulary of Proust's extended architectural metaphors frequently recalls the descriptions he translated from Ruskin, but two insistent points in such comparisons are peculiarly characteristic of the novelist's own vision: the possibility of creating a dialectic between inside and outside, a living space within which the artist can construct the world, an inner book that can be translated into articulated composition; and the possibility, usually represented by the gothic arch or the rose window, of bringing into immanent contact two apparently opposed views or ways of life.

At the conclusion of "Notre-Dame d'Amiens" ("Journées de pèlerinage") Proust returns to his own education before the gothic cathedral, "une sorte de livre ouvert, écrit dans un langage solennel où chaque caractère est une oeuvre d'art, et que personne ne comprend plus" (*CSB*, p. 104; p. 27 below). As pilgrim and student faced with the challenge of deciphering these hieroglyphs of an old language based on an even older Text, Proust first alludes to Emerson's advice about hitching one's wagon to a star ("Civilization") and then confesses how Ruskin stands for him among the Major Prophets as the gateway to this new language and mode of feeling:

Comprenant mal jusque-là la portée de l'art religieux au moyen âge, je m'étais dit, dans ma ferveur pour Ruskin: Il m'apprendra, car lui aussi, en quelques parcelles du moins, n'est-il pas la vérité? Il fera entrer mon esprit là où il n'avait pas accès, car il est la *porte*. Il me purifiera. . . . [*CSB*, p. 104; p. 27 below]

Et maintenant nous avons beau nous arrêter devant les statues d'Isaïe, de Jérémie, d'Ezéchiel et de Daniel en nous disant: "Voici les quatre grands prophètes," il y en a un de plus qui n'est pas ici et dont pourtant nous ne pouvons pas dire qu'il est absent, car nous le voyons partout. C'est Ruskin: si sa statue n'est pas à la porte de la cathédrale, elle est à l'entrée de notre coeur. Ce prophète-là a cessé de faire entendre sa voix. Mais c'est qu'il a fini de dire toutes ses paroles. C'est aux générations de les reprendre en choeur. [*CSB*, p. 105; p. 28 below]

While the essay on Amiens in the *Mercure* is probably the clearest prefiguration of Proust's metaphorics of the cathedral and the book, the long essay that concludes this stage of his critical apprenticeship, "John Ruskin," is an extended discussion of the character and obligations of the artist-critic. It is also, as we move from the first part of the essay to the second, the most compelling record of the ways in which Proust's reading had progressed from an initial reliance on his French predecessors—Milsand and La Sizeranne[17]—to an immersion in the interactive life of the original texts, the point where the words of the dead Englishman find a new resonance in the imagination of the French apprentice. "John Ruskin," which had been announced in both the obituary notice and the *Figaro* article, appeared in successive numbers of the *Gazette des beaux-arts*, the journal founded by Charles Ephrussi, one of the precursors of Swann. The first part, published in April, possibly written as early as the preceding summer, stays close with due acknowledgment to texts available in the French translations of Milsand and La Sizeranne

17. Joseph-Antoine Milsand (1817–1886), critic and philosopher, author of *L'Esthétique anglaise: étude sur M. John Ruskin* (Paris: Germer Baillère, 1864); Robert de La Sizeranne (1866–1932), critic and author of *La Peinture anglaise contemporaine* (Paris: Hachette, 1895) and *Ruskin et la religion de la beauté*, cited in note 7 above.

(the two exceptions being quotations from a passage in *The Bible of Amiens* and another from *The Seven Lamps*). The second part, published in the August issue of the *Gazette,* ranges much more widely over Ruskin's *oeuvre* and includes passages available only in the original texts of *The Pleasures of England, Lectures on Architecture and Painting, The Seven Lamps of Architecture, The Stones of Venice, Val d'Arno, Lectures on Art,* and *Saint Mark's Rest.* Proust had clearly passed through the portal into the freedom of Ruskin's writings. The two sections of this essay (called "Sur Ruskin" in the original periodical form) were combined, as noted above, into the third part of the Preface to *La Bible d'Amiens* (with some minor corrections and a number of supplementary notes). They later formed the third part of "En mémoire des églises assassinées" in *Pastiches et mélanges,* with the suppression of some of the quotes from Ruskin and the addition of an important four-page note (*CSB,* pp. 105–15, 115–29; pp. 29–49 below).

Proust begins the essay with a critical discussion of Ruskin's aesthetics as presented by Milsand and La Sizeranne. He contrasts the death of the artist with the survival—and translation—of his works, apparently reflecting his reading of Emerson (whom he had considered translating) and the doctrine of representative men: "Car l'homme de génie ne peut donner naissance à des oeuvres qui ne mourront pas qu'en les créant à l'image non de l'être mortel qu'il est, mais de l'exemplaire d'humanité qu'il porte en lui" (*CSB,* p. 106; p. 29 below). While he acknowledges his debt to his French predecessors, he is anxious to liberate Ruskin from the epicurean or dilettante overtones that may attach to the titles of the books by his French disciples—*L'Esthétique anglaise* and *La Religion de la beauté.* Although accepting their emphasis on the primacy of perception in Ruskin and his favorite artists, Proust is anxious to place the stress in "the religion of beauty" on the first term:

> Que l'adoration de la Beauté ait été, en effet, l'acte perpétuel de la vie de Ruskin, cela peut être vrai à la lettre; mais j'estime que le but de cette vie, son intention profonde, secrète et constante était autre, et si je le dis, ce n'est pas pour prendre le

contre-pied du système de M. de La Sizeranne, mais pour empêcher qu'il ne soit rabaissé dans l'esprit des lecteurs par une interprétation fausse, mais naturelle et comme inévitable. [*CSB,* pp. 109–10; p. 32 below]

Ruskin's religion was, Proust insists, "la religion tout court." For him happiness can be achieved only by looking beyond happiness; the esthesis is but a by-product of a consecration of the author's powers to values that are quite other than those of immediate pleasure. He associates Ruskin with the breed of genius whom Carlyle saw as deciphering and translating an "inner reality":

Et, très loin d'avoir été un dilettante ou un esthète, Ruskin fut précisément le contraire, un de ces hommes à la Carlyle, averti par leur génie de la vanité de tout plaisir et, en même temps, de la présence auprès d'eux d'une réalité éternelle, intuitivement perçue par l'inspiration. Le talent leur est donné comme un pouvoir de fixer cette réalité à la toute-puissance et à l'éternité de laquelle, avec enthousiasme et comme obéissant à un commandement de la conscience, ils consacrent, pour lui donner quelque valeur, leur vie éphémère. [*CSB,* p. 110; p. 33 below]

This is the sort of genius dedicated to the reading of that "inner book" that was to play such a crucial role in Proust's own aesthetics. While written the first time by experience, it could achieve, in the artist's translation, a coherence and permanence that would gather together the innumerable glosses and marginal inscriptions in a "message" that was, for Ruskin as for Carlyle, transpersonal and enduring:

Le poète étant pour Ruskin, comme pour Carlyle, une sorte de scribe écrivant sous la dictée de la nature une partie plus ou moins importante de son secret, le premier devoir de l'artiste est de ne rien ajouter de son propre cru à ce message divin. De cette hauteur vous verrez s'évanouir, comme les nuées qui se traînent à terre, les reproches de réalisme aussi bien que d'intellectualisme adressés à Ruskin. . . . Il y a dans ces critiques erreur d'altitude. La réalité que l'artiste doit enregistrer est à la fois matérielle et intellectuelle. La matière est réelle parce qu'elle est une expression de l'esprit. [*CSB,* p. 111; p. 34 below]

This insistence on "realism" and "intellectualism" in a very special sense comes close to the mature formulations of Proust's own aesthetic, at once rooted in affective experience and, freed from extraneous intrusions "de son propre cru," translated into an architecture accessible only through the imagination. Speaking of the range of Ruskin's writings, both achieved and left incomplete, Proust remarks upon their startling novelty and underlying identity: they give "l'idée de quelque chose de plus qu'humain, ou plutôt l'impression que chaque livre est d'un homme nouveau qui a un savoir différent, pas la même expérience, une autre vie" (*CSB,* p. 115; pp. 37–38 below). But this recurrent novelty is bound together and blended in the memory of the attentive reader.

As already noted, the second part of the essay draws much closer to the texts of Ruskin themselves and to the author's unique way of seeing. While proclaiming the primacy of vision, Ruskin has a retrospective as well as a prospective dimension; often the object can only be fully comprehended by the imagination when it is absent, adumbrating the "law" that Proust suggests in *Le Temps retrouvé:* "on ne [peut] imaginer que ce qui est absent":

> If the imagination is called to take delight in any object, it will not always be well, if we can help it, to put the *real* object there, before it. The imagination would on the whole rather have it *not* there;—the reality and the substance are rather in the imagination's way: it would think a good deal more of the thing if it could not see it. Hence that strange and sometimes fatal charm, which there is in all things as long as we wait for them, and the moment we have lost them; but which fades while we possess them. [*Modern Painters, CW,* V, 181–82]

Things have to be seen, and seen clearly, but they are often fully accessible to the Scribe only *after* they have been seen. Proust recognized that Ruskin's career was one of compounding losses, renunciations, and final, occluding vision. Yet he also recognized the peculiar powers that these departures liberated; it could be said of *Praeterita* as well as of Combray that the only true paradises are those that we have lost.

The concluding pages of "John Ruskin" are devoted to the moving account of the pilgrimage that Proust had made with the Yeatmans to Rouen in search of the tiny figure on the "portail des Libraires," a figure given a certain kind of immortality, as noted above, by Ruskin's attentive recreation of it in *The Seven Lamps*. Through the happy intervention of his Madeleine (Yeatman), the pilgrim is able to translate the art of the anonymous sculptor and the English critic into his own imaginative redaction: "I was moved to find him still there, because I realized that nothing dies that once has truly lived, neither the thought of the sculptor nor that of Ruskin" (*CSB,* p. 126; p. 46 below).

The essay, which opens with a meditation on the mortality of artists and the immortality of their works, closes with Proust appropriating Ruskin's tribute to Turner, dead in 1851, to the master who had died at the opening of the new century: "Through those eyes, now filled with dust, generations yet unborn will learn to behold the light of nature" (*Lectures on Architecture, CW,* XII, 128; *CSB,* p. 129; p. 49 below).

The appearance of the second part of "John Ruskin" in the August 1900 issue of the *Gazette des beaux-arts* marked the end of the first, intensive phase of Proust's apprenticeship to Ruskin. The major work that lay ahead was the patient labor of the translator (and his network of collaborators), first the text of *The Bible of Amiens* (appearing in part serially during 1903 and as a book in February 1904) and then that of *Sesame and Lilies* (the introductory essay appearing serially during 1905 and the book in 1906). This labor was complicated and enriched by Proust's characteristic scrupulosity in supplementing the texts with a web of footnotes, not only clarifying the references but also serving as an "improvised memory" of *other* passages from Ruskin in dialogue with the primary text. The years of these labors were difficult ones for the author still without an *oeuvre;* they were darkened by the death of his father (1903) followed by the death of his mother and collaborator in the translations (1905), by the progressive deterioration of his own health, and finally by the traumatic removal from the family apartment to the "temporary" settlement in his cell at 102, boulevard Haussmann.

But Proust, like Ruskin, could not bear to let a text enter the world without trying to recapture it through revision, marginal alteration, or cannibalization into some later project. We have seen the outline at least of the rather complicated bibliographic history of the essays from 1900—footnotes added, citations suppressed or substituted in the successive incarnations of the text. The most important critical essay to appear during the years of translation, "Sur la lecture" (the Preface for *Sésame et les lys*), begins, in fact, with an extended passage evoking a child's world of reading in a proto-Combray; and this passage, where the most "unnoticed" details are most vividly remembered, is actually cannibalized from the pages of the abandoned novel, *Jean Santeuil* (1895–99), that had preceded the discovery of Ruskin. There were also some occasional reviews of Ruskiniana that allowed him to rework or reiterate the arguments first raised in the essays of 1900: these briefer notes included reviews of Marie von Bunsen's *John Ruskin, sein Leben und sein Wirken,* which appeared in the *Chronique des arts et de la curiosité* for 7 March 1903; the *Chronique* reviews of Charlotte Broicher, *John Ruskin und sein Werk: Puritaner, Künstler, Kritiker* and the same author's German translation of *Modern Painters* I and II, both under the date 2 January 1904; as well as a review of a French translation by Mathilde Crémieux of *The Stones of Venice* in the *Chronique* of 5 May 1906. To these should be added the much more substantial article on his friend and sometime patron Robert de Montesquiou, published in *Les Arts de la vie* (15 August 1905) under the title "Un Professeur de beauté," since this exercise in literary politics includes some extended commentary on Ruskin's clarity of vision (a gift that he allegedly shared with Montesquiou). (These minor specimens of Ruskiniana were supplemented by a publication in quite another key—a pastiche of the earnestly didactic Ruskin apparently intended for inclusion in the cycle of "L'Affaire Lemoine"; something of its tone comes through in the full citation of the title: "La Bénédiction du sanglier. Etudes des fresques de Giotto représentant l'affaire Lemoine à l'usage des jeunes étudiants et étudiantes du Corpus Christi qui se soucient encore d'elles, par John Ruskin" [*CSB*, pp. 201–05].)

By far the most important "revision" or gloss on the Ruskin essays of 1900, however, is the "Post-Scriptum" written for the publication of *La Bible d'Amiens* and following in the Preface immediately on the "John Ruskin" essay from the *Gazette des beaux-arts* (*CSB*, pp. 129–41; pp. 49–61 below). This text, which strenuously raises the question of Ruskin's "idolatry," is frequently taken as Proust's recantation of his earlier passion for Ruskin and the precise end of his discipleship to the Sage of Coniston. But Proust's discussion of what he identifies here as a pervasive failure of "sincerity" on Ruskin's part is not so easily adjudicated. At the simple biographical level any reading of a definitive break with Ruskin leaves the important question of why his critic, in the more than two years following the completion of the "Post-Scriptum," continues his Ruskin studies and undertakes the translation of another major work, *Sesame and Lilies*, after this "repudiation." (Walter Strauss suggests that the continuation of the Ruskin projects was an act of piety to please his mother; George Painter, on the other hand, argues that the persistence was an effort to exorcise a spiritual "father.")[18]

18. Walter Strauss, *Proust and Literature: The Novelist as Critic* (Cambridge: Harvard University Press, 1957), pp. 184–86; George D. Painter, *Marcel Proust: A Biography* (London: Chatto and Windus, 1965), II, 1–2. Gary Wihl in the final chapter of his *Ruskin and the Rhetoric of Infallibility* (New Haven and London: Yale University Press, 1985) offers the most lucid and detailed discussion of Ruskin and Proust on the subject of idolatry. Wihl, in exploring the semantic fields of words such as *error* (both idolatrous and "sincere"), *lie*, and *idol*, demonstrates some of the profound ambivalences in these words when used by each author. Proust, as is evident from the final part of the Amiens Preface, sees Ruskin as a *false translator* when the latter subordinates "vividness" of perception to a "swarm of only superficially related symbols." Wihl (p. 134) underlines the shift in the use of the

Actually, taken within the context of the complete Preface to *La Bible d'Amiens*, Proust's indictment of Ruskin's motives seems less final when measured against the earlier defense of the same author against a charge of *naïve* "aestheticism" in the discussion of Milsand and La Sizeranne. What is more important, Proust's description of an interior struggle between the rival claims of esthesis and truth is cast in such a way as to suggest that it is an inevitable division for any deeply serious artist. And in the course of the commentary the reader with the retrospective advantage of Proust's own novel realizes that he is also describing under the rubric of "idolatry" the great temptation of his own narrator.

Proust characteristically begins his "Post-Scriptum" by allowing Ruskin to draw up the terms of the indictment himself, in language—as indicated earlier in the Preface—that is inescapably religious. Both Ruskin and Proust are fully aware of both the seductiveness of the temptation and the rigor of the charge. " 'Sous quelles formes magnifiques et tentatrices le mensonge a pu se glisser jusqu'au sein de sa sincérité intellectuelle. . . . ' ": he takes as his text his own words from the now adjacent essay of August 1900, a qualification within an encomium, and then quickly adds, "il y a une sorte d'idolâtrie que personne n'a mieux définie que Ruskin dans une page de *Lectures on Art*":

> Such I conceive generally, though indeed with good arising out of it, for every great evil brings some good in its backward eddies—such I conceive to have been the deadly function of art in its ministry to what, whether in heathen or in Christian lands, and whether in the pageantry of words, or colours, or fair forms, is truly, and in the deep sense, to be called idola-

---

word *idolatry:* "If Ruskinian idolatry is the reduction of an object or work of art followed by an elevation, then Proustian idolatry is the reverse—the wasting of passion on the worship of the hollow." Wihl also acknowledges Proust's originality in seeing Ruskin, contrary to popular opinion, as a far from literal-minded or narrowly mimetic critic; rather, for Proust, Ruskin was a powerful rhetorician who succumbed to his own rhetorical inventiveness in translating the figurative into the literal.

try—the serving with the best of our hearts and minds, some dear or sad fantasy which we have made for ourselves, while we disobey the present call of the Master, who is not dead, and who is not now fainting under His cross, but requiring us to take up ours. [*Lectures on Art, CW*, XX, 66; quoted by Proust *CSB*, p. 129]

The tragedy of misplaced priorities was, in Ruskin's doctrine of sacrifice, always a present danger. In the simplest sense Proust had already underlined this risk as early as the *Mercure* essay (which became an integral part of the Preface) where he sought to distinguish his notion of Ruskinian pilgrimage from mere fetishism: "un fétichisme qui n'est qu'illusion" (*CSB*, p. 70). (And no Ruskinian could contemplate the extraordinary incremental clutter—illustrating what was perhaps the widest-ranging mind of the century—of the Museum at Coniston without weighing the word "fetishism.") But in the "Post-Scriptum" the interrogation of motives, the possibility of the aesthetic asserting a subtle priority over the ethic, is much more deeply and universally put:

Mais il est un dilettantisme plus intérieur que le dilettantisme de l'action (dont il avait triomphé) et le véritable duel entre son idolâtrie et sa sincérité se jouait non pas à certaines heures de sa vie, non pas dans certaines pages de ses livres, mais à toute minute, dans ces régions profondes, secrètes, presque inconnues à nous-mêmes, où notre personnalité reçoit de l'imagination les images, de l'intelligence les idées, de la mémoire les mots, s'affirme elle-même dans le choix incessant qu'elle en fait, et joue en quelque sorte incessamment le sort de notre vie spirituelle et morale. Dans ces régions-là, j'ai l'impression que le péché d'idolâtrie n'ait cessé d'être commis par Ruskin. Et au moment même où il prêchait la sincérité, il y manquait lui-même, non en ce qu'il disait, mais par la manière dont il le disait. [*CSB*, p. 130; pp. 50–51 below]

Having thus implicated Ruskin in a struggle faced by every writer at the innermost arcanum of his imaginative life, Proust suggests that Ruskin never successfully resolved this duel between sincerity and idolatry despite the unambiguously moral character of his own teachings: "Les doctrines qu'il professait étaient des doctrines morales et non des doctrines esthétiques, et pourtant il les choisissait pour leur beauté. Et comme il ne voulait pas les présenter comme belles, mais comme vraies, il était obligé de se mentir à lui-même sur la nature des raisons qui les lui faisaient adopter" (*CSB,* p. 130; p. 51 below). This is especially poignant because, for Proust, Ruskin had clearly chosen the terms of his own "religion de la beauté," and his own greatest gifts as a critic were grounded in his intense perception of the beauty of objects. The indictment is also intimately related to the special role that texts (visual as well as literal) enjoyed in Ruskin's development. (Proust himself had earlier emphasized the significance for Ruskin in the work he was translating of the Bible taken literally rather than figuratively as a first text. Ruskin had, however, in the discussion of "idolatry" in *Aratra Pentelici,* identified a source of contemporary "frivolity" as "two forms of deadly Idolatry which are now all but universal in England" (*CW,* XX, 240). The first of these is "the worship of the Eidolon, or the Phantasm of Wealth," which was hardly a serious temptation for Ruskin himself. The second transgression, though, cuts much closer to Proust's indictment of Ruskin; it is "the Worship of the Letter, instead of the Spirit . . . the apprehension of a healing sacredness in the act of reading the Book whose primal commands we refuse to obey" (*CW,* XX, 240). The examples of Ruskin's "idolatry" that Proust brings forward are significantly drawn from "misreadings" for rhetorical purposes of the Bible itself (Egypt as "l'éducatrice de Moïse et l'Hôtesse du Christ," *CSB,* p. 134) and from "misreading" of Venice's history figured against the Biblical pageantry of her art ("Jamais cité n'eut une Bible plus glorieuse," *CSB,* p. 131).

At this crucial point, however, Proust implicates his own affective history while introducing the difficult question of how far aesthetic pleasure is imbricated in any discovery of truth. The event, which ultimately judges Proust rather than Ruskin, involves the former's reading precisely the seductive passage in *The Stones of Venice*

(*CW*, X, 141–42), itself based on a "misprision" of a verse from Ecclesiastes that formed part of the "text" of St. Mark's. Having submitted Ruskin's ringing denunciation of the sins of the Venetians to an ethical deconstruction, Proust then confesses to the suspect pleasure that this very text brought him when he first read it, within the figured confines of St. Mark's itself. Speaking of the page marred by "idolatry," he allows:

> Elle est elle-même mystérieuse, pleine d'images à la fois de beauté et de religion comme cette même église de Saint-Marc où toutes les figures de l'*Ancien* et du *Nouveau Testament* apparaissent sur le fond d'une sorte d'obscurité splendide et d'éclat changeant. Je me souviens de l'avoir lue pour la première fois dans Saint-Marc même, pendant une heure d'orage et d'obscurité où les mosaïques ne brillaient plus que de leur propre et matérielle lumière et d'un or intense, terrestre et ancien, auquel le soleil vénitien, qui enflamme jusqu'aux anges des campaniles, ne mêlait plus rien de lui; l'émotion que j'éprouvais à lire là cette page, parmi tous ces anges qui s'illuminaient des ténèbres environnantes, était très grande et n'était pourtant peut-être pas très pure. Comme la joie de voir les belles figures mystérieuses s'augmentait, mais s'altérait du plaisir en quelque sorte d'érudition que j'éprouvais à comprendre les textes apparus en lettres byzantines à côté de leurs fronts nimbés, de même la beauté des images de Ruskin était avivée et corrompue par l'orgueil de se référer au *texte sacré*. Une sorte de retour égoïste sur soi-même est inévitable dans ces joies mêlées d'érudition et d'art où le plaisir esthétique peut devenir plus aigu, mais non rester aussi pur. [*CSB*, p. 133; p. 53 below]

Though Proust has indicted Ruskin for his reading of the Venetian and Biblical texts earlier, he has here summoned himself to judgment in the profoundly ambiguous act of reading Ruskin; the temptations of "le texte sacré" (whether that of others or one's own) and of the "joies mêlées" will remain central concerns of Proust and his fictional narrator down to the last pages of the novel that had become their common life. And "the scene of reading" will become, again and again, the locus of the question of idolatry.

Proust's postscriptural reproof of the master is thus inseparable from a self-questioning of the disciple and translator. Proust, in translating a sentence from Ruskin on the hazards of interpreting Scripture ("There is no possibility of attaching the idea of infallible truth to any form of human language in which even these exceptional passages have been delivered to us," *CW*, XXXIII, 116), gives the duplicity of language an even more overt formulation: "Il n' y a pas de forme de langage humain où l'erreur n'ait pu se glisser" (*CSB*, p. 135).

Again, touching yet another affinity that he shared with Ruskin, Proust speaks toward the end of the "Post-Scriptum" of the profound materiality and topographical specificity of the latter's thought. (This can, of course, be both a rectifying "realism" and an occasion of "idolatry.")

> Car la pensée de Ruskin n'est pas comme la pensée d'un Emerson par exemple, qui est contenue tout entière dans un livre, c'est-à-dire un quelque chose d'abstrait, un pur signe d'elle-même. L'objet auquel s'applique une pensée comme celle de Ruskin et dont elle est inséparable n'est pas immatériel, il est répandu çà et là sur la surface de la terre. Il faut aller le chercher là où il se trouve, à Pise, à Florence, à la National Gallery, à Rouen, à Amiens, dans les montagnes de la Suisse. [*CSB*, p. 138; pp. 58–59 below]

The last instance returns us to where we first found Proust in pursuit of Ruskin, writing for his copy of La Sizeranne so that he could experience the Alps "through the eyes of this great man." By this stage in his development, Proust has not so much parted company with his English mentor as he has discovered that, distant as they are in certain formal doctrinal ways, they share common temptations as well as common affections. Thus, Proust—who continually slips into the first-person singular—asserts that despite his love for the hawthorn (which he shared with Ruskin and Walter Pater), a key to his affective *temps perdu,* "sincerity" compels that he distinguish the subject matter of a work of art from its more profound "content," that he frequent objects but not idolize them:

> Non, je ne trouverai pas un tableau plus beau parce que l'artiste aura peint au premier plan une aubépine, bien que je ne connaisse rien de plus beau que l'aubépine, car je veux rester sincère et que je sais que la beauté d'un tableau ne dépend pas des choses qui y sont représentées. Je ne collectionnerai pas les images de l'aubépine. Je ne vénère pas l'aubépine, je vais la voir et la respirer. [*CSB,* p. 137; p. 57 below]

The same might be said, on balance, of Proust's attitude at this stage of his career toward masters and "directeurs de conscience." In discerning the rounds that Ruskin lost in the continuing struggle against idolatry, Proust acquired insight into his own susceptibilities—his penchant for "sacred texts" and idolatrous pursuits. The analysis of these temptations whether under the guise of *snobisme,* or love, or erudition, or a mystified conception of art, became the major deconstructive activity of the novel he was yet to write but was already gathering into the "inner book." The last pages of the Preface return to the question of discipleship, taken not as burden but as a liberation. ("Les personnes médiocres croient généralement que se laisser guider . . . par les livres qu'on admire, enlève à notre faculté de juger une partie de son indépendance. 'Que peut vous importer ce que sent Ruskin: sentez par vous-même.' ") This line of argument is founded, Proust argues, on a basic psychological error common to those ignorant of genuine discipleship; they fail to recognize that those who have accepted "une discipline spirituelle sentent que leur puissance de comprendre et de sentir en est infiniment accrue, et leur sens critique jamais paralysé" (*CSB,* p. 140; p. 60 below). These last pages do not read like an act of repudiation. Rather than "exorcising a father" in Ruskin, Proust seems to have found a deeper insight into himself, into his weaknesses as well as his potential. The ultimate paragraph of the Preface is a complex and precursal meditation on the power of memory to resurrect that which is absent and seemingly lost forever. As noted above by Ruskin himself, certain powers of the imagination seem to operate effectively only in the absence of the object. In one sense Ruskin had become a part of Proust's own past; in another sense the master was removed just far enough so that the task of translation could begin: "C'est quand Ruskin est bien loin de nous que nous traduisons ses livres et tâchons de fixer dans une image ressemblante les traits de sa pensée" (*CSB,* p. 141; p. 61 below).

The translation of *La Bible d'Amiens* was completed in 1901, save for some late revisions. According to Marie Nordlinger, Proust relied on the literal versions of the Ruskin text that his mother prepared during the daylight hours as the point of departure for the accomplished translations that he labored over through the night. The circle of his collaboration extended further when it came to the pursuit of nuances, including not only Mlle. Nordlinger but also Robert d'Humières, Reynaldo Hahn, Robert de Billy, and François d'Oncieu among his informants. Georges de Lauris in the Preface to his collection of Proust correspondence, *A un ami,* tells the anecdote of the prince de Brancovan (the editor of *La Renaissance latine,* which published parts of *La Bible d'Amiens* serially) approaching the translator in some bewilderment: "Comment faites-vous, Marcel, puisque vous ne savez pas l'anglais?"[19] Lauris adds that, although Proust would have had difficulty ordering a mutton chop in an English restaurant and knew all the other English authors whom he loved only in French translation, he did indeed know the one who mattered most with genuine intimacy: "De fait, il ne connaissait que l'anglais de Ruskin mais alors dans toutes ses nuances."

The labor, however, that delayed the publication of *La Bible* and occupied more than a year of additional research was the creation of what Proust styled "an improvised memory," a gloss on the single text of Ruskin that brought into play the resonances of echoes from

---

19. Georges de Lauris, ed., *Marcel Proust: A un ami: correspondance inédite, 1903–1922* (Paris: Amiot-Dumont, 1948), p. 22.

the rest of the *oeuvre*. Recognizing that Ruskin above all other writers seemed to require this "echo chamber," he constructed through his footnotes an internal lexicon for reading in context. In a long footnote that begins with a passage from *Praeterita*, he outlined the rationale for his system of echoing footnotes in terms that sound like the compositional system of repetitions finally articulated in *A la recherche*:

> En mettant une note au bas des passages cités de *La Bible d'Amiens*, chaque fois que le texte éveillait par des analogies, même lointaines, le souvenir d'autres ouvrages de Ruskin, et en traduisant dans la note le passage qui m'était ainsi revenu à l'esprit, j'ai tâché de permettre au lecteur de se placer dans la situation de quelqu'un qui ne se trouvait pas en présence de Ruskin pour la première fois, mais qui, ayant déjà eu avec lui des entretiens antérieurs, pourrait, dans ses paroles, reconnaître ce qui est chez lui, permanent et fondamental. Ainsi j'ai essayé de pourvoir le lecteur comme d'une mémoire improvisée où j'ai disposé des souvenirs des autres livres de Ruskin,—sorte de caisse de résonance, où les paroles de *La Bible d'Amiens* pourront prendre quelque retentissement en y éveillant des échos fraternels. Mais aux paroles de *La Bible d'Amiens* ces échos ne répondront pas sans doute, ainsi qu'il arrive dans une mémoire qui s'est faite elle-même, de ces horizons inégalement lointains, habituellement cachés à nos regards et dont notre vie elle-même a mesuré jour par jour les distances variées. Ils n'auront pas, pour venir rejoindre la parole présente dont la ressemblance les a attirés, à traverser la résistante douceur de cette atmosphère interposée qui a l'étendue même de notre vie et qui est toute la poésie de la mémoire. ["Préface du traducteur," *La Bible d'Amiens; CSB*, pp. 75–76; pp. 5–6 below]

Elsewhere, Proust speaks of Balzac and Wagner as "self-contemplating" artists who gave their work retrospective unity through the interplay of echoes and anticipations. But Ruskin is even more clearly an artist who is constantly escaping unity—both through incompletion and accretion; even his most retrospective and radically selective effort, *Praeterita,* not only reached back toward his origins through multiple layers of text but generated an ongoing commentary in the margin through the uncompletable *Dilecta.* The same need for a "memory" to contain the absent texts, to achieve through juxtaposition the simultaneity that eludes the linear text, is stressed again in one of Proust's liminal notes for the second volume of translation, *Sésame et les lys:*

> Mais c'est le charme précisément de l'oeuvre de Ruskin qu'il y ait entre les idées d'un même livre, et entre les divers livres des liens qu'il ne montre pas, qu'il laisse à peine apparaître un instant et qu'il a d'ailleurs peut-être tissés après coup, mais jamais artificiels cependant puisqu'ils sont toujours tirés de la substance toujours identique à elle-même de sa pensée. Les préoccupations multiples mais constantes de cette pensée, voilà ce qui assure à ces livres une unité plus réelle que l'unité de composition, généralement absente, il faut bien le dire. [*SL,* p. 62*n;* p. 145 below]

As in the case of Augustine's conversion, the crucial scene at the end of Proust's long apprenticeship to Ruskin is one of reading, taken both as a literal experience and as a theory of self-instantiation. Thus, Proust chose to call the Preface to the second volume of his translations "Sur la lecture" ("On Reading" in the present translation, pp. 99–129 below). When he collected and again redacted this essay for *Pastiches et mélanges* in 1919, he retitled it "Journées de lecture" (not to be confused with the 1907 review for which he used the same title), establishing a parallelism with the second section of the first Preface ("Ruskin à Notre-Dame d'Amiens," pp. 9–28 in this volume), which he retitled "Journées de pèlerinage." But while the "journées" of the *Bible* Preface are a sociable pilgrimage with Ruskin to the monument of Amiens, itself "an open book" (p. 27 below) to which the English critic is the portal, the meditation on reading evoked by *Sesame and Lilies* is an altogether different matter, an exercise in reflective innerness. In fact, Proust specifically contrasts his own sense of reading as a solitary and privileged moment (clearly erotic in its subtext) with Ruskin's more traditional notion of reading as an invitation to a conversation with great minds.

The structure of the *Sesame* Preface is, in fact, a double meditation: first the delicately nuanced evocation of childhood memories of reading (pp. 99–110 below) that prefigures similar scenes in "Combray," and then an extended, analytic reflection on the innerness and solitude of the experience for which the book itself can only be an "incitement" (*CSB*, pp. 176f; pp. 114f below). Speaking of the role that reading can play in our spiritual life, Proust notes that what for the author are "Conclusions" become "Incitations" for the reader. By what he calls "a peculiar law of mental optics," what was for the author the end of his wisdom appears to us but the beginning of ours (*CSB*, p. 177; pp. 114–15 below). As Ruskin was the portal for the pilgrim of Amiens, so reading is here at the "threshold to spiritual life"; but while it can introduce us into this ultimately solitary domain, it does not in itself constitute it. ("La lecture est au seuil de la vie spirituelle; elle peut nous y introduire: elle ne la constitue pas." *CSB*, p. 178; p. 116 below). In this sense Proust's final extended essay on Ruskin is both terminal and liminal, opening on the "allegory of reading" (a term that he first uses in a footnote to the *Sesame* translation), a figural process that would be exfoliated in *A la recherche du temps perdu*. [20]

Proust's reflections on reading are intimately related to his central concern with "possession-taking," a concept that he borrowed from Ruskin. One recent and subtle critic, David Ellison, describes the ways in which the psychological analysis of the act of reading can be seen as a *mise-en-scène* that in the novel generates the narrative structure itself. [21] Enlisting both semiotic and rhetorical elements in

20. For a discussion of Proustian beginnings and endings, see Richard Macksey, "'Conclusions' et 'Incitations': Proust à la recherche de Ruskin," *MLN* 96 (1981): 1113–19.

21. David R. Ellison, *The Reading of Proust* (Baltimore: Johns Hopkins University Press, 1984). Ellison's argument with respect to idolatry and reading is discussed in a review by Richard Macksey, *MLN* 99 (1984): 1273–82.

the work, Ellison argues (p. 94) that "if Proust 'goes beyond' Ruskin, it is not because he has a better theory, but because he sinks into the abyss of possession/dispossession and assumes the desperate task of imprisoning a forever escaping sign." The dramatised first part of "Sur la lecture" is thus an exemplary text, where the description of a central scene of reading also demonstrates the apparently effortless transition from the isolated privileged moment to the narrative enactment of that moment as "an allegory of reading." Here the successive recognition of and fall into "idolatrous rhetoric" actually assumes the structure of a fiction. In the movement from the analytic to the narrative the germ of the *Recherche* comes into being.

At the end of his affair with Odette, after years of suffering and dedication to his "grand amour," Swann reflects that all his sacrifices were made "pour une femme . . . qui n'était pas mon genre!" The reader of Proust as dévoté, translator, and critic of Ruskin may be tempted to look back over the six years of intense work that punctuates his long apprenticeship to the English writer and conclude similarly that this passionate affair, too, was all offered up to an author who was, in the final analysis, not Proust's type. The superficial differences in background and temperament separating Proust from Ruskin are all to obvious: Ruskin's puritanical, Scottish-Evangelical inheritance, his moralizing, his ultimate role as a prophet of social and ethical renovation all contrast markedly with Proust's Mediterranean and Cartesian heritage, his indifference to doctrinal concerns, his detachment as a demi-Juif in a profoundly secular society, his role as the worldly chronicler of the Faubourg Saint-Germain, the pitiless, illusion-free critic of human passions and obsessions. All these persistent lines of character suggest an unbridgeable chasm between the two authors. Even the external records of their careers tend to reinforce this distance; Ruskin the restless traveler, dedicated until late in life to annual circuits of the Continent and its monuments; Proust, after a brief period of "Ruskinian pilgrimages," cloistered in an almost monastic consecration to the exploration of his own cork-lined cell; Ruskin, the author of a large and diverse body of writings that does not easily yield its essential unity; Proust, the architect of a single vast text into which he attempted to draw all that he had earlier experienced and written.

Beneath these dramatic differences, however, lie bonds of consanguinity that both account for the initial appeal across language and culture and explain as well those aspects of Ruskin's achievement that were permanently and subtly assimilated into Proust's imagination. These affinities are much more profound than the memories of a childhood organized and extended by overprotective parents; they touch a community of feeling that goes beyond a common love for the cathedrals of France, for Venice, for Giotto, Tintoretto, and Turner. These deeper affinities that bind the careers of Ruskin and Proust, the lessons that the French writer garnered from his English predecessor, can be broadly summarized in terms of three characteristic modes of the imagination: similar ways of seeing (precisions of the critical eye), similar ways of feeling (resonances of the literary and affective memory), and similar ways of writing (a constant struggle with digression, a syntax of complex subordination, "the cadence of mitigated authority," and a proliferating network of interactive images). During his apprenticeship to Ruskin, Proust discovered that he saw, that he felt, and—ultimately— that he wrote like Ruskin. Like the author of *Praeterita,* he was to be engaged in a constant search to unite through successive revisions the living self and the writing self. Both strove ultimately to bring together the associative and penetrative imaginations in a single critical act.

And whatever the vast distances that separated their careers, both writers were marked by similar division and haunted by common fears. Both Ruskin and Proust bear a resemblance to Isaiah Berlin's characterization of that other great "directeur de conscience," Leo Tolstoy: a polymathic "fox" in search of a vocation as unifying "hedgehog." Both were plagued by demons of incompletion and digression; both were tempted, in the comprehensive sense suggested in Proust's "Post-Scriptum," by the artist's sin of idolatry.

Both had, in Leo Spitzer's characterization of the mature Proust, the double face of calm sage and nervous seeker, of the intellectual and the impressionist. Maurice Blanchot spoke of Proust's life work as "une oeuvre achevée-inachevée." The same might be said of the vast monument assembled by Ruskin's editors, Cook and Wedderburn. Many of Proust's perceptive critics have remarked of his great novel, whose parts must be read both "tour à tour" and "à la fois," that it is the product of a double discourse, one undoing (or completing) the work of the other. Walter Benjamin speaks of Proust's "Penelope-work" of weaving and unweaving, of recollection and forgetting; Ernst Robert Curtius, in terms reminiscent of Proust on Ruskin, speaks of the "braiding" of "intellect" and "impression"; Roland Barthes describes the two discourses in more purely linguistic terms as that of the "decoder" and the "encoder"; Gérard Genette argues that *A la recherche* must be seen at once "comme oeuvre" and "comme approche de l'oeuvre." All of these deeply duplicitous characterizations could, with important qualifications, be applied to Ruskin's work as well. It is these resonances that perhaps go furthest toward explaining the affinities between the two writers, how the example of the English prophet was assimilated into the sensibility of the French novelist.

One of Proust's most profound readers, Georges Poulet, chooses at the conclusion of his study of Proustian space the image of a bookcase in Marcel's bedroom at Balbec as the most explicit emblem of the novelist's struggle to contain multiplicity within the unity of the work. The glass panes of the bookcase reflect a series of scenes, part of the sunset that was outside the room, but also—framed figuratively—the moments of the novel itself that contains this scene. For Poulet this juxtaposition in space enacts the "solid geometry in time" of Proust's novel. One would like to imagine that behind the panes of the bookcase (which Proust translates into the predellas of an altar reredos), as behind the Arena frescoes of Giotto, stand the books of John Ruskin.[22]

22. Georges Poulet, *L'Espace proustien* (Paris: Gallimard, 1963), pp. 128–36.

Both writers had to come to terms with incompletion. By projecting the "texte sacré" into the future, beyond the provisional monument of his immense novel, Proust (in his prospective stage) finally escapes the "idolatry" of provisional origins, making of his work's very incompleteness its overarching virtue. This may have been a strategy that he learned from Ruskin's occluded example. But Proust also situated, close to the end of his "unfinished," probationary monument, a "coup de théâtre" that evokes his apprenticeship to Ruskin and the scene where he first read *The Stones of Venice.* The narrator, desolate of any hope for redeeming the time and achieving his vocation, passes through the courtyard of the Hôtel Guermantes and stumbles against an uneven paving-stone. Suddenly, out of the wastes of lost time, he recovers "un peu de temps à l'état pur" (III, 872), and the simultaneous experience in the present of a moment before the façade of St. Mark's in a Venice long since fallen into the oblivion of his own past. This experience is the beginning of a series of centripetal "moments" that bring together the strands of a life seemingly frayed beyond repair. It is the Venice of John Ruskin that contributes to this resurrection (tentative, to be sure), and it was the author's "pèlerinage ruskinien" that first made a place for the stone that is at once a stumbling block and the keystone of the novelistic arch. In the same subtle and almost forgotten way Ruskin himself had become a part of Proust's life and had emerged in *A la recherche,* translated into aspects of Proust's portraits of the artist (Elstir, Vinteuil, Bergotte, the narrator himself). The duty and task of the writer had thus, in the fullest sense, become that of a translator; and the vast fictional edifice that this vocation generated was erected over the partially effaced signs of a cemetery.

Marcel Proust

Preface to John Ruskin's
Bible of Amiens

Translated and Edited by
Jean Autret and Phillip J. Wolfe

Translator's
Preface

I. Foreword

Ioffer here a translation of *The Bible of Amiens* by John Ruskin. But it seemed to me that this was not enough for the reader. To read only one book by an author is to see that author only once. True, in a single conversation with someone we can discern particular traits. But it is only through repeated encounters in varied circumstances that we can recognize these traits as characteristic and essential. For a writer, for a musician, or for a painter, this variation of circumstances that enables us to discern, by a sort of experimentation, the permanent features of character is found in the variety of the works themselves. We meet again in a second book, in another painting, the peculiarities which we might have thought the first time belonged to the subject matter as much as to the writer or the painter himself. By comparing different works, we distinguish common traits which, taken together, reveal the moral character of the artist. When several portraits by Rembrandt, painted from different models, are gathered in a room, we are immediately struck by what is common to all of them, what constitutes the very features of the Rembrandt face. By inserting a footnote to the text of *The Bible of Amiens* each time this text evoked, through even remote analogies, the recollection of other works of Ruskin, and by translating in the note the passage which had come to my mind, I have tried to put the reader in the position of one who would not find himself in Ruskin's presence for the first time but who, having had previous conversations with Ruskin, would be able to recognize in his words what is permanent and fundamental in him. Thus I have tried to provide the reader with, so to speak, an improvised memory in which I have arranged recollections of other works of Ruskin—a kind of sounding board against which the words of *The Bible of Amiens* will be able to ring more deeply by awakening fraternal echoes. But these echoes will undoubtedly not correspond to the words of *The Bible of Amiens,* as they penetrate a memory which is itself composed of horizons generally hidden from our sight and whose various distances our life itself has measured day by day. In order to come into focus with the present word whose resemblance evoked them, these echoes will not have to go through the gentle resistance of that interposed atmosphere which is the span of our life and all the poetry of memory.

Fundamentally, the first part of every critic's task should be to help the reader appreciate these special traits by drawing his attention to similar traits that enable him to recognize them as the essential features of the genius of a writer.

If the critic is aware of this and has helped others to awareness, his function is almost fulfilled. If he has not perceived it, he can write all the books in the world on Ruskin: the Man, the Writer, the Prophet, the Artist, the Influence of his Thought, the Errors of his Doctrine, and all these works may perhaps reach a very high level of excellence, but skirt the subject. They may exalt the reputation of the critic but, as regards the true understanding of the work, they will be of less value than the exact perception of a correct nuance, however insignificant it might seem.

I am conscious, though, that the critic should then go further. He should try to reconstruct what the unique spiritual life of a writer haunted by such special realities could have been, his inspiration being the measure of his vision of those realities, his talent the measure of his ability to recreate them in his work, his ethics, finally, the instinct which, making him consider them from a viewpoint of eternity (however particular these realities appear to us), impelled him to sacrifice to the need of perceiving them and to the necessity of reproducing them, in order to ensure their lasting and clear image, all his pleasures, all his duties, and even his own life, which has no raison d'être except as the only possible way of entering into contact with those realities and has no value except that which an instrument indispensable to his experiments may have for a physicist. I need not say that I have not attempted to fulfill this second part of the critic's duty here with regard to Ruskin. That can be the object of subsequent studies. This is only a translation, and in the notes I have contented myself for the most part with giving the quotation that seemed to me appropriate without adding commentaries. Some notes, however, are more developed. These might have been better placed if, instead of leaving them here and there as footnotes, I had incorporated them into the body of my preface, which they complete and rectify on several points. But I did not put them there because this preface, save the foreword and a more recent postscript, simply reproduces articles I had given to the *Mercure de France* and the *Gazette des Beaux-Arts* at the time of Ruskin's death.

Other notes are of a different character. Those in chapter IV are mostly archeological. Every time that Ruskin, by way of quotation, but more often by way of allusion, incorporates into the structure of his sentences some biblical recollection, as the Venetians inserted in their monuments the sacred sculptures and precious stones they brought from the Orient, I have always looked up the exact reference so that the reader might see to what changes Ruskin would submit a verse before using it, and thus might better realize the mysterious yet unchanging chemistry of his mind, the originality and precision of his thought. Seeking the references, I could trust neither the index of *The Bible of Amiens* nor the Misses Gibbs' book, *The Bible References of Ruskin,* which are excellent but far too incomplete. So I used the Bible itself.

The text translated here is that of *The Bible of Amiens* in extenso.

In spite of the different suggestions I have received and which perhaps I should have followed, I have not omitted a single word of it. But having come to this decision, so that the reader might have a complete version of *The Bible of Amiens,* I must confess that there are many tedious passages in this book, as in all those Ruskin wrote toward the end of his life. Furthermore, during this period of his life, Ruskin lost all respect for syntax and all concern for clarity, more so than the reader will often believe. He will then very unjustly blame the translator for these mistakes.

For the same reasons, I have given all the appendices, save the Alphabetical Index and the List of Photographs of the Cathedral by Mr. Kaltenbacher, photographs which one could formerly buy with *The Bible of Amiens.* Finally, the English edition is adorned with four engravings which are not reproduced here, *Cimabue's Madonna, Amiens on All Soul's Day* (I describe this engraving further on [. . .]), *The Northern Porch before Restoration.* Since photographs were sold with the book, one understands why Ruskin chose for his engravings subjects relating only by a sort of allusion to the description he gives of the cathedral and why he did not needlessly repeat the photographs. Those who are familiar with the books of Ruskin will more readily see in the somewhat singular choice of the subjects of these engravings an effect of the eccentric, one might almost say humorous, disposition of his mind—which in a sense always led him to avoid what was expected, to put opposite a description of the Baptism of Christ by Giotto an engraving representing the Baptism of Christ not by Giotto but such as one might see in an old psalter, or else, in a study of the church of St. Mark, not to describe any of its important features but to devote numerous pages to the description of a bas-relief which one would never notice, or would distinguish with difficulty, and which besides is of no interest; but these are defects of Ruskin's mind which his admirers recognize with pleasure when encountering them because they know that, even though these are mannerisms, they are an integral part of the particular physiognomy of a great writer.

It remains for me to express my most profound gratitude, from among so many persons whose advice has been valuable to me, to Mr. Alfred Valette, who has given this edition infinitely generous and competent attention that does him the greatest honor; to Mr. Charles Ephrussi, who with his usual thoughtfulness has facilitated all my research by putting at my disposal the library of the *Gazette des Beaux-Arts,* and to Mr. Robert d'Humières. Whenever I was puzzled by a linguistic difficulty, I would consult the remarkable translator of Kipling, and he would immediately resolve the problem with his astonishing understanding of English texts, into which his intuition as much as his erudition enters. Thus was he often and tirelessly helpful to me. I offer him here my affectionate thanks.

II. Notre-Dame d'Amiens According to Ruskin [1]

I would like to give the reader the desire and the means to spend a day in Amiens on a sort of Ruskinian pilgrimage. It is not worth the trouble to begin by asking him to go to Florence or Venice when Ruskin has written a whole book on Amiens. [2] On the other hand, it seems to me that it is thus that the "cult of the Heroes" should be celebrated—I mean in spirit and in truth. We visit the place where a great man was born and the place where he died; but does he not inhabit even more the places he admired above all others, whose beauty is the very thing we love in his books?

We honor with a fetishism which is no more than a delusion a tomb in which there lies merely that part of Ruskin which was not his [essential] self, and yet we would not go to kneel before the stones of Amiens, to which he came seeking ideas and which preserve them still, like those of a tomb in England where only the heart remains of a poet whose body had been consumed—snatched from the flames in a sublime and tender gesture by another poet. [3]

No doubt snobbery, which makes everything it touches seem reasonable, has not yet reached these aesthetic excursions (for the French at least) and has thereby saved them from ridicule. Say that you are going to Beyreuth to hear an opera by Wagner, to Amsterdam to visit an exposition, and people will regret not being able to accompany you. But if you admit that you are going to see a storm at the Pointe du Raz, apple trees in bloom in Normandy, a statue at Amiens beloved by Ruskin, people cannot keep from smiling. I hope, nevertheless, that you will go to Amiens after reading this.

When we work in order to please others, we may fail to succeed, but the things we have done to satisfy ourselves always have a chance of interesting someone else. It is impossible that there should be no one who takes any pleasure in what has given me so much. For no one is unique, and fortunately for the sympathy and understanding which are such great pleasures in our life, our individualities are shaped within a universal framework. If we could analyze the soul as we analyze matter, we would see that under the apparent diversity of minds as well as of things there are but a few simple substances and irreducible elements, and that into the composition of what we believe to be our personality enter elements that are quite common and that are met again to some degree everywhere in the universe.

The indications that writers give us in their works of the places they have loved are often so vague that the pilgrimages we try to make there inherit from them something uncertain and hesitating, as though we feared a certain deception. Like Edmond de Goncourt's character searching for a tomb which was unmarked by a cross, we are reduced to praying at random. This is a kind of disappointment you will not have to fear with Ruskin, particularly at Amiens; you will not run the risk of coming to spend an afternoon there without knowing how to find him in the cathedral: he has come to fetch you at the railway station. He will find out not only how capable you are of appreciating the beauties of the cathedral but also how much time the train you plan to take for your return trip will allow you to devote to them. He will not only show you the way which leads to Notre-Dame but will also indicate alternative routes, according to how much of a hurry you may be in. And since he wants you to follow him in the carefree frame of mind which comes from satisfaction of the body, perhaps also in order to show you that in the manner of the saints whom he prefers he is not contemptuous of "honest" pleasure,[4] before taking you to the church he will lead you to the pastry cook's. If you should stop at Amiens with an aesthetic purpose in mind, you are already welcome, for many do not do as you do; "The intelligent English traveller, in this fortunate age for him, is aware that, half-way between Boulogne and Paris, there is a complex railway-station, into which his train, in its relaxing speed, rolls him with many more than the average number of bangs and bumps prepared, in the access of every important French *gare,* to startle the drowsy or distrait passenger into a sense of his situation. He probably also remembers that at this halting-place in mid-journey there is a well-served buffet, at which he has the privilege of 'Dix minutes d'arrêt.' He is not, however, always so distinctly conscious that these ten minutes of arrest are granted to him within not so many minutes' walk of the central square of a city which was once the Venice of France. Putting the lagoon islands out of question, the French River-Queen is nearly as large in compass as Venice herself," etc. {1:1–2; *CW* 33:25}

But enough has been said to you about the traveler for whom Amiens is only a stopping place; you, who are coming to see the cathedral and who deserve that someone see to it your time is well spent, you will be escorted to Notre-Dame, but by which route?

"I have never been able to make up my mind which was really the best way of approaching the cathedral for the first time. If you have plenty of leisure, and the day is fine,[5] the really right thing to do is to walk down the main street of the old town, and cross the river, and proceed quite out to the chalk hill out of which the citadel is half quarried. Hence you will understand the real height and relation of tower and town, then, returning, find your way by any narrow streets or chance bridges you can—the more winding and dirty the streets, the better; and whether you come first on the west front or apse,[6] you will think them worth all the trouble you have had to reach them.

"But if the day be dismal, as it may sometimes be, even in France, or if you cannot or will not walk, which may also chance, for all our athletics and lawn-tennis,—or if you must really go to Paris this

afternoon, and only mean to see all you can in an hour or two,—
then, supposing that, notwithstanding these weaknesses, you are
still a nice sort of person, for whom it is of some consequence which
way you come to a pretty thing, or begin to look at it—I think the
best way is to walk up the Street of Three Pebbles. Stop a little as you
go, so as to get into a cheerful temper, and buy some bonbons or
tarts in one of the charming patissiers' shops on the left. Just past
them, ask for the theatre and go straight up to the south transept,
which has really something about it to please everybody. Everybody
must like the transparent fretwork of the flèche above, which seems
to bend to the west wind,—though it doesn't—at least, the bend-
ing is a long habit, gradually yielded into, with grace and sub-
missiveness, during the last three hundred years. And, coming
quite up to the porch, everybody must like the pretty French
Madonna in the middle of it, with her head a little aside, and her
nimbus a little aside, too, like a becoming bonnet. A Madonna in
decadence she is, though, for all, or rather by reason of all, her
prettiness, and her gay soubrette's smile; and she has no business
there either, for this is St. Honoré's porch, not hers; and grim and
grey St. Honoré used to stand there to receive you,—he is banished
now to the north porch, where nobody ever goes in. This was done
long ago, in the fourteenth-century days, when the people first
began to find Christianity too serious, and devised a merrier faith for
France, and would have bright-glancing, soubrette Madonnas everywhere—letting their own dark-eyed Joan of Arc be burned for a
witch. And thenceforward, things went their merry way, straight
on, 'ça allait, ça ira,' to the merriest days of the guillotine. But they
could still carve, in the fourteenth century, and the Madonna and
her hawthorn-blossom lintel are worth your looking at,—and even
more the sculptures, just as delicate and more calm, that are above
and tell St. Honoré's own story, little talked of now in the faubourg
in Paris that bears his name.

"But you will be impatient to go into the church. Put a sou in
every beggar's box who asks it there,—it is none of your business
whether they should be there or not, nor whether they deserve to

have the sou,—be sure only that you yourself deserve to have it to give; and give it prettily, and not as if it burnt your fingers." [4:6–8; *CW* 33:126–29, with minor emendations by Proust.]

It is this second itinerary, the simplest one and, I suppose, the one you will prefer, that I followed the first time I went to Amiens; and the moment I caught sight of the south portal, I saw in front of me, on the left, at the same place indicated by Ruskin, the beggars he talks about, and so old that perhaps they were still the same ones. Happy to begin following Ruskinian directions so quickly, I went first of all to give them alms, with the delusion, into which entered some of that fetichism I was blaming just now, that I was performing a lofty act of piety toward Ruskin. I thought I felt him directing my gesture, a partner in my charity, with a half share in my offering. I knew, at less expense, the state of mind of Frédéric Moreau in *l'Education sentimentale,* when on the boat, in the presence of Mme. Arnoux, he extends his closed hand toward the cap of the harpist and "opening it with bashfulness" drops a twenty-franc coin into it. "It was not," says Flaubert, "vanity that urged him to give these alms in front of her, but a consecrated thought of which he made her a party, an almost religious impulse of the heart."

Then, being too close to the portal to see its general effect, I retraced my steps, and having arrived at the distance I thought proper, only then did I look. The day was splendid, and I had arrived at the hour when the sun, at this time of year, pays its daily visit to the Virgin, once gilded and which the sun alone gilds today during the moments when it restores to her, on the days when it shines, a different, fleeting, and sweeter brilliance. Besides, there is no saint the sun does not visit, giving to the shoulders of one a mantle of warmth, to the face of another a halo of light. It never ends its day without having gone all around the immense cathedral. It was the hour of its visit to the Virgin, and it was to its momentary caress that she seemed to direct her centuries-old smile, the smile which Ruskin considers, as you have seen, that of a soubrette, to which he prefers the queens of the royal porch of Chartres, [examples] of a more unaffected and more serious art. Here I refer the reader to the

pages of *The Two Paths,* which I have mentioned farther on in a note
[. . .], and in which Ruskin compares the Vierge Dorée to the
queens of Chartres. If I allude to it here it is because, *The Two Paths*
dating from 1858 and *The Bible of Amiens* from 1885, a comparison
of the texts and the dates shows how much *The Bible of Amiens* differs
from all those books which we write on matters we have studied in
order to talk about them (supposing that we have even taken that
trouble) rather than talking of those things which we have long been
studying to satisfy a disinterested taste, never dreaming that they
might later be the subject of a book. I thought you would prefer *The
Bible of Amiens,* feeling that as you leafed through it you were
becoming aware that here were things upon which Ruskin meditated continually, those things which therefore express most profoundly his thought; that the gift he was making to you was one of
those which are most precious to those who love, and which consist
of objects one has used a long time oneself, and only for oneself, with
no intention of ever parting with them. In writing his book, Ruskin
did not have to labor for you; he merely divulged his recollections
and opened his heart to you. I thought that the Vierge Dorée would
acquire some importance in your eyes when you saw that almost
thirty years before *The Bible of Amiens* she had a place in Ruskin's
memory where, when he needed to give an example to his listeners,
he knew he could find her, full of grace and endowed with those
solemn thoughts which he often sought out in her presence. Even
then she already numbered among those manifestations of beauty
which not only gave to his sensitive eyes a more vivid delight than he
had ever known, but by which Nature, in giving him this aesthetic
orientation, had predestined him to go forth and seek, as in her most
moving expression, all that can be gathered together on earth of the
True and the Divine.

No doubt, if, as has been asserted, Ruskin's mind wandered in
his extreme old age (as with that mysterious bird which in Gustave
Moreau's famous painting does not wait for the arrival of death to
flee the house), among the familiar forms that still ran through the
confused reverie of the aged man without his being able to reflect

upon them as they passed by, the Vierge Dorée must surely have been present. Maternal again, as the sculptor of Amiens portrayed her, holding the divine child in her arms, she must have been like the nurse whom alone the one she rocked in the cradle for so long allows to remain at his bedside. And as old people experience their last pleasures almost without realizing it, in their contact with familiar pieces of furniture and in the tasting of well-loved dishes, joys recognizable as such only by the often fatal pain they would suffer if deprived of these, so Ruskin must have felt an obscure pleasure at beholding the casting of the Vierge Dorée, lowered by the invincible forces of time from the heights of his thought and the inclinations of his taste into the depths of his unconscious existence and the satisfactions of habit.

There with her unique smile, which not only makes a person of the Virgin, but an individual work of art of the statue, she seems to dismiss this doorway out of which she leans as being merely the museum to which we must go to see her, as foreigners must go to the Louvre to see the Mona Lisa. But if the cathedrals, as has been said, are the museums of the religious art of the Middle Ages, they are living museums with which Mr. André Hallays* would find no fault. They were not constructed for the purpose of housing works of art, but it is the works of art—however individual they may be— that were made for them and could not without sacrilege (I am speaking only of aesthetic sacrilege) be placed anywhere else. There with her unique smile, how I love the Vierge Dorée, with her smile of the mistress of the celestial mansion; how I love her welcome at this door of the cathedral in her simple and exquisite adornment of hawthorn. Like the rosebushes, the lilies, and the fig trees of another porch, this sculptured hawthorn is still in bloom. But this medieval springtime, prolonged for so long, will not be eternal, and the wind of the centuries has already stripped from the front of the church, as on the solemn day of a Corpus Christi without fragrance, some of its

---

*Ed. note: Born in 1859, Hallays was an art critic and historian whose two best-known books are on Avignon and Nancy in the series Les Villes d'Art.

stone roses. One day, no doubt, the smile of the Vierge Dorée (which has already, however, lasted longer than our faith)[7] will also cease, because of the erosion of the stones which it gracefully scatters, to spread beauty for our children, as it once poured out courage to our believing fathers. I feel I was wrong to call it a work of art: a statue that is thus forever part of a particular place on earth, of a certain city, that is to say a thing which has a name as a person has, which is an individual, of which no other exactly alike can ever be found on the face of the continents, of which even the railway employees at the place where we must inevitably come in order to see it, in announcing its name seem unwittingly to tell us: "Love that which you will never see twice"*—such a statue perhaps has something less universal than a work of art; it holds us, at any rate, by a tie stronger than that of the work of art itself, one of those ties such as persons and countries hold us by. The Mona Lisa is the Mona Lisa of [da] Vinci. Without wishing to offend Mr. Hallays, what does her birthplace matter to us, what does it even matter to us that she is naturalized French?—She is rather like a wonderful woman "without a country." Nowhere where thoughtful looks meet hers could she ever be a "displaced person." We cannot say as much of her smiling and sculptured sister, the Vierge Dorée (need we say, moreover, how inferior she is?). Coming no doubt from the quarries near Amiens, having made only the one trip in her youth to come to the porch of Saint Honoré, not having moved since, having been weather-beaten little by little by the damp wind of the Venice of the North which bent the spire above her, gazing for so many centuries on the inhabitants of this city of whom she is the oldest and most sedentary,[8] she is truly an Amiénoise. She is not a work of art. She is a beautiful friend we must leave at the melancholy provincial square from which no one has ever succeeded in taking her away, and where, for eyes other than ours, she will continue to receive directly on her face the wind and sun of Amiens and to let the little sparrows

---

*Ed. note: "Aimez ce que jamais on ne verra deux fois." The line is from Alfred de Vigny's *La Maison du Berger*.

alight with a sure instinct of scenic effect in the hollow of her welcoming hand, or pick at the stone stamens of the antique hawthorn that has been her youthful attire for so many centuries. In my room a photograph of the Mona Lisa retains only the beauty of a masterpiece. Near her a photograph of the Vierge Dorée takes on the sadness of a souvenir. But let us not wait until, followed by its countless retinue of rays and shadows resting on the relief of the stone, the sun has ceased to silver the gray old porch, at once sparkling and tarnished. It has been too long since we lost sight of Ruskin. We had left him at the feet of this same virgin, before whom he will have waited with patient forbearance till we had addressed our personal homage to her in our own way. Let us enter the cathedral with him.

"We cannot enter it to better advantage than by this south door. For all cathedrals of any mark have nearly the same effect when you enter at the west door; but I know no other which shows so much of its nobleness from the south interior transept; the opposite rose is exquisite and lovely, and the shafts of the transept aisles forming a wonderful group with those of the choir and nave; also, the apse shows its height better, as it opens to you when you advance from the transept into the mid-nave. Looking from the west end of the nave, however, it is just possible for an irreverent person to think the nave narrow, than the apse high. And if you have no wonder in you for that choir and its encompassing circlet of light, when you look up into it from the cross-centre, you need not travel farther in search of cathedrals, for the waiting-room of any station is a better place for you;—but, if it amaze you and delight you at first, then, the more you know of it, the more it will amaze. For it is not possible for imagination and mathematics together, to do anything nobler or stronger than that procession of windows, with material of glass and stone—nor anything which shall look loftier.

"Whatever you wish to see, or are forced to leave unseen, at Amiens, if the overwhelming responsibilities of your existence, and the inevitable necessities of precipitate locomotion have left you so much as one quarter of an hour, not out of breath, for the contemplation of the capital of Picardy, give it wholly to the cathedral choir. Aisles and porches, lancet windows and roses, you can see elsewhere as well as here—but such carpenter's work, you cannot. It is fully developed flamboyant just past the fifteenth century, and has some Flemish stolidity mixed with the playing French fire of it; but wood-carving was Picardy's joy; and so far as I know, there is nothing else so beautiful cut out of the goodly trees of the world.

"Sweet and young-grained wood it is: oak, trained and chosen for such work, sound* now as four hundred years since. Under the carver's hand it seems to cut like clay, to fold like silk, to grow like living branches, to leap like living flame, . . . and it shoots and wreathes itself into an enchanted glade, inextricable, imperishable, fuller of leafage than any forest, and fuller of story than any book."9 [4:8, 5; *CW* 33:129–130, 125]

Now famous the world over, reproduced in museums by castings which the attendants will not allow to be touched, these choir stalls, so old, so illustrious, and so beautiful continue to exercise in Amiens their modest functions as choir stalls, as they have been doing for several centuries to the great satisfaction of the Amiénois—like those artists who, having achieved glory, continue nevertheless to hold some trifling post or to give lessons. These functions consist, even before the instructing of souls, of providing support for the body; and to that end, turned down for each service and showing their backs, they devote themselves upretentiously.

Through continual rubbing, the wood of these stalls has little by little taken on, or rather revealed, the dark purple which is at its heart and which the eye that was once enchanted by it prefers to all else—to the point, even, where it can no longer look at the colors of paintings, finding these coarse by comparison. It is then with a kind of intoxication that one enjoys the glow of that wood, ever more vivid, which is like the sap of the living tree overflowing with the passage of time. The simplicity of the figures sculpted here seems to take on, from the material in which they live, a certain

---

*Ed. note: Proust has "qui résonne," i.e., "which resounds."

quality which makes them doubly natural. And as for "those fruits, those flowers, those leaves and those branches," all motifs taken from the local vegetation, which the Amiénois sculptor carved from Amiens wood, the diversity of the planes here having resulted in different degrees of chafing in the wood, one sees some wonderful contrasts of color—as where a leaf stands out in a shade other than that of its stem, recalling those lofty strains which Mr. Gallé* could evoke from the melodious heart of oak trees.

But it is time to arrive at what Ruskin refers to in particular as the Bible of Amiens, the West Porch. "Bible" is taken here in the literal and not the figurative sense. This porch of Amiens is not merely a stone book, a stone Bible, in the vague sense in which Victor Hugo[10] would have understood it: it is "the Bible" in stone. No doubt, before you realize this, when you see the western façade of Amiens for the first time, blue in the mist, brilliant in the morning, sunsoaked and sumptuously gilded in the afternoon, rosy and already softly nocturnal at sunset, at whatever hours its bells ring out in the skies as Claude Monet has captured them on his sublime canvases,[11] where this creation of man reveals its very life, yet which nature has reclaimed by enveloping it, a cathedral, whose life, like that of the earth in its double revolution, unfolds down the centuries while renewing itself and maturing daily—at that moment, if you release it from the changing colors in which nature clothes it, you will receive in front of this façade a confused but powerful impression. Upon seeing this colossal and lacelike swarming of human figures in stone which rise skyward, holding their crosses in their hands, their banderoles or scepters, this company of saints, these generations of prophets, this train of apostles, this host of kings, this line of sinners, this assembly of judges, this flight of angels, side by side, one above the other, standing near the door and looking down at the city from the niches high above or from the ledge of the even higher galleries, receiving only the vague and dazzled looks of the

*Ed. note: Emile Gallé (1846–1904) was a well-known glass and furniture designer.

men at the foot of the towers, you feel, at the ringing out of the bells, and no doubt in the warmth of your emotion, that this magnificent pile, motionless and thrilling, is a stirring sight. But a cathedral is not only a beauty to be felt. Even if it is no longer for you a teaching to be followed, it is at least still a book to be understood. The porch of a Gothic cathedral, and more particularly the porch of Amiens, the Gothic cathedral par excellence, is the Bible. Before I explain it to you I would like, with the help of a quotation from Ruskin, to make you understand that, whatever your beliefs may be, the Bible is something real, of the present, and we have to find in it something else besides the flavor of its archaism and the entertainment of our curiosity.

"The 1st, 8th, 12th, 15th, 19th, 23rd, and 24th psalms, well learned and believed, are enough for all personal guidance and have in them the law and the prophecy of all righteous government: and every real triumph of natural science is anticipated in the 104th. Consider what other group of historic or didactic literature has a range comparable with that of the Bible.

"Think if you can match that table of contents in any other—I do not say 'book' but 'literature.' Think, so far as it is possible for any of us—either adversary or defender of the faith—to extricate his intelligence from the habit and the association of moral sentiment based upon the Bible, what literature could have taken its place, or fulfilled its function, though every library in the world had remained unravaged? I am no despiser of profane literature. So far from it, that I believe no interpretations of Greek religion have ever been so affectionate, none of Roman religion so reverent, as those which will be found at the base of my art teaching, and current through the entire body of my works. But it was from the Bible that I learned the symbols of Homer, and the faith of Horace: the duty enforced upon me in early youth of reading every word of the gospels and prophecies as if written by the hand of God, gave me the habit of awed attention which afterwards made many passages of profane literature, frivolous to an irreligious reader, deeply grave to me.

"That there is a Sacred classic literature, running parallel with that of the Hebrews, and coalescing in the symbolic legends of medieval Christendom, is shown in the most tender and impressive way by the independent, yet similar, influence of Virgil upon Dante, and upon Bishop Gawaine Douglas. And the story of the Nemean Lion, with the aid of Athena in its conquest, is the real root-stock of the legend of St. Jerome's companion, conquered by the healing gentleness of the Spirit of Life. I call it a legend only. Whether Heracles ever slew, or St. Jerome ever cherished, the wild or wounded creature, is of no moment to us. But the legend of St. Jerome takes up the prophecy of the Millennium, and foretells, with the Cumaean Sibyl, and with Isaiah, a day when the Fear of Man shall be laid in benediction, not enmity, on inferior beings, when they shall not hurt or destroy in all the holy Mountain, and the Peace of the Earth shall be as far removed from its present sorrow, as the present gloriously animate universe from the nascent desert, whose deeps were the places of dragons, and its mountains, domes of fire.

"Of that day knoweth no man; but the Kingdom of God is already come to those who have tamed in their own hearts what was rampant of the lower nature, and have learned to cherish what is lovely and human, in the wandering children of the clouds and fields. Dated Avallon, August 28, 1882." [3:50–54; *CW* 33:117–20]

And perhaps now you will be willing to follow the résumé of the Bible written at the west porch of Amiens, which I am going to try to give you according to Ruskin.

At the center is the statue of Christ which is, not in the figurative but in the literal sense, the cornerstone of the structure. To His left (that is, to the right for us who are facing the Christ as we look at the porch, but we shall use the terms *left* and *right* with regard to the statue of Christ), six apostles: near Him Peter, then beyond Him James the Greater, John, Matthew, Simon. To His right Paul, then James the bishop, Philip, Bartholomew, Thomas, and Jude.[12] Following the apostles are the four major prophets. After Simon, Isaiah and Jeremiah; after Jude, Ezekiel and Daniel; then, on the piers of the entire west façade, come the twelve minor prophets, three on each of the four piers, and beginning with the pier farther to the left: Hosea, Joel, Amos, Micah, Jonah, Obadiah, Nahum, Habakkuk, Zephaniah, Haggai, Zechariah, Malachi. So that the cathedral, always in the literal sense, rests on Christ and on the prophets who foretold Him as well as on the apostles who declared Him. The prophets of Christ and not those of God the Father:

"The voice of the entire building is that of Heaven at the Transfiguration, 'This is my beloved Son, hear ye Him.' Though Moses was an apostle not of Christ but of God, though Elijah was a prophet not of Christ but of God, they are not here." But, exclaims Ruskin, "There is yet another and greater prophet still, who, as it seems at first, is not here. Shall the people enter the gates of the temple, singing 'Hosanna to the Son of David'; and see no image of His father, then?—Christ himself declare, 'I am the root and the offspring of David'; and yet the Root have no sign near it of its Earth? Not so, David and his Son are together. David is the pedestal of the Christ. He holds his sceptre in his right hand, the scroll in his left.

"Of the statue of Christ, itself, I will not speak here at any length, as no sculpture would satisfy, or ought to satisfy, the hope of any loving soul that has learned to trust Him; but at the time it was beyond what till then had been reached in sculptured tenderness; and was known far and near as the 'Beau Dieu d'Amiens.' Yet understood, observe, just as clearly to be no more than a symbol of the Heavenly Presence and not an idol, in our sense of the word— only a letter, or sign of the Living Spirit,—which, however, was indeed conceived by every worshipper as here meeting him at the temple gate: the Word of Life, the King of Glory, and the Lord of Hosts. 'Dominus Virtutum,' 'Lord of Virtues,' is the best single rendering of the idea conveyed to a well-taught disciple in the thirteenth century by the words of the twenty-fourth Psalm." [4:30–36; *CW* 33:144–48]

We cannot stop at each of the statues of the west porch. Ruskin will explain to you the meaning of the bas-reliefs placed below them (two quatrefoil bas-reliefs, one under the other below each of them), the upper one under each apostle representing the virtue he taught or manifested in his life, the lower one, the opposite vice. Under the prophets the bas-reliefs represent their prophecies.

Under St. Peter is Courage with a leopard on its shield; under Courage, Cowardice is depicted as a man who, frightened by an animal, drops his sword, while a bird sings on, "The coward has not the heart of a thrush." Under St. Andrew is Patience, whose shield bears a bull on it (never retreating).

Under Patience, Anger: a woman stabbing a man with a sword (anger being essentially a feminine vice which has no connection with indignation). Under St. James, Gentleness, whose shield bears a lamb, and Rudeness, a woman kicking over her cupbearer, "the forms of ultimate French rudeness being in the gesture of the cancan."

Under St. John, Love, divine Love, not human love: "I in them, and thou in me." Its shield bears a tree with branches grafted onto a cut-off trunk: "In those days shall Messiah be cut off, but not for Himself." [4:41; *CW* 33:153] Under Love, Discord: a man and a woman quarreling; she has dropped her distaff. Under St. Matthew, Obedience. On its shield, a camel: "Today the most disobedient and ill-tempered of all serviceable beasts," says Ruskin, "but the northern sculptor knew little of its character. Since, in spite of all, it spends its life in the most painful of services, I think he has chosen it as the symbol of passive obedience, without joy or sympathy, such as the horse, and on the other hand incapable of hurting, such as the ox. It is true that its bite is dangerous enough, but it is very probable that this was not known in Amiens, even by the Crusaders, who would ride their horses only, or nothing." [4:41; *CW* 33:153]

Under Obedience, Rebellion, a man snapping his fingers in front of his bishop "(as Henry VIII before the Pope and the English and French cockneys before all priests whatever)."

Under St. Simon, Perseverance caresses a lion and holds its crown. "Hold fast that which thou hast, that no man take thy crown." [4:41; *CW* 33:154] Below, Atheism leaves its shoes at the church door. "The infidel fool is always represented, in the XIIth and

XIIIth centuries, as barefoot, Christ having his feet shod with the preparation of the gospel of Peace. 'How beautiful are thy feet with shoes, oh Prince's Daughter.'" [4:41; *CW* 33:154]

Under St. Paul is Faith. Under Faith is Idolatry, worshiping a monster. Under St. James the bishop is Hope, holding a standard with crown; under Hope, Despair, stabbing herself.

Under St. Philip is Charity, giving a mantle to a naked beggar.

Under St. Bartholomew, Chastity with the phoenix, and under [Chastity], Lust, represented by a young man kissing a woman holding a scepter and a mirror. Under St. Thomas, Wisdom (a shield with an edible root meaning temperance as the beginning of wisdom). Under [Wisdom], Folly: the type used in all early psalters of a glutton armed with a club. "The fool has said in his heart: 'There is no God, he devours my people as a piece of bread.'" (Psalm LIII, quoted by Mr. Mâle). Under St. Jude, Humility, bearing a shield with a dove, and Pride, falling from its horse. [Cf. 4:41; *CW* 33:155] "Note," says Ruskin, "that the Apostles are all tranquil, nearly all with books, some with crosses, but all with the same message: 'That peace be in this house and if the Son of Peace be there,' etc. But the prophets—all seeking, or wistful, or tormented, or wondering, or praying, except Daniel. The most tormented is Isaiah. No scene of his martyrdom is depicted, but the bas-relief under him shows him seeing the Lord in his temple, and yet feeling he has unclean lips. Jeremiah also carries his cross—but more serenely." [4:38; *CW* 33:148–49]

Unfortunately, we cannot stop at the bas-reliefs under the prophets which depict the verses of their chief prophecies: Ezekiel sitting before two wheels,[13] Daniel holding a book supported by lions,[14] then, sitting at Belshazzar's feast, the fig-tree and the leafless vine, the sun and the moon lightless as prophesied by Joel,[15] Amos gathering the leaves of the unfruitful vine, to feed the sheep, who find no grass,[16] Jonah, escaping from the sea, then sitting under a gourd, Habakkuk, whom an angel holds by the hair to visit Daniel, who strokes a young lion,[17] the prophesies of Zephaniah; the beasts of Nineveh, the Lord with a lantern in each hand, the hedgehog and bittern,[18] etc. [Cf. 4:39; *CW* 33:149–50]

I do not have time to take you to the two secondary doors of the west porch, the one of the Virgin[19] (which contains, beside the statue of the Virgin: to her left, the statues of the angel Gabriel, the Virgin Annunciate, the Virgin Visitant, St. Elizabeth, the Virgin presenting the Child seen by St. Simeon, and to the right, the three Magi-Kings, Herod, Solomon, and the Queen of Sheba, under each statue, as under those of the main porch, are bas-reliefs whose subjects relate to each)—and the door of St. Firmin, which contains the statues of the saints of the Diocese. No doubt it is because of this, because they are "friends of the Amiénois," that the bas-reliefs under them represent the signs of the zodiac and the labors of the months, that Ruskin admires them above all. You will find castings of these bas-reliefs of the porch of St. Firmin[20] in the Museum of the Trocadéro, and, in Mr. Mâle's book, charming commentaries on the local and climatic truth of these little genre scenes.

"But into questions respecting the art of these bas-reliefs," says Ruskin, "I do not here attempt to enter. They were never intended to serve as more than guides of thought. And if the reader follows this guidance quietly, he may create for himself better pictures in his heart; and at all events may recognize these following truths, as their united message.

"First, that throughout the sermon on this Amiens Mount, Christ never appears, or is for a moment thought of, as the Crucified, nor as the Dead: but as the Incarnate Word—as the present Friend—as the Prince of Peace on Earth,—and as the Everlasting King in Heaven. What His life is, what His commands are, and what His judgment will be, are the things here taught: not what He once did, nor what He once suffered, but what He is now doing—and what He requires us to do. That is the pure, joyful, beautiful lesson of Christianity; and the fall from that faith, and the corruptions of its abortive practice, may be summed briefly as the habitual contemplation of Christ's death instead of His life, and the substitution of His past suffering for our present duty.

"Then, secondly, though Christ bears not His cross, in the mourning prophets,—the persecuted apostles—and the martyred disciples do bear theirs. For just as it is well for you to remember what your undying Creator is doing for you—it is well for you to remember what your dying fellow-creatures have done: the Creator you may at your pleasure deny or defy—the Martyr you can only forget; deny, you cannot. Every stone of this building is cemented with His blood.

"Keeping, then, these things in your heart, look back now to the central statue of Christ, and hear His message with understanding. He holds the book of the Eternal Law in His left hand; with His right He blesses,—but blesses on condition. 'This do, and thou shalt live;' nay, in stricter and more piercing sense, This be, and thou shalt live: to show mercy is nothing—thy soul must be full of mercy; to be pure in act is nothing—thou shalt be pure in heart also.

"And with this further word of the unabolished law—'This if thou do not, this if thou art not, thou shalt die.' Die (whatever meaning you would give the word)—totally and irrevocably.

"The Life, and Gospel, and Power of it, are all written in the mighty works of its true believers: in Normandy and Sicily, on river islets of France and in the river glens of England, on the rocks of Orvieto, and by the sands of Arno. But of all, the simplest, completest, and most authoritative in its lessons to the active mind of North Europe, is this on the foundation stones of Amiens.

"All human creatures, in all ages and places of the world, who have had warm affections, common sense and self-command, have been, and are, Naturally Moral. The knowledge and enforcement of those things have nothing to do with religion.

"But if, loving well the creatures that are like yourself, you feel that you would love still more dearly, creatures better than yourself—were they revealed to you;—if striving with all your might to mend what is evil, near you and around, you would fain look for a day when some Judge of all the Earth shall wholly do right, and the little hills rejoice on every side; if, parting with the companions that have given you all the best joy you had on earth, you desire ever to meet their eyes again and clasp their hands,—where eyes shall no more be dim, nor hands fail;—if, preparing yourselves to lie down beneath the grass in silence and loneliness, seeing no more beauty, and feeling no more gladness—you would care for the promise to you of a time when you should see God's light again, and know the things you have longed to know, and walk in the peace of everlasting Love—then, the Hope of these things to you is religion, the substance of them in your life is Faith. And in the power of them, it is promised us, that the kingdoms of this world shall yet become the kingdoms of our Lord and of His Christ." [4:51–55, 57, 59–60; *CW* 33:169–74]

Here ends the teaching that men of the thirteenth century came to seek at the cathedral, a teaching which, with a useless and bizarre luxury, it continues to offer in a kind of open book, written in a solemn language where each letter is a work of art, a language no longer understood. Giving it a meaning less literally religious than during the Middle Ages or even an aesthetic meaning only, you have been able, nevertheless, to relate it to one of those feelings that appear to us as the true reality beyond our lives, to one of "those stars to which it is well that we hitch our wagon."* Not appreciating until then the import of religious art in the Middle Ages, I had said to myself, in my enthusiasm for Ruskin: He will teach me, for he too, in some portion at least, is he not the truth? He will make my spirit enter where it had no access, for he is the door. He will purify me, for his inspiration is like the lily of the valley. He will intoxicate me and will give me life, for he is the vine and the life. Indeed, I have felt that the mystic perfume of the rose trees of Sharon has not vanished forever, since one still breathes it, at least in his words. And now indeed the stones of Amiens have acquired for me the dignity of the stones of Venice, and almost the grandeur the Bible had, when it was still the truth in the hearts of men and solemn beauty in their works. *The Bible of Amiens* was intended by Ruskin to be but the first book of a series entitled *Our Fathers Have Told Us,* and

---

*Ed. note: Compare Emerson: "Now that is the vision of man, in every instance of his labor, to hitch his wagon to a star, and see his chore done by the gods themselves." *Civilization* in *The Complete Works of Ralph Waldo Emerson* (Boston and New York: Houghton Mifflin Company, 1922), p. 28.

in fact if the old prophets of the porch of Amiens were sacred for Ruskin, it was because the soul of the thirteenth-century artists was still in them. Even before knowing whether I would find it, it was the soul of Ruskin I went to seek there, which he imparted to the stones of Amiens as deeply as their sculptors had imparted theirs, for the words of genius can give, as well as does the chisel, an immortal form to things. Literature, too, is a "lamp of sacrifice," consuming itself to light the coming generations. I was complying unconsciously with the spirit of the title, *Our Fathers Have Told Us,* when I went to Amiens with these thoughts and with the desire to read the Bible of Ruskin there. For Ruskin, having believed in those men of another time because in them was faith and beauty, also happened to write his Bible as they had written theirs, believing in the prophets and apostles. For Ruskin, the statues of Jeremiah, Ezekiel, and Amos perhaps no longer had exactly the same meaning as they had for the sculptors of the past; yet they were at least works full of instruction from great artists and men of faith, and the eternal meaning of forgotten prophecies. For us, if their being the work of those artists and the meaning of these words are no longer sufficient to make them precious, let them at least be for us the things in which Ruskin found this spirit, the brother of his own and father of ours. Before we arrived at the cathedral, was it not for us above all the one he had loved? And did we not feel that there were such things as the Holy Scriptures, since we were reverently looking for Truth in his books? And now we stop in vain before the statues of Isaiah, Jeremiah, Ezekiel, and Daniel, saying to ourselves, "Here are the four great prophets, and the other prophets after them are minor, for there are only four great prophets," there is one more who is not here and of whom, moreover, we cannot say that he is absent, for we see him everywhere. It is Ruskin: if his statue is not at the cathedral door,[21] it is at the entrance to our heart. That prophet's voice is no longer heard. But it is because he has finished uttering his words. It is for the coming generations to take them up again in chorus.

III. *John Ruskin*

Like *The Muses Leaving Apollo Their Father to Enlighten the World*,[22] the ideas of Ruskin had one by one left the sublime head that carried and incarnated them in living books and had gone forth to teach the nations. Ruskin had retired into that solitude where prophetic beings often go until it pleases God to call to Himself the cenobite or the ascetic whose superhuman task is finished. And one can only guess, through the veil held by pious hands, the mystery which was being accomplished, the slow destruction of a perishable brain that had sheltered an immortal legacy.

Today, death has let humanity take possession of the immense legacy left by Ruskin. For the man of genius cannot give birth to immortal works except by creating them in the image, not of his mortal being, but of the humanity he bears within himself. His thoughts are, in a way, lent to him for his lifetime, of which they are the companions. At his death they return to humanity and teach it. It is like that imposing and familiar dwelling on the rue de la Rochefoucauld that was called Gustave Moreau's house so long as he lived and that has been called, since he died, the Gustave Moreau Museum.

For a long time there has been a John Ruskin Museum.[23] Its catalogue is a summary of all the arts and of all the sciences. Adjoining each other are photographs of paintings by masters and collections of minerals, as in Goethe's house. Like the Ruskin Museum, the work of Ruskin is universal. He sought the truth, and found beauty even in chronological tables and social laws. But logicians having defined the "Fine Arts"[24] in a way that excludes mineralogy as well as political economy, it is only of that part of Ruskin's work that relates to the "Fine Arts" as generally understood, of Ruskin the aesthetician and art critic that I shall have to speak here.

At first he was called a realist. And, indeed, he has often repeated that the artist must adhere to the pure imitation of nature, "without rejecting, despising, choosing anything." [*Modern Painters, CW* 3:624]

But it has also been said that he was an intellectual, because he wrote that the best painting was the one that contained the loftiest thoughts. Speaking of a group of children who, in the foreground of Turner's *Building of Carthage,* play with toy sailing boats, he concluded: "The exquisite choice of this incident, as expressive of the ruling passion which was to be the source of future greatness, is quite as appreciable when it is told as when it is seen, it has nothing to do with the technicalities of painting; a scratch of the pen would have conveyed the idea and spoken to the intellect as much as the elaborate realizations of colour. Such a thought is something far above all art: it is epic poetry of the highest order." [*Modern Painters, CW* 3:113] "Likewise," adds Milsand,[25] who quotes this passage in analyzing the *Holy Family* by Tintoretto, "the features which allowed Ruskin to recognize the great master are a ruined wall and the beginning of a new structure, by which the artist symbolically makes us understand that the birth of Christ was the end of the Jewish order and the coming of the new covenant." In a composition by the same Venetian, a *Crucifixion,* Ruskin sees a masterpiece of painting because the author, by means of the apparently insignificant incident of an ass feeding on palm leaves in the background of Calvary [cf. *Modern Painters, CW* 4:271; *Stones of Venice, CW* 11:385], knew how to assert the profound idea that "it was Jewish materialism, with its expectation of a wholly temporal Messiah, and with the confounding of its hopes at the time of the entry into Jerusalem, that had been the cause of the hatred unleashed against the Savior and hence of his death."

It has been said that he suppressed the role of imagination in art by giving too large a share to science. Did he not say that "every class of rock, every kind of earth, every form of cloud, must be studied and rendered with equal precision? . . . Every geological formation has features entirely peculiar to itself; definite lines of fracture, giving rise to fixed resultant forms of rocks and earth; peculiar vegetable products, among which still farther distinctions are wrought out by climate and elevation. In the plant, the painter observes every character of colour and form, . . . seizes on its lines of rigidity or repose, . . . observes its local habits, its love or fear of peculiar places, its nourishment or destruction by particular influences; he associates it . . . with all the features of the situation it inhabits . . ." [*Modern Painters, CW* 3:34–48] He must "render the delicate fissure, and descending curve, and undulating shadow of the mouldering soil with gentle and fine finger, like the touch of the rain itself . . ." [*Ibid., CW* 3:483] "The greatest picture is that which conveys to the mind of the spectator the greatest number of the greatest ideas." [*Ibid., CW* 3:92]

It has been said on the other hand that he ruined science by giving imagination too large a part in it. In fact, one cannot help but think of the naïve finalism of Bernardin de Saint-Pierre, who said that God had divided melons into segments so that men could eat them more easily, when one reads such pages as this: "God has employed colour in His creation as the unvarying accompaniment of all that is purest and most precious; while for things precious only in material uses, or dangerous, common colours are reserved. Look at a dove's neck, and compare it with the grey back of a viper. The crocodile and alligator are grey, but the innocent lizard green and beautiful." [*Ibid., VI,* 68]

If it has been said that he reduced art to be but a vassal of science, because he put forth the theory that a work of art should be considered as information on the nature of things, so far as to declare that "a Turner discovers more on the nature of rocks than any academy will ever know,"* and "a Tintoretto has but to let his hand go to reveal on the play of muscles a multitude of truths that will baffle all the anatomists on earth," it has also been said that he humiliated science before art [*Eagle's Nest, CW* 22:211 and *Stones of Venice, CW* 11:49–50].

---

*Ed. note: Ruskin's original in *Eagle's Nest* reads: "Turner had drawn his mountains rightly, long before their structure was known to any geologist in Europe."

Finally, it has been said that he was a pure aesthetician and that Beauty was his sole religion, because in fact he loved it all his life.

But on the other hand, it has been said that he was not even an artist, because he introduced into his appreciation of beauty considerations which were perhaps superior, but at any rate foreign to aesthetics. The first chapter of *The Seven Lamps of Architecture* prescribes to the artist the use of the most precious and durable material, and makes this duty derive from the sacrifice of Jesus, and the long-standing conditions for the sacrifice well-pleasing to God, conditions which must not be considered as abrogated, since God never informed us expressly that they were [cf. *The Seven Lamps, CW* 8:30–34]. And in *Modern Painters,* to settle the question of who is right, the partisans of color or the adepts of chiaroscuro, here is one of the arguments: "Take a wider view of nature, and compare generally rainbows, sunrises, roses, violets, butterflies, birds, goldfish, rubies, opals, and corals, with alligators, hippopotami, lions, wolves, bears, swine, sharks, slugs, bones, fungi, fogs, and corrupting, stinging, destroying things in general, and you will feel then how the question stands between the colourists and chiaroscurists, — which of them have nature and life on their side, and which have sin and death." [*Modern Painters, CW* 6:69]

And since so many contrary things have been said about Ruskin, it has been concluded that he was himself contradictory.

Of so many aspects of Ruskin's character, the one that is most familiar to us, because it is the one of which we possess (if one may so put it) the most beautiful portrait, the most studied and the most effective one, the most striking and the most famous,[26] and in fact thus far the only one,[27] is the Ruskin who during his whole life knew but one religion: that of Beauty.

That the adoration of Beauty was, in fact, the perpetual act of Ruskin's life may be true literally; but I think the aim of that life, its profound, secret, and constant intention, was something else, and if I say this, it is not to take a position contrary to Mr. de la Sizeranne's belief, but to prevent it from being depreciated in the minds of the readers by a false, but natural and almost inevitable interpretation.

Religion itself was not only Ruskin's principal religion (and I shall return to this point in a while, for it dominates and characterizes his aesthetics), but, considering for the moment only the "Religion of Beauty," we should warn our contemporaries that they cannot use this term correctly with reference to Ruskin unless they rectify the meaning that their aesthetic dilettantism is prone to give it. In fact, for an age of dilettantes and aesthetes, an adorer of Beauty is a man who practices no other cult and who, recognizing no other god, spends his life in the voluptuous contemplation of works of art.

However, for reasons whose metaphysical nature exceeds the bounds of a simple study of art, Beauty cannot be loved fruitfully if it is loved only for the pleasures it gives. Just as the pursuit of happiness for happiness' sake leads but to ennui, and as in order to find it we must look for something else, so too aesthetic pleasure is given to us in addition if we love Beauty for itself as something real existing outside of us, and infinitely more important than the joy it gives us. Far from having been a dilettante or an aesthete, Ruskin was precisely the opposite, one of those men who, like Carlyle, were warned by their genius of the vanity of pleasure and, at the same time, of the presence near them of an eternal reality, intuitively perceived by inspiration. Talent is given them as a power to relate this reality to the all-powerful and eternal to which, with enthusiasm and as if obeying a command of conscience, they dedicate their ephemeral life in order to give it some value. Such men, attentive to and eager about the universe to be explored, are made aware of the parts of reality which their special gifts provide them with a particular understanding of, by a kind of demon that guides them, a voice they hear, the eternal inspiration of men of genius. Ruskin's special gift was the feeling for beauty, in nature as in art. It was in Beauty that his nature led him to seek reality, and his entirely religious life received from it an entirely aesthetic use. But this Beauty to which he thus happened to dedicate his life was not conceived of by him as an object of enjoyment made to charm, but as a reality infinitely more important than life, for which he would have given his own life. From this, as you will see, the whole aesthetic system of Ruskin follows. First, you will understand that the years when he became acquainted with a new school of architecture or of painting were the principal landmarks in the development of his ethics. He would speak of the years when Gothic art presented itself to him with the same gravity, the same emotional nostalgia, the same serenity with which a Christian speaks of the day the truth was revealed to him. The events of his life are intellectual and the important dates are those on which he comprehends a new form of art: the year he understands Abbeville, the year he understands Rouen, the day Titian's painting and the shadows in Titian's painting appear to him as nobler than Rubens's painting, than the shadows in Rubens's painting.

You will then understand that, the poet being for Ruskin, as for Carlyle, a sort of scribe writing at nature's dictation a more or less important part of its secret, the artist's first duty is to add nothing of his own to the sublime message. From this eminence you will see vanish, like low-lying mists, the accusations of realism as well as of intellectualism levelled at Ruskin. If these objections are off the mark, it is because they do not aim high enough. There is an error of altitude in these criticisms. The reality that the artist must record is both material and intellectual. Matter is real because it is an expression of the mind. As for mere appearance, no one has ridiculed better than Ruskin those who see in its imitation the aim of art. "The simple pleasure in the imitation would be precisely of the same degree (if the accuracy could be equal), whether the subject of it were the hero or his horse. We may consider tears as the result of agony or of art, whichever we please, but not of both at the same moment. If we are surprised by them as an attainment of the one, it is impossible we can be moved by them as a sign of the other." [*Modern Painters, CW* 3:101–02] If he attaches so much importance to the aspect of things, it is because this alone reveals their deep nature. Mr. de la Sizeranne has admirably translated a page in which Ruskin shows that the principal lines of a tree indicate what other pernicious trees have come in its way and pushed it aside, what winds have tormented it, etc. The configuration of an object is not merely the image of its nature, it is the expression of its destiny and the outline of its history. [Cf. *The Elements of Drawing, CW* 15:91]

Another outcome of this conception of art is this: if reality is one and if the man of genius is he who sees it, what does it matter what medium he represents it in, be it in paintings, statues, symphonies, laws, or acts? In his *Heroes,* Carlyle does not discriminate between Shakespeare and Cromwell, between Mohammed and Burns. Emerson counts Swedenborg as well as Montaigne among his *Representative Men of Humanity.* The weakness of the system is that, because of the unity of the reality expressed, it does not differentiate deeply enough between the various modes of expression. Carlyle says it was inevitable that Boccaccio and Petrarch should be good diplomats, since they were good poets. Ruskin commits the same error when he says that "a painting is beautiful in the measure the ideas it translates into images are independent of the language of the images."* [*Modern Painters, CW* 3:89] It seems to me that if Ruskin's system errs in any direction, it is in this. For painting can attain the unique reality of things, and thus rival literature only so long as it is not literary itself.

If Ruskin has declared that the duty of the artist is to obey scrupulously those "voices" of genius which tell him what is real and must be transcribed, it is because he has himself experienced what is true in inspiration, unerring in enthusiasm, and fruitful in admiration. However, although what excites enthusiasm, what commands respect, and what arouses inspiration is different for each individual, each attributes to it a character more privately sacred. One might say that for Ruskin this revelation, this guide, was the Bible: "I would read every passage of it as if written by the hand of God. And this state of mind, fortified with the years, made many passages of the profane writers, frivolous to an irreligious reader, deeply grave to

---

*Ed. note: Ruskin's original in *Modern Painters* reads: "The art is greatest which conveys to the spectator, by any means whatsoever, the greatest number of the greatest ideas."

me. It is from the Bible that I learned the symbols of Homer, and the faith of Horace." [4:52; *CW* 33:118–19]

Let us pause here as at a fixed point, at the center of gravity of Ruskinian aesthetics. It is thus that his religious feeling directed his aesthetic feeling. To begin with, let us reply to those who might believe that his religious feeling altered his aesthetic feeling, that to the artistic appreciation of monuments, statues, and paintings he added religious considerations that had no business there, by asserting that the case was, in fact, quite to the contrary. That something of the divine which Ruskin felt was the basis of the feeling which works of art inspired in him was precisely what was profound and original in this feeling and which imposed itself on his taste without being susceptible to modification. And the religious veneration with which he expressed this feeling, his fear of distorting it in the slightest degree when translating it, prevented him, contrary to what has often been thought, from ever mixing any artifice of reasoning that would be foreign to his impression when faced with works of art. So that those who see in him a moralist and an apostle enjoying in art what is not art are as mistaken as those who, neglecting the profound essence of his aesthetic feeling, confuse it with a voluptuous dilettantism. So that, in short, his religious fervor, which had been the sign of his aesthetic sincerity, strengthened it further and protected him from any foreign encroachment. Whether some of these conceptions of his supernatural aesthetics be false is a matter which, in our opinion, is of no importance. All those who have any understanding of the laws governing the development of genius know that its force is measured more by the force of its beliefs than by what may be satisfying to common sense in the object of those beliefs. But, since Ruskin's Christianity resulted from the very essence of his intellectual nature, his artistic preferences, equally profound, must have had some relation to it. Therefore, just as the love of Turner's landscapes corresponded in Ruskin to that love of nature which gave him the greatest joys, so to the thoroughly Christian nature of his thinking corresponded his permanent attraction, which dominates his whole life and work, to what one may call

Christian art: French medieval architecture and sculpture, Italian medieval architecture, sculpture, and painting. You need not look for traces in his life of the disinterested passion with which he loved those works, you will find the proof of it in his books. His experience was so vast, that very often the most profound knowledge of which he gives evidence in one work is neither utilized nor mentioned, even by a mere allusion, in those other works of his where it would belong. He is so rich that he does not lend us his words; he gives them to us and does not take them back. You know, for instance, that he wrote a book on the cathedral of Amiens. From this you might conclude that this was the cathedral he liked most or which he knew best. Yet in *The Seven Lamps of Architecture,* where the cathedral of Rouen is mentioned forty times as an example, and that of Bayeux nine times, Amiens is not mentioned once. In *Val d'Arno,* he confesses to us that the church which gave him the greatest enthusiasm for the Gothic is Saint-Urbain at Troyes. Now neither in *The Seven Lamps* nor in *The Bible of Amiens* is there a single reference to Saint-Urbain. [28] With regard to the absence of references to Amiens in *The Seven Lamps,* you might think that perhaps he came to know Amiens only at the end of his life. Not so. In 1859, in a lecture given at Kensington, he compares at length the Vierge Dorée of Amiens with the statues of an art less skillful, but of deeper feeling, which seem to support the west porch of Chartres. Yet in *The Bible of Amiens,* where we might think he had gathered all his thoughts on Amiens, not once, in those pages where he speaks of the Vierge Dorée, does he make allusion to the statues at Chartres. Such is the infinite richness of his love, of his knowledge. Generally, in a writer, the recurrence of certain favorite examples, if not even the repetition of certain developments, reminds you that you are dealing with a man who had a particular life, a particular body of knowledge as opposed to another, a limited experience from which he draws all the profit he can. The mere consultation of the indexes of Ruskin's various works, the perpetual newness of the works cited, and still more the disdain for the information of which he availed himself once and, very often, abandoned forever, give the idea of something more than human, or rather the impression that each book is by a new man, who has a different knowledge, not the same experience, another life.

It was the charming play of his inexhaustible richness to pull out from the marvelous jewel case of his memory treasures that were always new: one day the precious rose window of Amiens, the next the golden lacework of the porch of Abbeville, to join them with the dazzling jewels of Italy.

In fact, he could pass thus from one country to another, for the same soul he had adored in the stones of Pisa was also the one that had given to the stones of Chartres their immortal form. No one has felt as he did the unity of Christian art during the Middle Ages, from the banks of the Somme to those of the Arno, and he realized in our hearts the dream of the great popes of the Middle Ages: "Christian Europe." If, as has been said, his name must remain attached to Pre-Raphaelitism, one should understand by that not what followed Turner, but what preceded Raphael. Today we may forget the services he rendered to Hunt, to Rossetti, to Millais, but what he has done for Giotto, for Carpaccio, for Bellini, we cannot. His sublime work was not to rouse the living, but to raise the dead.

Does not this unity of Christian art of the Middle Ages constantly appear in the viewpoint of those pages where his imagination illuminates here and there the stones of France with a magic reflection of Italy? See him telling you in *The Pleasures of England*: "While the Charity of Giotto at Padua presents her blazing heart in her hand to God, and tramples at the same instant on bags of gold, the treasures of the world, and gives corn and flowers, that on the west porch of Amiens is content to clothe a beggar with a piece of the staple of the manufacture of the town." [*The Pleasures of England*, 4:95, *CW* 33:486] In *The Nature of Gothic*, see him comparing the manner in which the flames are treated in the Italian Gothic and in the French Gothic, of which the porch of Saint-Maclou at Rouen is taken as an example. [Cf. *The Stones of Venice, CW* 10:232–33] And, in *The Seven Lamps of Architecture*, see again a little of the colors of Italy playing on the gray stones of this same porch.

"The subject of the typanum bas-relief [of the porch of Saint-Maclou in Rouen] is the Last Judgment, and the sculpture of the Inferno side is carried out with a degree of fearful grotesqueness I can only describe as a mingling of the minds of Orcagna and Hogarth. The demons are perhaps even more awful than Orcagna's; and, in some expression of debased humanity in its utmost despair, the English painter is at least equalled. Not less wild is the imagination which gives fury and fear even to the placing of the figures. An evil angel, poised on the wing, drives the condemned troops from before the Judgment seat; but they are urged on by him so furiously, that they are driven not merely to the extreme limit of that scene, which the sculptor confined elsewhere within the tympanum, but out of the tympanum and *into the niches* of the arch; while the flames that follow them, bent by the blast, as it seems, of the angel's wings, rush into the niches also, and burst up *through their tracery,* the three lower-most niches being represented as all on fire, while, instead of their usual vaulted and ribbed ceiling, there is a demon in the roof of each, with his wings folded over it, grinning down out of the black shadow." [*The Seven Lamps of Architecture, CW* 8:211–12]

This comparison of different kinds of arts and of different countries was not the farthest he went. He must have been struck by the similarity of certain religious ideas in pagan and Christian symbols.[29] Mr. Ary Renan[30] has commented, with profundity, on the elements of Christ already in Gustave Moreau's Prometheus. Ruskin, whose devotion to Christian art never made him contemptuous of paganism,[31] has compared, in an aesthetic and religious manner, the lion of St. Jerome to the lion of Nemea, Virgil to Dante, Samson to Hercules, Theseus to the Black Prince, the prophecies of Isaiah to the prophecies of the Cumaean Sibyl. There is no good cause for comparing Ruskin to Gustave Moreau, but one may say that a natural tendency, developed through familiarity with Primitives, had led both to proscribe the expression of violent feelings in art, and, in as much as this was applied to the study of symbols, to proscribe a certain fetishism in the worship of the symbols themselves, not a very dangerous fetishism for minds so attached in reality to the feeling symbolized that they could pass from one symbol to another without being hindered by superficial diversity. With respect to the systematic prohibition from expressing violent emotion in art, the principle which Mr. Ary Renan has called the principle of Beautiful Inertia, where can one find it better defined than in the pages of *Relation between Michael Angelo and Tintoretto*.[32] [Cf. *CW* 22:84 *seq.*] As for the somewhat exclusive worship of symbols, was not the study of French and Italian medieval art inevitably bound to lead to it? And since, through works of art, he was seeking the spirit of an age, the resemblance of these symbols of the porch of Chartres to the frescoes of Pisa would necessarily strike him as proof of the originality typical of the spirit which then animated the artists, and their differences as evidence of its versatility. In any one else the aesthetic sensations would have run the risk of being chilled by reasoning. But in him everything was love, and iconography, as he understood it, would better have been called iconolatry. Furthermore, art criticism makes room in a timely way for something possibly greater; it almost has the methods of science, it contributes to history. The appearance of a new element in the porches of cathedrals alerts us to changes no less profound in the history, not only of art, but of civilization, than those announced to geologists by the appearance of a new species on earth. The stone sculpted by nature is no more instructive than the stone sculpted by the artist, and we do not derive a greater profit from the one which has preserved an ancient monster for us than from the one which shows us a new god.

From this point of view, the drawings that accompany the writings of Ruskin are very significant. In the same plate you will be able to see an identical motif of architecture, as it is treated at Lisieux, at Bayeux, at Verona, and at Padua, as if it were a matter of variations within the same species of butterfly under different skies. Yet never do these stones he loved so much become abstract examples for him. On each stone you see the nuance of the hour united with the color of centuries. "To run to St. Wulfran [of Abbeville]," he tells us, "*before the sun was off the towers,* [is a thing] to cherish the past for—to the end." [*Praeterita, CW* 35:157] He went even farther; as in a primitive painting, he did not separate the cathedrals from that background of rivers and valleys where they appear to the traveler who approaches them. One of his most instructive drawings in this respect is the one reproduced as the second engraving of *Our Fathers Have Told Us,* and which is entitled: *Amiens, le jour des Trépassés.* In these cities of Amiens, Abbeville, Beauvais, Rouen, which a visit from Ruskin consecrated, he would spend his time drawing, at times in the churches ("without being disturbed by the sacristan"), at times in the open air. And the company of draughts-men and engravers he took with him must have formed most delightful passing colonies in these cities, like the scene Plato shows us of the sophists following Protagoras from town to town, similar also to the swallows, in imitation of which they liked to stop at the old roofs and ancient towers of the cathedrals. Perhaps one might still be able to find some of those disciples of Ruskin who accom-panied him to the banks of this newly evangelized Somme, as if the days of St. Firmin and of St. Salve had returned; disciples who, as the new apostle spoke and explained Amiens as a Bible, made drawings instead of taking notes, gracious notes whose collection is no doubt in some English museum, and where I imagine reality has been slightly rearranged according to Viollet-le-Duc's taste. The engrav-ing, *Amiens le jour des Trépassés,* seems to lie a little with regard to beauty. Is it perspective alone that thus brings the cathedral and the church of Saint-Leu close to the banks of a widened Somme? It is true that Ruskin could answer us, drawing support from the words of Turner which he quoted in *Eagle's Nest* and which Mr. de la Siz-eranne has translated: "Turner, in his early life, was sometimes good-natured, and would show people what he was about. He was one day making a drawing of Plymouth harbour, with some ships at the distance of a mile or two, seen against the light. Having shown this drawing to a naval officer, the naval officer observed with surprise, and objected with very justifiable indignation, that the ships of the line had no port-holes. 'No,' said Turner, 'certainly not. If you will walk to Mount Edgecumbe, and look at the ships against the sunset, you will find that you can't see the port-holes.' 'Well, but,' said the naval officer, still indignant, 'you know the port-holes are there.' 'Yes,' said Turner, 'I know that well enough; but my business is to draw what I see, and not what I know is there.' " [*Eagle's Nest, CW* 22:210]

If, being in Amiens, you go in the direction of the slaughter-house, you will have a view which is not different from that of the engraving. You will see distance arranging, in the deceitful but happy manner of the artist, the monuments, which, as you approach, will resume their original, but wholly different, position; for instance, you will see inscribed on the front of the cathedral the outline of one of the town's water hydrants, making solid geometry into plane geometry. Should you nevertheless find this landscape, tastefully composed by perspective, a little different from the one that Ruskin's drawing records, you could blame above all the changes that have been brought about in the aspect of the town during the almost twenty years since Ruskin's stay there, and, as he said about another site he loved, "Since I last composed, or meditated there various *improvements* have taken place." [33] [*Praeterita, CW* 35:48]

But at least this engraving from *The Bible of Amiens* will have associated in your memory the banks of the Somme with the cathedral, better perhaps than your sight would have done, no matter in what part of the town you might have placed yourself. It will prove to you, better than anything I could have said, that Ruskin did not separate the beauty of the cathedrals from the charm of the regions from which they sprang, and which everyone who visits them still enjoys in the particular poetry of the region and in the remembrance of the misty or golden afternoon he spent there. Not only is the first chapter of *The Bible of Amiens* called: *By the Rivers of Waters,* but the book Ruskin intended to write on the cathedral of Chartres was to be entitled: *The Sources of the Eure.* It was not, therefore, only in his drawings that he set the churches by the riverbanks and that he associated the grandeur of the Gothic cathedrals with the charm of the French sites. [34] And we would feel more vividly the charm inherent in a region if we did not have at our disposal those seven-league boots that express trains are, and if, as formerly, to arrive at some spot we were obliged to pass through countrysides increasingly like those to which we were going, like zones of graduated harmony which, by making this harmony less easily penetrable to what differs from it, by protecting it gently and with mystery from fraternal resemblances, not only envelop it in nature, but prepare our minds for it.

These studies by Ruskin of Christian art were for him like the verification and proof of his ideas on Christianity and of other ideas we have not been able to mention here, the most famous of which we shall let Ruskin define presently: his horror of mechanization and industrial art. "All the beautiful things were made when men of the Middle Ages *believed* the pure, joyful, beautiful lesson of Christianity." [4:58, 52; *CW* 33:173, 169] And he saw art later declining with faith, skill taking the place of feeling. Seeing the power of achieving beauty, which was the privilege of the ages of faith, his belief in the goodness of faith must have been strengthened. Each volume of his last work, *Our Fathers Have Told Us* (only the first was written), was to comprise four chapters, of which the last was to be dedicated to the masterpiece which was the culmination of the faith whose study formed the object of the first three chapters. Thus Christianity, which had cradled Ruskin's aesthetic sense, received from it a supreme consecration. And as he was about to take his Protestant reader before the statue of the Madonna, and after having scoffed at her "who should understand that no Lady-worship of any sort was ever pernicious to humanity," or before the statue of St. Honoré, after deploring that he is so little spoken of "in the faubourg of Paris that bears his name," [*ibid.*, 4:48, 7; *CW* 33:164, 129] he could have said, as he did at the end of *Val d'Arno*:

"If you will fix your minds only on the conditions of human life which the Giver of it demands, 'He hath showed thee, O man, what is good; and what doth the Lord require of thee, but to do justly, and to love mercy, and to walk humbly with thy God?' (Micah 6:8), you will find that such obedience is always acknowledged by temporal blessing. If you summon to your thoughts the state of unrecorded multitudes, who laboured in silence, and adored in humility, as the snows of Christendom brought memory of the Birth of Christ, or her spring sunshine, of His Resurrection, you may know that the promise of the Bethlehem angels has been literally fulfilled; and will pray that your English fields, joyfully as the banks of Arno, may still dedicate their pure lilies to St. Mary of the Flowers." [*CW* 23:164]

Finally, Ruskin's medieval studies confirmed, with his belief in the goodness of faith, his belief in the necessity of free, joyful, and personal work without the intervention of mechanization. In order that you might realize this better, it would be best to transcribe here a very characteristic page of Ruskin. He is speaking of a figurine a few centimeters in size, lost in the midst of hundreds of such tiny figurines, of the porch of the Booksellers of the Rouen cathedral.

"The fellow is vexed and puzzled in his malice; and his hand is pressed hard on his cheek bone, and the flesh of the cheek is wrinkled under the eye by the pressure. The whole, indeed, looks wretchedly coarse, when it is seen on a scale in which it is naturally compared with delicate figure etchings; but considering it as a mere filling of an interstice on the outside of the cathedral gate, and as one of the more than three hundred, it proves very noble vitality in the art of the time. [*The Seven Lamps of Architecture, CW* 8:217]

"We have certain work to do for our bread, and that is to be done strenuously; other work to do is for our delight, and that is to be done heartily: neither is to be done by halves and shifts, but with a will; and what is not worth this effort is not to be done at all. Perhaps all that we have to do is meant for nothing more than an exercise of the heart and of the will, and is useless in itself; but, at all events, the little use it has may well be spared if it is not worth putting our hands and our strength to. It does not become our immortality to take an ease inconsistent with its authority, nor to suffer any instruments with which it can dispense, to come between it and the thing it rules. There is dreaming enough, and earthiness enough, and sensuality enough in human existence without our turning the few glowing moments of it into mechanism, and since our life must at best be but a vapour that appears for a little time and then vanishes away, let it at least appear as a cloud in the height of Heaven, not as the thick darkness that broods over the blast of the Furnace, and rolling of the Wheel." [*Ibid.*, 219–220]

I confess that when I reread this page at the time of Ruskin's death, I was seized with the desire to see the little man he speaks of. And I went to Rouen, as if obeying a dying wish, and as if Ruskin, upon dying, had in some way entrusted to his readers the poor creature to which he had given life again by speaking of it, and which, unknowingly, had just lost forever the person who had done for it as much as its first sculptor. But when I arrived near the huge cathedral in front of the portal where the saints were warming themselves in the sun, saw higher up the galleries where the kings radiated up to those supreme heights of stone I believed uninhabited, and where here a sculptured hermit lived in isolation, letting the birds rest on his forehead, while there a gathering of apostles listened to the message of an angel poised near them, folding his wings, under a flight of pigeons spreading theirs, and not far from a personage who, receiving a child on his back, turned his head in a sudden and secular motion; when I saw, lined up before its porches or leaning over the balconies of its towers, all the stone hosts of the mystic city breathing the sun or the morning shadow, I understood it would be impossible to find a figurine of but a few centimeters in the midst of this superhuman multitude. I nevertheless went to the porch of the Bookseller's. But how to recognize the figurine among hundreds of others? All of a sudden, a talented and promising young sculptress, Mrs. L. Yeatman, said to me, "Here is one that looks like it." We looked farther down, and . . . there it was. It scarcely measures ten centimeters. It is crumbling, and yet the look is the same, the stone still has the hole that raises the eyeball and gives it that expression which made me recognize it. The artist, who died centuries ago, left there, among thousands of others, this little person who dies a little more each day, and has been dead for a really long time, forever lost in the midst of the crowd. But he had put it there. One day, a man for whom there is no death, for whom there is no material infinity, no oblivion, a man who, casting away from him that nothingness which oppresses us to follow purposes which dominate his life, purposes so numerous that he will not be able to attain them all, while we seemed to have none, this man came, and, among those waves of stone where each lacelike effervescence seemed to resemble the others, seeing there all the laws of life, all the thoughts of the soul, naming them by their names, he said, "See, it is this, it is that." As on the Day of Judgment, which is represented near by, his words resound like the archangel's trumpet, and he says, "Those who have lived will live, matter is nothing." And, in fact, like the dead whom, not far away, the tympanum represents awakening at the sound of the archangel's trumpet, arising, having recovered their forms, recognizable, alive, the figurine is now alive again and has recovered its look, and the Judge has said, "You have survived; you will live." As for him, he is not an immortal judge, his body will die; but what does it matter! as if he were not destined to die he performs his immortal task, unconcerned at the size of the thing that occupies his time, and, having but one human life to live, he spends several days in front of one of ten thousand figures of a church. He made a drawing of it. It corresponded for him to those ideas that exercised his mind, indifferent to approaching old age. He made a drawing of it; he spoke of it. And the harmless and monstrous little figurine will have come back to life, against all hope, from that death which seems more total than the others, which is the disappearance into the midst of infinite numbers and the leveling down of similarities, but from which genius quickly rescues us. Finding the figurine there again, one cannot help but be touched. It seems to live and to gaze, or rather to have been caught by death at the very moment of its gaze, like the Pompeians whose movements remain suspended. It is a single thought of the sculptor, in fact, that has been arrested here in its movement by the immobility of the stone. I was touched on finding the figurine there again; nothing therefore dies that has survived, no more the sculptor's thought than Ruskin's thought.

On encountering the figurine there, an object necessary to Ruskin, who dedicated to it one of the few engravings illustrating his book[35] because it was an actual and enduring part of his thought, and agreeable to us because his thought is necessary to us, guides ours which met it on the way, our state of mind was closer to that of the artists who carved the Final Judgment on the tympana and who thought that what is individual, what is most original in a person, in an intention, does not die, it persists in the memory of God and will be resurrected. Who is right, the grave digger or Hamlet, when the one sees but a skull where the other recalls a fantasy? Science may say: the grave digger; but it has reckoned without Shakespeare, who will make the memory of that fantasy last beyond the dust of the skull. At the call of the angel, each corpse will be found still there, in his place, when we believed him dust long ago. At the call of Ruskin, we see the smallest figurine framing a miniscule quatrefoil resurrected in its proper form, looking at us with the same look that seems to be contained in but one millimeter of stone. No doubt, poor little monster, I would not have been skilled enough, among the millions of stones of the cities, to find you, to make out your face, to rediscover your personality, to call you, to bring you back to life. But it is not that the infinity, the number, the nothingness which oppress us are very strong; it is that my imagination is not really strong. Indeed, there was nothing truly beautiful in you. Your poor face, which I might never have noticed, does not have a very interesting expression, although evidently it has, like any person, an expression no one else ever had. But, since you lived enough to continue gazing with that same oblique glance for Ruskin to notice you and, after he had said your name, for his reader to be able to recognize you, are you living enough now, are you loved enough? And one cannot help thinking of you with emotion, though you do not seem to be attractive, because you are a living creature, because, through so many centuries, you were dead without hope of resurrection, and because you are resurrected. And one of these days, perhaps, someone else will go to find you at your porch, looking with emotion at your mischievous and slanted resurrected face, because what emerged from one man's thought can alone one day capture another thought, which in turn has fascinated ours. You were right to remain there, unlooked at, crumbling. You could not expect anything from matter where you were but nothingness. But the small have nothing to fear, nor do the dead. For sometimes the Spirit visits the earth; at his passage, the dead arise, the forgotten figurines reawaken and capture the attention of the living who, for them, foresake the living who are not alive and go seeking life only where the Spirit has revealed it to them, in stones that are already dust and yet still intellect.

He who enveloped the old cathedrals in more love and more joy than even the sun bestows on them when it adds its fleeting smile to their centuries-old beauty cannot, if well understood, have been mistaken. It is the same with the world of spirits as with the physical universe, where a jet of water cannot rise above the height of the place from which the water first descended. Things of great literary beauty correspond to something, and it is perhaps enthusiasm in art that is the criterion of truth. Supposing that Ruskin sometimes made mistakes, as a critic, in the exact appraisal of the value of a work; the beauty of his erroneous judgment is often more interesting than the beauty of the work being judged and corresponds to something which, in spite of being something other than the work, is no less precious. That Ruskin was wrong when saying that the *Beau Dieu* of Amiens "was beyond what till then had been reached in sculptured tenderness, though any representation of Christ must eternally disappoint the hope of any loving soul that has learned to trust in Him" [4:36; *CW* 33:147], and that Mr. Huysmans was right when calling this same *Dieu* of Amiens "a fop with an ovine face," is something we do not believe, but it is a matter of little import. "I call it a legend only," says Ruskin, speaking of the story of St. Jerome. "Whether Heracles slew, or St. Jerome ever cherished, the wild or wounded creature, is of no moment to us." [4:54; *CW* 33:120] We can say as much of Ruskin's judgments on art whose justness might be contested. Whether the *Beau Dieu* of Amiens was or was not what Ruskin believed is of no moment to us. As when Buffon says that "all the intellectual beauties found [in a beautiful style], all the relationships of which it is composed, are so many truths, as useful and perhaps more precious for the public mind than those which may be the essence of the subject," the truths of which the beauty of the pages of the *Bible* on the *Beau Dieu* of Amiens are composed have a value which is independent of the beauty of that statue, and Ruskin would not have found it had he spoken of them with contempt, for enthusiasm alone could give him the power to discover them.

To what extent this wonderful soul faithfully reflected the universe, and under what touching and tempting forms falsehood may have crept, in spite of everything, into the heart of his intellectual sincerity, is something we will perhaps never know, and it is, at any rate, something we cannot look for here. "How far," he said, "my mind has been paralyzed by the faults and sorrow of my life,—how far short its knowledge may be of what I might have known, had I more faithfully walked in the light I had, is beyond my conjecture or confession." [4:52; *CW* 33:119] At any rate, he would have been one of those "geniuses" of whom even those among us who were born with the gifts of the fairies have need in order to be initiated into the knowledge and love of a new part of Beauty. Many of the words used by our contemporaries for exchanging ideas bear his mark, as one sees on coins the effigy of the sovereign of the day. Dead, he continues to enlighten us, like those dead stars whose light reaches us still, and one may say of him what he said on the occasion of Turner's death, "Through those eyes, now filled with dust, generations yet unborn will learn to behold the light of nature." [*Lectures on Architecture, CW* 12:128]

IV. P.-S.

"Under what magnificent and tempting forms falsehood may have crept into his intellectual sincerity. . . ." Here is what I meant: there is a kind of idolatry which no one has better defined than Ruskin in a page of *Lectures on Art*: "Such I conceive generally, though indeed with good arising out of it, for very great evil brings some good in its backward eddies—such I conceive to have been the deadly function of art in its ministry to what, whether in heathen or Christian lands, and whether in the pageantry of words, or colours, or fair forms, is truly, and in the deep sense, to be called idolatry— the serving with the best of our hearts and minds some dear and sad fantasy which we have made for ourselves, while we disobey the present call of the Master, who is not dead, and who is not fainting under His cross, but requiring us to take up ours."[36] [*CW* 20:66] It seems to me that at the very basis of Ruskin's work, at the root of his talent, is found precisely this idolatry. No doubt he never let it completely overlay—even in order to embellish it—immobilize, paralyze, and finally kill his intellectual and moral sincerity. At every line in his works, as in every moment of his life, one feels this need for sincerity struggling against idolatry, proclaiming its van- ity, humiliating beauty before duty, even if it were unaesthetic. I shall not give examples of this in his life (which is not like the life of a Racine, of a Tolstoi, of a Maeterlinck, aesthetic at first and moral afterward, but where at the outset morality claims its rights within the very heart of aesthetics—never perhaps freeing itself from aesthetics as completely as in the lives of the Masters I have just mentioned). It is sufficiently well known that I need not recall its phases, from the first scruples he feels about drinking tea while looking at Titians to the moment when, having sunk in philan- thropic and social works the five million his father left him, he decides to sell his Turners. But there is a more inward dilettantism of action (which he overcame), and the true conflict between his idolatry and his sincerity took place not at certain hours of his life, not in certain pages of his books, but at every moment, in those profound, secret regions almost unknown to us, where our person- ality receives images from imagination, ideas from intelligence, words from memory, asserts itself in the continual choices it must make, and in some way without respite decides the fate of our spiritual and moral life. In those regions, it seems that Ruskin never ceased to commit the sin of idolatry. At the very moment he was preaching sincerity, he was himself lacking in it, not by what he said, but by the way in which he said it. The doctrines he professed were moral doctrines and not aesthetic doctrines, and yet he chose them for their beauty. And since he did not wish to present them as beautiful but as true, he was forced to deceive himself about the nature of the reasons that made him adopt them. Hence there was such a continual compromising of conscience, that immoral doctrines sincerely professed would perhaps have been less dangerous for the integrity of the mind than those moral doctrines in which affirmation is not absolutely sincere, as they are dictated by an unavowed aesthetic preference. And the sin was constantly committed, in the very choice of each explanation given of a fact, of each appreciation given of a work, in the very choice of the words he used—and it finally gave a deceitful attitude to the mind ceaselessly addicted to it. To put the reader in a better position to judge the kind of trickery that a page of Ruskin is for each one of us and evidently was for Ruskin himself, I am going to quote one of those pages which I find most beautiful and yet in which this defect is at its most flagrant. We shall see that though the beauty in it is *in theory* (that is to say, in appearance, the basis of the writer's thought having always been appearance, and the form, reality) subordinated to moral feeling and truth, in reality truth and moral feeling are there subordinated to aesthetic feelings, and to an aesthetic feeling somewhat warped by that perpetual compromising. The passage is from the *Causes of the Fall of Venice*.[37]

"Not in the wantonness of wealth, not in vain ministry to the desire of the eyes or pride of life, were those marbles hewn into transparent strength, and those arches arrayed in the colours of the iris. There is a message written in the dyes of them, that once was written in blood; and a sound in the echoes of their vaults, that one day shall fill the vault of heaven—'He shall return to do judgment and justice.' [Cf. Genesis 18:19] The strength of Venice was given her, so long as she remembered this; her destruction found her when she had forgotten this; and it found her irrevocably, because she forgot it without excuse. Never had city a more glorious Bible.

Among the nations of the North, a rude and shadowy sculpture filled their temples with confused and hardly legible imagery; but, for her, the skill and treasures of the East had gilded every letter, and illuminated every page, till the Book-Temple shone from afar off like the star of the Magi. In other cities, the meetings of the people were often in places withdrawn from religious association, subject to violence and to change; and on the grass of the dangerous rampart, and in the dust of the troubled street, there were deeds done and counsels taken, which, if we cannot justify, we may sometimes forgive. But the sins of Venice, whether in her palace or in her piazza, were done with the Bible at her right hand. The walls on which its testimony was written were separated but by a few inches of marble from those which guarded the secrets of her councils, or confined the victims of her policy. And when in her last hours she threw off all shame and all restraint, and the great square of the city became filled with the madness of the whole earth, be it remembered how much her sin was greater, because it was done in the face of the House of God, burning with the letters of His Law. Mountebank and masquer laughed their laugh, and went their way; and a silence has followed them, not unforetold; for amidst them all, through century after century of gathering vanity and fostering guilt, that white dome of St. Mark's had uttered in the dead ear of Venice, 'Know thou, that for all these things God will bring thee into judgment.'" [Cf. Ecclesiastes 11:9] [*The Stones of Venice, CW* 10:141–42]

Now, had Ruskin been entirely sincere with himself, he would not have thought that the crimes of the Venetians had been more inexcusable and more severely punished than those of other men because they possessed a church in multicolored marble instead of a cathedral in limestone, because the palace of the Doges was near St. Mark's instead of at the other end of town, and because in Byzantine churches the biblical text, instead of being represented as in the sculpture of the northern churches, is accompanied, in the mosaics, by letters that form a quotation from the Gospel or from the prophecies. It is nevertheless true that this passage from *The Stones of*

Venice is of great beauty, rather difficult though it be to give an account of the reasons for this beauty. It seems to us that it rests on something false and we feel some scruples in giving in to it.

And yet there must be some truth in it. Properly speaking, there is no beauty that is entirely deceitful, for aesthetic pleasure is precisely what accompanies the discovery of a truth. To what kind of truth may correspond the very vivid aesthetic pleasure we experience when reading such a page is rather difficult to say. The page itself is mysterious, full of images both of beauty and of religion, like this same church of St. Mark where all the figures of the Old and New Testaments appear against the background of a sort of splendid obscurity and scintillating brilliance. I remember having read it for the first time in St. Mark's itself, during a dark and tempestuous hour, when the mosaics shone only by their own physical light and with an internal, ancient, and earthly gold to which the Venetian sun, which sets even the angels of the campaniles ablaze, mingled nothing of its own; the emotion I felt, as I was reading this page, among all those angels which shone forth from the surrounding darkness, was great, and yet perhaps not very pure. In the same manner as the joy of seeing the beautiful, mysterious figures increased, but was altered in some way by the pleasure of erudition that I experienced upon understanding the text that had appeared in Byzantine letters around their haloed brows, so in the same way the beauty of Ruskin's images was intensified and corrupted by the pride of referring to the sacred text. A sort of egotistical self-evaluation is unavoidable in those joys in which erudition and art mingle and in which aesthetic pleasure may become more acute, but not remain as pure. And perhaps this page of *The Stones of Venice* was more beautiful chiefly because it gave me precisely those mixed joys I experienced in St. Mark's, this page which, like the Byzantine church, also had in the mosaics of its style that dazzled in the shadows, next to its images, its biblical quotation inscribed near by. Furthermore, was this page not like those mosaics of St. Mark's which professed to teach and cared little about their artistic beauty? Today they give us pleasure only. Yet the pleasure their didacticism gives the scholar is selfish, and the most disinterested is still that given the artist by this beauty little thought of, or even unknown, by those who merely intended to teach the masses and who in addition gave them beauty.

In the last page of *The Bible of Amiens,* truly sublime, the line "if you would care for the promise to you" [4:60; *CW* 33:174] is an example of the same kind. When, again in *The Bible of Amiens,* Ruskin closes the piece on Egypt by saying: "She was the Tutress of Moses; and the Hostess of Christ" [3:27; *CW* 33:103], we may grant him "Tutress of Moses": to educate, certain values are needed. But, in a considered judgment of the qualities of Egyptian genius, can the fact of having been "*the hostess*" of Christ really be taken into account, even if it does add beauty to the sentence?

It is with my most cherished aesthetic impressions that I have tried to struggle here, trying to push intellectual sincerity to its utmost and cruelest limits. Need I add that if I make this general reservation, in rather an absolute sense, less on the works of Ruskin than on the essence of their inspiration and the quality of their beauty, for me he is nevertheless one of the greatest writers of all times and of all countries. I have tried to capture in Ruskin, as in a "subject" particularly favorable to this observation, an infirmity essential to the human mind, rather than wanting to denounce a personal fault. Once the reader has understood what this "idolatry" consists of, he will come to understand the excessive importance Ruskin attaches in his art studies to the literalness of the works (an importance of which I have given too summarily another cause in the preface, see page 39 above) and also that abuse of the words "irreverent," "insolent," and "difficulties which we should be insolent in desiring to solve, a mystery which we are not required to unravel" (*Bible of Amiens,* p. 239). [3:49; *CW* 33:117] "Let therefore the young artist beware of the spirit of choice; it is an insolent spirit" (*Modern Painters*) [*CW* 4:60], "it is just possible for an irreverent person rather to think the nave narrow" (*Bible of Amiens*) [4:8; *CW* 33:129], etc., etc.,—and the state of mind that they reveal. I was thinking about that idolatry (I was thinking also about that pleasure Ruskin feels in balancing his sentences in an equilibrium that seems to impose on the thought, rather than receiving from it, a symmetrical ordering)[38] when I said, "Under what touching and tempting forms falsehood may have crept, in spite of everything, into the heart of his intellectual sincerity is what I do not have to seek." But quite the contrary, I should have sought it and would indeed be guilty of idolatry were I to take refuge behind that essentially Ruskinian formula of respect.[39] It is not that I am unable to recognize the virtues of respect, it is the very condition of love. But it must never, where love ceases, be substituted for it, allowing us to believe without enquiry and to admire on faith. Besides, Ruskin would have been the first to applaud us for not granting to his writings an infallible authority, since he refused it even to the Holy Scriptures. "There is no possibility of attaching the idea of infallible truth to any form of human language" (*The Bible of Amiens*, III, p. 49). [3:49; *CW* 33:116] But the attitude of "reverence" that believes it to be "insolent to solve a mystery" [3:49; *CW* 33:117] pleased him. To have done with idolatry and to make sure no misunderstanding on this matter remains between the reader and me, I would like, here, to call upon one of our most justly famous contemporaries* (as different, moreover, as one can be from Ruskin) but who in his conversations, not in his books, shows this defect carried to such extremes that it is easier to recognize and show it in him without further need to take such pains to magnify it. When he speaks, he is afflicted—deliciously—with idolatry. Those who have heard him once will consider very crude an "imitation" where nothing remains of his charm, but they will know, however, of whom I mean to speak, whom I take here as an example, when I tell them that he recognizes admirably in the material with which a tragic actress drapes herself, the very fabric seen on *la Mort* in *Le Jeune homme et la Mort,* by Gustave Moreau, or in the garb of one of his lady friends, "the very dress and coiffure worn by the princess de Cadignan the day she saw d'Arthez for the first time." And looking at the actress's draped costume or at the society lady's dress, touched

---

*Ed. note: The contemporary in question is Robert de Montesquiou.

by the nobility of his recollection he exclaims: "It is truly beautiful!" not because the fabric is beautiful, but because it is the fabric painted by Moreau or described by Balzac and is thus forever sacred . . . to the idolaters. In his room you will see, alive in a vase or painted in frescoes on the wall by some of his artist friends, bleeding hearts, because it is the very flower one sees represented at the Madeleine in Vézelay. As for an object that belonged to Baudelaire, to Michelet, to Hugo, he surrounds it with a religious respect. I enjoy too deeply, even to the point of intoxication, the witty improvisations to which a particular kind of pleasure he finds in this veneration leads and inspires our idolater, to want to quarrel with him in the least.

But at the height of my pleasure, I wonder whether the incomparable talker—and the listener who gives in—do not sin equally through insincerity; whether because a flower (the passion flower) resembles in some of its parts the instruments of the crucifixion, it is sacrilegious to make a present of it to a person of another religion; and whether the fact that a house may have been inhabited by Balzac (if, moreover, nothing remains in it that may inform us about him) makes it more beautiful. Must we really, other than to pay her an aesthetic compliment, honor a person because her name is Bathilde, like the heroine of Lucien Leuwen?

Mme. de Cadignan's dress is a delightful invention of Balzac because it gives us an idea of Mme. de Cadignan's art, because it lets us know what impression she wants to make on d'Arthez and some of her "secrets." But once stripped of the spirit that is in it, it is no more than a sign deprived of its meaning, that is to say, nothing; and to keep on adoring it so much as to be enraptured upon encountering it in real life on a woman's body is, properly speaking, idolatry. It is the favorite intellectual sin of artists and one to which but very few have not succumbed. *"Felix culpa!"* one is tempted to say upon seeing how very fertile it has been for them in charming inventions. But at least they must not succumb without having struggled. There is not in nature any particular form, no matter how beautiful, that is worth anything in any other way than by the hint of infinite beauty incarnated in it: not even the blossom of the apple tree, not even the blossom of the pink hawthorn. My love for them is infinite, and the suffering (hay fever) that their proximity causes me permits me each spring to give them proofs of love which are not within the common reach. But even for them, so nonliterary, so unconnected with an aesthetic tradition, not being "the very flower in such and such a painting by Tintoretto," as Ruskin would say, "or in such and such a drawing by Leonardo," as our contemporary would say (he who has revealed to us, among so many other things about which everyone is now talking and which no one looked at before him—the drawings at the Academy of Fine Arts in Venice), I shall always guard against an exclusive cult that would attach to them anything but the joy they give us, a cult in the name of which, by an egotistical inward movement, we would make of them "our" flowers, and would take care to honor them by adorning our rooms with works of art in which they figure. No, I shall not find a painting more beautiful because the artist has painted a hawthorn in the foreground, though I know of nothing more beautiful than the hawthorn, for I wish to remain sincere and because I know that the beauty of a painting does not depend on the things represented in it. I shall not collect images of hawthorn. I do not venerate hawthorn, I go to see and smell it. I have permitted myself this short incursion—which is in no sense an offensive—into the terrain of contemporary literature, because it seemed to me that the traits of idolatry seen in the bud in Ruskin would appear more clearly to the reader here where they are magnified, and so much the more so since here they are also differentiated. At any rate, I beg our contemporary, if he has recognized himself in this clumsy sketch, to think that it was done without malice and that, as I have said, I had to reach the utmost limits of sincerity toward myself to reproach Ruskin thus and to find this fragile part in my otherwise absolute admiration for him. Now, not only "sharing with Ruskin is no dishonor,"* but I could also

---

*Ed. note: Parody of "Un partage avec Jupiter—N'a rien du tout qui déshonore," from Molière's *Amphitryon,* ll. 1898–99.

find no higher praise for this contemporary than to reproach him in the same manner as I have reproached Ruskin. And if I have been discreet enough not to name him, I almost regret it. For when one is admitted near Ruskin, be it in the posture of the giver, and only to support his book and help in a closer reading of it, "on n'est pas à la peine mais à l'honneur."*

I return to Ruskin. I am today so accustomed to Ruskin that I have to search my innermost self to understand the source and study the nature of this idolatry and the little artificialities which at times it mingles with the more vivid literary pleasures he gives us. But this idolatry must have shocked me often when I began to love his books, before closing my eyes little by little to their defects, as happens with any love. Infatuation for living creatures sometimes has a base origin which is later purified. A man becomes acquainted with a woman because she may help him reach a goal other than herself. Then once he knows her, he loves her for herself and sacrifices to her without hesitation that goal which it was merely her function to help him attain. Likewise, with my love for Ruskin's books was mingled, in the beginning, something of a selfish interest, the joy of the intellectual benefit I was going to draw from them. It is certain that when I read the first pages, feeling their power and their charm, I tried not to resist them, not to argue too much within myself, because I felt that if one day the charm of Ruskin's thought should, for me, permeate everything it had touched upon, in a word, if I were entirely captivated by his thought, the universe would become enriched by all that I had not known until then, Gothic cathedrals and innumerable paintings of England and Italy, which had not yet roused in me that longing without which there is never true knowledge. For Ruskin's thought is not like that of

*Ed. note: Well-known saying referring to an episode in Joan of Arc's life. When asked why she had carried her standard into the church at the coronation of Charles VII in Rheims, she answered, "Il avait été à la peine, il était juste qu'il fût à l'honneur." Mark Twain translated these famous words thus: "It had borne the burden, it had earned the honor" [Cf. Mark Twain, *Personal Recollections of Joan of Arc* (New York: Harper and Row, 1924), Book III, p. 187.]

Emerson, for example, which is entirely contained in a book, that is to say, an abstract thing, a pure sign of itself. The object to which thought such as Ruskin's is applied, and from which it is inseparable, is not immaterial, it is scattered here and there over the surface of the earth. One must seek it where it is, in Pisa, Florence, Venice, the National Gallery, Rouen, Amiens, the mountains of Switzerland. Such thought which has an object other than itself, which has materialized in space, which is no longer infinite and free, but limited and subdued, which is incarnated in bodies of sculptured marble, in snowy mountains, in painted countenances, is perhaps less sublime than pure thought. But it makes the universe more beautiful for us, or at least certain individual parts, certain specifically named parts of the universe, because it touched upon them, and because it introduced us to them by obliging us, if we want to understand it, to love them.

And so it was, in fact; all at once the universe regained an infinite value in my eyes. And my admiration for Ruskin gave such an importance to the things he had made me love that they seemed to be charged with a value greater even than that of life. This was literally the case, and at a time when I believed my days to be numbered, as I left for Venice in order to be able before dying to approach, touch, and see incarnated in decaying but still-erect and rosy palaces, Ruskin's ideas on domestic architecture of the Middle Ages. What importance, what reality in the eyes of one who must soon leave the earth, can be possessed by a city so special, so fixed in time, so specific in space as Venice, and how could the theories on domestic architecture which I could study and verify there on living examples be those "truths which are more powerful than death, which prevent us from fearing it, and which almost make us love it?"[40] It is the power of genius to make us love a beauty more real than ourselves in those things which in the eyes of others are as particular and perishable as ourselves.

"I will say that they are beautiful when your eyes say it too," said the poet, but this is not true if it refers to the eyes of a beloved woman. In a certain sense, and whatever may be, even in the domain

of poetry, the wonderful compensations it has for us, love depoetizes
nature. For the lover, the earth is no longer but "the carpet of the
beautiful, childish feet" of his mistress, nature is only "her temple."
Love, which makes us discover so many profound psychological
truths, on the contrary shuts us off from poetic feeling for nature,[41]
because it puts us in an egotistical frame of mind (love is the highest
form of selfishness, but is selfishness nonetheless) where it is difficult
for the poetic feeling to be produced. Admiration for a thought, on
the contrary, gives rise to beauty at each step because at each
moment it rouses in us the desire for it. Mediocre people generally
believe that to let oneself be guided by books one admires takes away
some of one's independence of judgment. "What is it to you how
Ruskin feels: feel for yourself." Such an opinion rests on a psychological error that will be treated as it deserves by all those who, having
thus adopted an intellectual discipline, feel that their power to
understand and feel is infinitely increased and their critical sense
never paralyzed. We are then simply in a state of grace in which all
our faculties, our critical sense as much as our other senses, are
strengthened. Therefore, this voluntary servitude is the beginning
of freedom. There is no better way of becoming aware of one's
feelings than to try to recreate in oneself what a master has felt. In
this profound effort it is our thought, together with his, that we
bring to light. We are free in life, but subject to purpose: the
sophism of freedom of indifference was picked apart long ago. The
writer who constantly creates a void in his mind, thinking to free it
from any external influence in order to be sure of remaining individual, yields unwittingly to a sophism just as naive. Actually the only
times when we truly have all our powers of mind are those when we
do not believe ourselves to be acting with independence, when we do
not arbitrarily choose the goal of our efforts. The subject of the
novelist, the vision of the poet, the truth of the philosopher are
imposed on them in a manner almost inevitable, exterior, so to
speak, to their thought. And it is by subjecting his mind to the
expression of this vision and to the approach of this truth that the
artist becomes truly himself.

But in speaking of this passion that I had for Ruskin's thought, a little artificial at first and then so deep, I speak with the help of memory, a memory that recalls only facts, "but from the distant past can recapture nothing." It is only when certain periods of our lives have come to a close forever, when, even during the hours in which power and freedom seem to have been given to us, we are forbidden to reopen their doors furtively, it is when we are incapable of placing ourselves again, even for an instant, in our former state, it is only then that we refuse to believe that such things might have been entirely abolished. We can no longer sing of them, having ignored the wise warning of Goethe that there is poetry only in those things which one still feels. But unable to rekindle the flames of the past, we want at least to gather its ashes. Lacking a resurrection we can no longer bring about, with the cold memory we have kept of those things—the memory of facts telling us, "you were thus," without permitting us to become thus again, affirming to us the reality of a lost paradise instead of giving it back to us through recollection—we wish at least to describe it and to establish its knowledge. It is when Ruskin is far away from us that we translate his books and try to create a fair likeness of the characteristics of his thought. Therefore, you will not know the sounds of our faith or of our love, and it is our piety alone that you will perceive here and there, cold and furtive, occupied, like the Theban Virgin, in restoring a tomb.

MARCEL PROUST

Proust's Notes to
the Preface

1. This part of the introduction was dedicated in the *Mercure de France,* where it first appeared [on April 1, 1900] in the form of an article, to Mr. Léon Daudet. I am happy to be able to renew to him here the testimony of my deep gratitude and of my admiring friendship.

2. Here, according to Mr. Collingwood, are the circumstances under which Ruskin wrote this book:

"Mr. Ruskin had not been abroad since the spring of 1877, and in August, 1880, he felt able to travel again. He went on a tour to the northern French cathedrals, staying at his old haunts—Abbeville, Amiens, Beauvais, Chartres, Rouen—and then returned with Mr. A. Severn and Mr. Brabanson to Amiens, where he spent the greater part of October. He was writing a new book—*The Bible of Amiens*—which was to be to the *Seven Lamps* what *St. Mark's Rest* was to *Stones of Venice.* Though he did not feel able to lecture to strangers at Chesterfield, he visited old friends at Eton, on November 6, 1880, to give an address on Amiens. For once he forgot his notes, but the lecture was no less brilliant and interesting. It was practically the first chapter of his new work, *The Bible of Amiens*—itself intended as the first volume of *Our Fathers Have Told Us: Sketches of the History of Christendom,* etc.

"The distinctly religious tone of the work was noticed as marking, if not a change, a strong development of a tendency that had been strengthening for some time past. He had come out of the phase of doubt into acknowledgment of the strong and wholesome influence of serious religion; into an attitude of mind in which, without unsaying anything he had said against narrowness of creed and inconsistency of practice, without stating any definite doctrine of the afterlife or adopting any sectarian dogma, he regarded the fear of God and the revelation of the Divine Spirit as great facts and motives not to be neglected in the study of history, as the groundwork of civilization and the guide of progress." (Collingwood, *The Life and Work of John Ruskin,* II, p. 206 and following). [Cambridge, Mass.: Houghton, Mifflin and Company, The Riverside Press, 1893, 2 vols., vol. II, pp. 507–10] With regard to the subtitle of *The Bible of Amiens,* which Mr. Collingwood recalls (*Sketches of the History of Christendom for Boys and Girls Who Have Been Held at Its Fonts*), I shall point out how much it resembles other of Ruskin's subtitles, for instance the one of *Mornings in Florence: Simple Studies of Christian Art for English Travellers* and still more the one of *St. Mark's Rest: The History of Venice, Written for the Help of the Few Travellers Who Still Care for Her Monuments.*

   3. The heart of Shelley, snatched from the flames in front of Lord Byron by Hunt, during the cremation. Mr. André Lebey (himself author of a sonnet on the death of Shelley) sent me an interesting correction on this subject. It was not Hunt but Trelawny who pulled the heart of Shelley out of the furnace, not without seriously burning his hand. I regret not being able to publish here Mr. Lebey's curious letter. It reproduces in particular this passage from Trelawny's memoirs: "Byron asked me to preserve the skull for him, but remembering that he had formerly used one as a drinking cup, I was determined that Shelley's should not be so profaned." The day before, while Williams's corpse was being identified, Byron told Trelawny: "Let me see the jaw. . . . I can recognize any one by the

teeth, with whom I have talked." But, taking into account Trelawny's report and without even considering the harshness Childe
Harold willingly affected in the presence of the Corsair, one must
remember that, a few lines farther on, Trelawny recounting Shelley's cremation declares: "Byron could not face this scene, he with-
drew to the beach and swam off to the 'Bolivar'." [Edward John
Trelawny, *The Last Days of Shelley and Byron* (New York: The
Philosophical Library, 1952), pp. 88–90]

4. See the admirable portrait of Saint Martin in Book I of *The
Bible of Amiens*: "Companionable even to the loving-cup,[. . .] he is
the patron of honest drinking; the stuffing of your Martinmas goose
is fragrant in his nostrils, and sacred to him the last kindly rays of
departing summer." [1:29; *CW* 33:44]

5. You will perhaps therefore have a chance, as I did (even if you
do not follow the way indicated by Ruskin), to see the cathedral,
which at a distance seems to be but of stone, suddenly transfigured,
and—the sun passing through its interior, making visible and
volatilizing its windows, on which there are no paintings—standing up against the sky, between its stone pillars, giant and immaterial apparitions of gold, green, and flame. You will also be able,
near the slaughterhouse, to look for the view from which the
engraving *Amiens, Jour des Trépassés* was taken.

6. The beauties of the cathedral of Amiens and of Ruskin's book
do not require the shadow of a notion of architecture in order to be
felt, and so that this article might be sufficient in itself, I have used
only the everyday technical terms which everybody knows, and only
when precision and conciseness made them necessary. In all events,
in order to answer those readers who are modest and would say, like
M. Jourdain, "Do as if I did not know it," I remind them that the
main façade of a cathedral always faces west. The doorway of the west
façade, or west porch, is generally composed of three porches, a main
one and two secondary ones. The opposite part of the cathedral, that
is to say, the east part, does not have any porch and is called the apse.
The south porch and the north porch are the porches of the north and
south façades. The passage which forms the arms of the cross in

cross-shaped churches is called the transept. A trumeau, says Viollet-le-Duc, is a pillar dividing a main doorway into two bays. The
same Viollet-le-Duc calls "quatrefoils" in architecture an ornamen-
tal foliation having four circular lobes.

7. Mr. Paul Desjardins has spoken at greater length of stones
which have remained intact longer than hearts.

8. And looked at by them: I can, at this moment, even see the
men hurrying toward the Somme swollen by the tide, passing in
front of the porch they have known for so long, raise their eyes
toward "the Star of the Sea."

9. Begun on July 3, 1508, the 120 choir stalls were completed
in 1522, on Saint John's Day. The beadle, Mr. Regnault, will let
you walk about in the midst of the life of all these personages who,
by the color of their bodies, the lines of their movements, their
worn-out cloaks, their strong broad shoulders, continue to uncover
the essence of the wood, to show its strength, and to sing its
softness. You will see Joseph traveling on the balustrade, Pharoah
sleeping on the crest where the figure of his dreams unfolds, while on
the lower misericords the soothsayers are engaged in interpreting.
He will let you pinch with no risk of any damage to them the long
ropes of wood, and you will hear them produce a sound like that of a
musical instrument, which seems to say, and proves, indeed, how
indestructible and fine they are.

10. Miss Marie Nordlinger, the eminent English artist, has
brought to my attention a letter from Ruskin in which Victor
Hugo's *Notre Dame de Paris* is called the dregs of French literature.
[See Ruskin's letter to F. J. Furnival, dated May 22, 1855: "Did
you ever read *The Hunchback of Notre-Dame*? I believe it to be simply
the most disgusting book ever written by man." (*Letters, CW*
36:212)]

11. *La Cathédrale de Rouen aux différentes heures du jour,* by Claude
Monet (Camondo Collection). For "interiors" of cathedrals, I am
aware only of those, so beautiful, by the great painter Helleu.

12. Mr. Huysmans says: "The Gospels insist that Saint Jude not
be confused with Judas, and yet he was; and because of the similarity

of his name with that of the traitor, during the Middle Ages Christians reviled him. . . . He comes out of his silence only to ask Christ a question on Predestination, and Jesus' answer is beside the point or, to speak more accurately, he does not answer him at all," and he goes on to speak of "the deplorable reputation he owes to his namesake Judas" (*La Cathédrale,* pp. 454–55).

13. Ezekiel 1:16.

14. Daniel 6:22.

15. Joel 1:7 and 2:10.

16. Amos 4:7.

17. Habakkuk 2:1.

18. Zephaniah 2:15; 1:12; 2:14.

19. Arriving at this door, Ruskin says: "If you come, good Protestant feminine reader—come civilly: and be pleased to recollect that [no] Lady-worship of any sort, whether of dead ladies or living ones, ever did any human creature any harm—but the Money-worship, Wig-worship, Cocked-Hat-and-Feather worship . . . have done, and are doing, a great deal—and that any of these, and all, are quite million-fold more offensive to the God of Heaven and Earth and Stars, than all the absurdest and lovingest mistakes made by any generations of His simple children, about what the Virgin-mother could, or would, or might do, or feel for them" [*CW* 33: 164–65]

20. And the castings of several statues mentioned here, and also the choir stalls.

21. Mr. André Michel, who did us the honor of mentioning this study in a *causerie* on art in the *Journal des Débats,* seems to have seen in these last lines a kind of regret at not finding the statue of Ruskin in front of the cathedral, almost a desire to see it there, and, in short, seems already to be hatching a plan asking that it be placed there some day. Nothing was farther removed from our thought. It suffices for us, and is more pleasing to us, to meet Ruskin every time we go to Amiens in the character of the "Mysterious Traveler" with whom Renan talked in the Holy Land. But, after all, since so many statues are erected (and since Mr. André Michel gives us the idea,

which would never have occurred to us), let us admit that a statue of Ruskin in Amiens would at least have, over another statue, the advantage of meaning something. We see him very well in one of the squares of Amiens "as a stranger come to the city," as Mr. Boislèves says of the bronze of Alfred de Vigny.

22. ["Les Muses quittant Apollon leur père pour aller éclairer le monde."] Title of a painting by Gustave Moreau which is in the Moreau Museum.

23. At Sheffield.

24. This part of the preface appeared first in the *Gazette des Beaux-Arts*.

25. Among the writers who have spoken of Ruskin, Milsand was one of the first, both in order of time and by the force of his thinking. He has been a sort of forerunner, an inspired and incomplete prophet, who did not live long enough to see the development of the work he had, in short, foretold.

26. The Ruskin of Mr. de la Sizeranne. Ruskin has been considered to this day, and with just claim, as the personal preserve of Mr. de la Sizeranne, and if at times I try to venture on his ground, it certainly will not be to ignore or usurp his right, which is not the first occupant's alone. As I enter this subject dominated on all sides by the magnificent monument he has erected to Ruskin, I must thus render homage and pay tribute to him.

27. Since these lines were written, Mr. Bardoux and Mr. Brunhes have published, one a considerable work, and the other a small book on Ruskin. I recently had the opportunity to say how well I thought of these two books, but too briefly not to wish to come back to them. All I can say here is that my very high esteem for Mr. Bardoux's beautiful effort does not prevent me from thinking that Mr. de la Sizeranne's book was too perfect, within the limits the author had set for himself, to have anything to lose from this competition and emulation that seems to take place on the subject of Ruskin, and to which we owe, among other things, some curious pages by Mr. Gabriel Mourey and some definitive words by Mr. André Beaunier. Messrs. Bardoux and Brunhes have given different

points of view, and thus have renewed the horizon. That is what, with all due allowance, I myself tried to do here a little earlier.

28. To be more exact, Saint-Urbain is mentioned once in *The Seven Lamps* and Amiens once also (but only in the preface to the second edition), while there are mentions of Abbeville, Avranches, Bayeux, Beauvais, Bourges, Caen, Caudebec, Chartres, Coutances, Falaise, Lisieux, Paris, Rheims, Rouen, and Saint-Lô, to speak of France only.

29. In *Saint Mark's Rest,* he goes so far as to say that there was but one Greek art from the battle of Marathon down to the day of the doge Selvo [*Saint Mark's Rest, CW* 24:281] (cf. the pages of *The Bible of Amiens,* in which he makes the builders who dug the ancient labyrinth of Amiens descend from Daedalus, "the first sculptor of imagery pathetic with human life and death") [5:19; *CW* 33:136]; and in the mosaics of the baptistry of St. Mark's he recognizes a harpy in a cherub, a canephora in a Herodias, a Greek vase in a golden dome, etc. [*Saint Mark's Rest, CW* 24:283–84]

30. In an admirable study, published in the *Gazette des Beaux-Arts.* Since Fromentin, no painter, we believe, has shown greater mastery as a writer. These lines had already appeared while Mr. Ary Renan was still living. Now that he is dead, I wonder if I did not understate the truth. It now seems to me that he was superior to Fromentin.

31. "So from it," he says, "that I believe no interpretations of Greek religion have ever been so affectionate, none of Roman religion so reverent, as those which will be found at the base of my teaching." [*The Bible of Amiens,* 4:52; *CW* 33:118]

32. Cf. Chateaubriand, preface to the first edition of *Atala*: "The muses are celestial women who do not disfigure their features by making faces; when they weep, it is with the secret design of embellishing themselves."

33. *Praeterita,* I, ch. 2. [*CW* 25:48].

34. What an interesting collection one could make with land-scapes of France seen through English eyes: the rivers of France, by Turner; *Versailles,* by Bonnington; *Auxerre* or *Valenciennes, Vézelay* or

Amiens, by Walter Pater; *Fontainebleau,* by Stevenson; and so many others!

35. *The Seven Lamps of Architecture.* [*CW* 8:216–17, plate XIV: sculptures from the bas-reliefs of the North Door of the cathedral of Rouen]

36. Ruskin's sentence applies better to idolatry as I understand it if taken out of context than where it is found in *Lectures on Art.* I have, moreover, quoted the beginning of the development farther on in a note to pages 330, 331, and 332.

37. How could Mr. Barrès leave out Ruskin when, in an admirable chapter of his latest book, he was electing an ideal senate for Venice? Was he not more worthy to sit in it than Léopold Robert or Théophile Gautier, and would he not have been well placed between Byron and Barrès, between Goethe and Chateaubriand?

38. I do not have the time today to make myself clear on this defect, but it seems to me that through my translation, dull though it may be, the reader will be able to perceive, as through the rough, but suddenly illuminated glass of an aquarium, the rapid but visible channeling of the thought by the sentence and the immediate loss the thought undergoes.

39. Throughout *The Bible of Amiens,* the reader will often find similar formulas.

40. Renan.

41. I was still not quite sure that this idea was absolutely right, but my mind was soon relieved by the only means that exists for the verification of our ideas; I mean the chance encounter with a great mind. In fact, almost at the moment I had written these lines there appeared in the *Revue des Deux Mondes* the verses of the countess de Noailles which I give below. One will see that I had unknowingly, as Mr. Barrès said at Combourg, "set my steps in the footsteps of genius":

Children, look well at all the plains around;
The nasturtium surrounded by its bees;
Look well at the pond, the fields, before love;

For thereafter, one never again sees anything of the world.
Thereafter, one sees but one's heart before oneself;
One sees but a bit of flame on the road;
One hears nothing, one knows nothing, and one listens
To the feet of sad love which runs or sits.

Selected Notes of Proust
to His Translation of
La Bible d'Amiens

Each note given here is preceded by the passage from *The Bible of Amiens* (*CW* 33) to which it refers; the citation following each passage is to chapter and section number. The page and note number given with the note itself is a citation to *La Bible d'Amiens*, cinquième édition (see p. x above). These selected notes have been translated and edited by Phillip J. Wolfe.

"Let these noble words of tender Justice be the first example to my young readers of what all History ought to be. It has been told to them, in *The Laws of Fiesole*, that all great Art is Praise." [Preface: 4]

The Laws of Fiesole, I, 1–6. [Cf. *CW* 15:351] Compare the commentary and final dedication of these words at the end of *Modern Painters* [*CW* 7:463–64]: "All that is involved in these passionate utterances of my youth was first expanded and then concentrated into the aphorism given twenty years afterwards in my inaugural Oxford lectures, 'All great art is praise'; and on that aphorism, the yet bolder saying founded, 'So far from Art's being immoral, in the ultimate power of it, nothing but Art is moral: Life without Industry is sin, and Industry without Art, brutality' (I forget the words, but that is their purport): and now, in writing beneath the cloudless peace of the snows of Chamouni, what must be the really final words of the book which their beauty inspired and their strength guided, I am able with yet happier and calmer heart than ever heretofore, to enforce its simplest assurance of Faith, that the knowledge of what is beautiful leads on, and is the first step, to the knowledge of the things which are lovely and of good report; and that the laws, the life, and the joy of beauty in the material world of God, are as eternal and sacred parts of His creation as, in the world of spirits, virtue; and in the world of the angels, praise." (Chamouni, Sunday, September 16th, 1888.) [p. 102*n*1]

"St. Martin teazes nobody, spends not a breath in unpleasant exhortation, understands, by Christ's first lesson to himself, that undipped people may be as good as dipped if their hearts are clean; helps, forgives, and cheers (companionable even to the loving-cup), as readily the clown as the king; he is the patron of honest drinking. . . ." [1:29]

Ruskin is not the only one, it seems to me, who enjoys using these characteristics to depict a saint. The best of George Eliot's clergymen and Carlyle's prophets are no more "preaching saints" than they are "saints like John the Baptist." They "do not spend a breath in unpleasant exhortation." They are as kind "to the clown as [to] the king" and are also patrons "of honest drinking." [pp. 131– 32*n*2. Proust's note continues with quotations from Thomas Carlyle on Knox, Burns, Mohammed, and Luther (from *On Heroes*) and from George Eliot on Irwine (*Adam Bede*), Gilfil (*Scenes of Clerical Life*), and Farebrother (*Middlemarch*).]

"But the savage conqueror of Gaul was incapable of examining the proofs of a religion, which depends on the laborious investigation of historic evidence, and speculative theology. He was still more incapable of feeling the mild influence of the

Gospel, which persuades and purifies the heart of a genuine convert. His ambitious reign was a perpetual violation of moral and Christian duties: his hands were stained with blood, in peace as well as in war; and, as soon as Clovis had dismissed a synod of the Gallican Church, he calmly assassinated *all* the princes of the Merovingian race." [2:46]

In this whole portrait of Clovis, Ruskin reveals a tendency not to give too unfavorable a moral interpretation of harshness, a tendency that exists also, it seems to me, in Carlyle (see, in Carlyle, *Cromwell,* etc.). In this there are, I believe, two things. First, a sort of historical or sociological gift that is able to discover a different moral intention in apparently identical actions, according to the times and the culture, and to connect the extremely diverse forms which the same morality or immorality assumes through the ages. This gift exists to a very high degree in writers such as Ruskin, and still more in George Eliot. It also exists in Mr. Tarde. Secondly, a fine literary man may also, by a natural bent of his imagination, appreciate a primitive culture. At times, even in Ruskin's letters, this taste is recognized by a certain affectation of harshness or nonconformity. Read in Mr. de la Sizeranne's book, p. 61, Ruskin's answer to a priest in debt: "Try first begging—I don't mind if it's really needful—stealing. But don't buy things you can't pay for. And of all manners of debtors pious people building churches they can't pay for are the most detestable nonsense to me. And of all the sects of believers your modern English Evangelical is the most absurd, etc., etc." [p. 183*n*1. The quotation is from *Arrows of the Chace, CW* 34:595.]

———————

"I am alone, to my belief, among recent scholars, in maintaining Herodotus' statement of [Egypt's] influence on the archaic theology of Greece." [3:27]

"I am alone, to my belief, in maintaining Herodotus' statement." Anyone with a mind keen enough to be struck by the characteristic qualities of a writer's personality, and disregarding whatever he might have been told about Ruskin, that he was a prophet, a seer, a Protestant, and other things that make no sense, will feel that such qualities, although certainly secondary, are nevertheless very "Ruskinian." Ruskin lives in a sort of fraternal society with all the great minds of all times, and since he is interested in them only so far as they can answer eternal questions, there are for him neither ancients or moderns, and he can speak about Herodotus as he would of a contemporary. Since the ancients have no value for him, except in so far as they are "current" and can serve as illustrations for our daily meditations, he does not treat them at all as ancients. Then again all their words, not suffering from the passage of time and no longer considered as relating to a given period, are of greater importance to him, keeping in a way the scientific value they might have had, but which they had lost as time went on. From the way Horace speaks at the fountain of Bandusia, Ruskin concludes that he was pious "in the manner of Milton" [*Queen of the Air, CW* 19:348].* And already at the age of eleven, learning the odes of Anacreon for his own pleasure, he learned "with certainty, what in later study of Greek art it has proved extremely advantageous for me to know, that the Greeks liked doves, swallows, and roses just as well as I did" (*Praeterita,* § 81). [*CW* 35:74]. For an Emerson, "culture" evidently has the same value. But even without stopping at profound differences, let us first note, to emphasize the particular traits of Ruskin's character, that in his eyes there being no difference between science and art (see the preface, pp. 51–57), he speaks of the ancients as scholars with the same reverence as of the ancients as artists. He invokes Psalm 104 with reference to discoveries in the natural sciences, he sides with Herodotus (and would willingly oppose his opinion to that of a contemporary scholar) in a question of religious history, he admires a Carpaccio painting as an important contribution to the descriptive history of parrots (*St. Mark's Rest: The Shrine of the Slaves*). [*CW*

---

*Ed. note: Bandusiae Fons was a fountain in Apulia made famous by Horace in his ode III, 13, beginning with "O fons Bandusiae, splendidior vitro."

24:341] Evidently, here we would quickly encounter the idea of classical sacred art (see farther on, notes pp. 244–46, 338–39), "there is but one Greek art, etc., Saint Jerome and Hercules," etc., each of these ideas leading to the others. But for the moment we only have a Ruskin tenderly loving his library, making no distinction between science and art, therefore thinking that a scientific theory may remain true as a work of art may remain beautiful (he never expresses this idea explicitly, but it secretly governs all the others and, alone, could make them possible) and asking of an ancient ode or a medieval bas-relief some information on natural history or critical philosophy, persuaded that it is more useful to consult all wise men of all times and of all countries than fools of today. Of course, this inclination is repressed by a critical sense so just that we can trust him entirely, and he exaggerates it only for the pleasure of making little jokes on "the entomology of the XIIIth century," etc. etc. [pp. 212–14*n*2]

"Jerome's life by no means 'began as a monk of Palestine.' Dean Milman has not explained to us how any man's could; but Jerome's childhood, at any rate, was extremely other than recluse, or precociously religious. He was born of rich parents living on their own estate, the name of his native town in North Illyria, Stridon, perhaps now softened into Strigi, near Aquileia." [3:34]

The best place to read this chapter is in the church of San Giorgio dei Schiavoni in Venice. One takes a gondola and, in a quiet canal, a little before reaching the shimmering, sparkling infinity of the lagoon, one comes upon this "Shrine of Slaves" where one can see (when the sun illuminates them) the paintings Carpaccio devoted to Saint Jerome. One should bring along *Saint Mark's Rest* and read the entire chapter of which I give here a sizable extract, not because it is one of Ruskin's best, but because it clearly was written under the influence of the same preoccupations as chapter III ["The Lion Tamer"] of *The Bible of Amiens*—and to have with "The Lion Tamer" an illustration showing "The Lion." Ruskin had gone to Venice to study Carpaccio from September 1876 to May 1877, that is to say, two or three years before beginning *The Bible of Amiens*. [pp. 219–20*n*2. Proust's note continues with a passage from *Saint Mark's Rest, CW* 33:346–50]

"Fate had otherwise determined, and Jerome was so passive an instrument in her hands that he began the study of Hebrew as a discipline only, and without any conception of the task he was to fulfil. . . ." [3:38]

This sort of ignorance deep in their souls is at the base of Ruskin's idea of all the prophets, that is to say, of all men truly inspired. Speaking of himself, he says: "This, then, is the message which, knowing no more as I unfolded the scroll of it, what next would be written there, than a blade of grass knows what the form of its fruit shall be, I have been led year by year to speak, even to this end" (*Fors* [*Clavigera*], IV, letter LXXVIII, p. 121) [*CW* 19:138] and speaking of the last days of Moses: "The whole history of those forty years was unfolded before him, and the mystery of his own ministries revealed to him" (*Modern Painters*, IV, V, XX, 46 [*CW* 6:460–61], cited by Mr. Brunhes). But this future that men do not see is already contained in their hearts. And it seems to me that Ruskin never expressed it in a more mysterious and more beautiful fashion than in this sentence on Giotto as a child, when he saw Florence for the first time: "He saw . . . deep beneath, the innumerable towers of the City of the Lily, the depths of his own heart yet hiding the fairest of them all (the Campanile)." (*Giotto and His Work in Padua* [. . .].) [*CW* 24:18] [p. 227*n*1]

"Alas, no, Queen Sophia, neither old St. Jerome's nor any other human lips nor mind, may be depended upon in that function; but the Eternal Sophia. . . ." [3:47]

A typically Ruskinian allusion to the etymology of a word: Sophia; here it is hardly a pun, but the reader has been able to see in the previous chapter just how far Ruskin's etymological enthusiasm could take him, in the case of the meaning delicately "saline" of the word *salique,* and in the puns with "salted" and "salient." [2:31; *CW* 33:70] But taking into consideration the above passage only (Sophia—Wisdom), it finds its explanation (and with it, all of Ruskin's plays on words, even the most tiresome) in the following lines of *Sesame and Lilies, of Kings and Treasuries* 15 [*CW* 18:65]: "A well-educated gentleman is learned in the *peerage* of words; knows the words of true descent and ancient blood, at a glance, from words of modern canaille; remembers all their ancestry, their intermarriages, distant relationships, and the extent to which they were admitted, and the offices they held, among the national noblesse of words at any time, and in any country," etc. I have not the time to show that here again there is a form of idolatry, and one of those to which the temptation of a man of taste has the most difficulty not to succumb. [pp. 235–36*n*1]

"I am no despiser of profane literature. So far from it that I believe no interpretations of Greek religion have ever been so affectionate, none of Roman religion so reverent, as those which will be found at the base of my art teaching, and current through the entire body of my works. But it was from the Bible that I learned the symbols of Homer, and the faith of Horace. . . ." [3:52]

Compare "You are perhaps surprised to hear Horace spoken of as a pious person. Wise men know he is wise, true men know he is true. But pious men, for want of attention, do not always know he is pious. One great obstacle to your understanding of him is your having been forced to construct Latin verses, with introduction of the word Jupiter always, at need, when you were at a loss for a dactyl. You always feel Horace only used it also when *he* wanted a dactyl. Note, then, his piety, and accept his assured speech of it: "*Dis, pietas mea, et Musa, cordi est,*" etc. (*Val d'Arno,* chap. IX, § 219–21 and following). See also: "Horace is as true in his religion as Wordsworth; but all power of understanding the honest classic poets has been taken away from English gentlemen by the mechanical drill in verse-writing at school. Throughout the whole of their lives afterwards, they never can get themselves quit of the notion that all verses were written as an exercise, and that Minerva was only a convenient word for the last of a hexameter, and Jupiter for the last but one. It is impossible that any notion can be more fallacious. . . . Horace dedicates his favorite pine to Diana, and he chants his autumnal hymn to Faunus, guides the noble youths and maids of Rome in their choir to Apollo, and he tells the farmer's little girl that the Gods will love her, though she has only a handful of salt and meal to give them—just as earnestly as ever English gentleman taught Christian faith to English youth, in England's truest days" (*The Queen of the Air*, I, 47–48). And finally, "The faith of Horace in the spirit of the Fountain of Brundisium, in the Faun of his hillside, and in the protection of the greater gods is constant, vital, and practical." (*Fors Clavigera*, letter XCIII, 111). [pp. 241–42*n*1]

"The story of the Nemean Lion, with the aid of Athena in its conquest, is the real root-stock of the legend of St. Jerome's companion, conquered by the healing gentleness of the Spirit of Life." [3:53]

Likewise, in *Val d'Arno* [*CW* 23:119], the lion of Saint Mark descends directly from the Lion of Nemea, and the crest which crowns him is that which one sees on the head of Hercules of Camarina (*Val d'Arno*, I, § 16, p. 13) [Cf. *The Queen of the Air*, *CW* 19:416–17], with this difference indicated elsewhere in the same work (*Val d'Arno*, VIII, § 203, p. 169) [*CW* 23:119] that "Heraklès kills the beast, and makes a helmet and cloak of his skin; the Greek St. Mark converts the beast, and makes an evangelist of him."

It is not in order to find another sacred genealogy for the Lion of Nemea that we have quoted this passage, but to stress the whole theme of the end of this chapter of *The Bible of Amiens*, "that there is a sacred classic literature." Ruskin did not want Greek to be opposed to Christian, but to Gothic (*Val d'Arno*) [*CW* 23:119], for "Saint

Mark is Greek like Heraklès." We are touching here on one of Ruskin's most important ideas, or, more exactly, one of his most original feelings toward the contemplation and study of Greek and Christian works of art, and it is necessary, to make it well understood, to quote a passage from *Saint Mark's Rest,* which, we believe, is one of those in the works of Ruskin where is better shown, and better seen at work, that particular disposition of mind which made him take no heed of the coming of Christianity, recognize an already Christian beauty in pagan works, and follow the persistence of a Hellenic ideal in the works of the Middle Ages. That this disposition of mind which we believe to be wholly aesthetic, at least logically in its essence if not chronologically in its origin, was systematized in Ruskin's mind and that he extended it to historical and religious criticism is certain indeed. But even when Ruskin compares Greek dynasties with Gothic dynasties (*Val d'Arno,* chap. "Franchise"), when he declares in *The Bible of Amiens* [3:26; *CW* 33:102] that "Christianity has brought no great change to the human ideal of virtue and happiness," when, as we saw on the preceding page, he speaks of the religion of Horace, he simply draws theoretical conclusions from the aesthetic pleasure he experienced upon recognizing a canephora in Herodias' daughter, a harpy in a cherub, a Greek vase in a Byzantine dome. Here is the passage from *Saint Mark's Rest* [*CW* 24:280–81]: "And this is true, not of Byzantine art only, but of Greek art, pur sang. There is but one Greek art, from Homer's day down to the Doge Selvo's" (we could say from Theognis to the countess Mathieu de Noailles), "and these St. Mark's mosaics are as truly wrought in the power of Daedalus, with the Greek constructive instinct, and in the power of Athena, with the Greek religious soul, as ever chest of Cypselus or shaft of Erechtheum."

Then Ruskin enters the baptistry of Saint Mark's and says: "Over the door is Herod's feast. Herodias' daughter dances with St. John Baptist's head in the charger, on her head,—simply the translation of any Greek maid on a Greek vase, bearing a pitcher on her head. . . . Pass on now into the farther chapel under the darker

dome. Darker, and very dark;—to my old eyes, scarcely decipherable; to yours, if young and bright, it should be beautiful, for it is
indeed the origin of all those gold-domed backgrounds of Bellini
and Cima and Carpaccio; itself a Greek vase, but with new Gods.
That ten-winged cherub in the recess of it, behind the altar, has
written on the circle in its breast, 'Fulness of wisdom.' It is the type
of the Breath of the Spirit. But it was once a Greek Harpy, and its
wasted limbs remain, scarcely yet clothed with flesh from the claws
of birds that they were. Above, Christ Himself ascends, borne in a
whirlwind of angels; and, as the vaults of Bellini and Carpaccio are
only the amplification of the Harpy-Vault, so the Paradise of Tin-
toret is only the final fulfilment of the thought in this narrow cupola.

". . . These mosaics are not earlier than the thirteenth century.
And yet they are still absolutely Greek in all the modes of thought,
and forms of tradition. The Fountains of fire and water are merely
forms of the Chimera and the Peirene; and the maid dancing,
though a princess of the thirteenth century in sleeves and ermine, is
yet the phantom of some water-carrier from an Arcadian spring."
[*CW* 24:283–85]

For me, this page has not only the charm of having been read in
the baptistry of Saint Mark's, in those blessed days when, with some
other disciples "in spirit and in truth" of the master, we would go
about Venice in a gondola, listening to his teachings by the water's
edge, and landing at each one of the temples that seemed to spring
up from the sea to offer us the object of his descriptions and the very
image of his thought, to give life to his books, whose immortal
reflection shines on them today. But if these churches are the life of
Ruskin's books, they are also their spirit. (The line repeated by
Fantasio: "You call me your life, call me your soul" never had more
appropriate application.)* Undoubtedly, Ruskin's books have retained something of the beauty of these places. Undoubtedly, if
Ruskin's books had at first created in us a kind of fever and desire

---

*Ed. note: The quotation is from Musset's comedy in two acts, *Fantasio,* act I,
scene 2.

that, in our imagination, gave to Venice and to Amiens a beauty which, once in their presence, we did not find in them at first, the shimmering sun of the canal or the golden cold of a French autumn morning on which they were read has given these pages a charm we feel only later, less fascinating than that when they were first read, but deeper perhaps, and which they will keep as indelibly as if they had been dipped in some chemical preparation which leaves beautiful, verdant reflections on the pages, and which, here, is nothing but the special color of the past. Indeed, if this page from *Saint Mark's Rest* had no other charm, we would not have had to quote it here. But it seems to us that commenting on this ending of the chapter from *The Bible of Amiens* will make you understand its profound meaning and its uniquely "Ruskinian" character. And compared with similar pages (see notes, pages 213–14, 338–39), it will enable the reader to discover an aspect of Ruskin's thought which, even if he has read all that has been written to date on Ruskin, will have for him the charm, or at least the merit, of being shown, it seems to me, for the first time. [pp. 244–46*n*1]

"Of Gothic, mind you; Gothic clear of Roman tradition, and of Arabian taint; Gothic pure, authoritative, unsurpassable, and unaccusable;—its proper principles of structure being once understood and admitted." [4:1]

See the development of these ideas in Walter Pater's *Miscellanea* (article on "Notre-Dame of Amiens"). I do not know why Ruskin's name is never once mentioned. [p. 250*n*2]

"It was a universal principle with the French builders of the great ages to use the stones of their quarries as they lay in the bed; if the beds were thick, the stones were used of their full thickness—if thin, of their necessary thinness, adjusting them with beautiful care to directions of thrust and weight. The natural blocks were never sawn, only squared into fitting, the whole native strength and crystallization of the stone being thus kept unflawed—"*ne dédoublant jamais* une pierre. Cette méthode est excellente, elle conserve à la pierre toute sa force naturelle,—tous ses moyens de résistance." See M. Viollet le Duc, Article "Construction" (Matériaux), vol. iv, p. 129. He adds the very notable fact that, *to this day, in seventy departments of France, the use of the stone-saw is unknown.*" [4:2, footnote]

On stones used in the direction of the grain or against the grain, see Ruskin, *Val d'Arno,* chap. VIII, § 169. Essentially, for Ruskin, who establishes no dividing line between nature and art, between art and science, an uncut stone is already a scientific document, that is to say, in his eyes a work of art which must not be mutilated. "There is history in them,[. . .] in all their veins and zones, and their disconnected lines. Their colours write various legends, never untrue, of the former political states of the mountain kingdom to which this marble belonged, of its infirmities and fortitudes, convulsions and consolidations, from the beginning of time" (*The Stones of Venice,* III, 1, 42, quoted by Mr. de la Sizeranne). [p. 251*n*1]

"The architectural form can never be well delighted in, unless in some sympathy with the spiritual imagination out of which it rose." [4:4]

Compare the contrary idea in Léon Brunschwig's beautiful book, *Introduction à la vie de l'Esprit,* chap. III: "In order to experience an aesthetic joy, to appreciate the edifice, no longer as well built but as truly beautiful, one must . . . feel it in harmony, no longer with some external purpose, but with the intimate state of actual consciousness. That is why ancient monuments that no longer serve the purpose for which they were built or whose purpose fades more quickly from our memory lend themselves so easily and so completely to aesthetic contemplation. *A cathedral is a work of art when one no longer sees in it the instrument of salvation, the center of social life in a city*; for the believer who sees it another way, it is something else" (page 97). And page 112: "The cathedrals of the Middle Ages . . . may have for some people a certain charm their authors did not suspect." The preceding sentence is not in italics in the text. But I wanted to isolate it because it seems to me that it is the very counterpart of *The Bible of Amiens* and, more generally, of all the studies of Ruskin on religious art in general. [p. 254*n*1]

". . . And, coming quite up to the porch, everybody must like the pretty French Madonna in the middle of it, with her head a little aside, and her nimbus switched a little aside too, like a becoming bonnet. A Madonna in decadence she is, though, for all, or rather by reason of all, her prettiness. . . . [4:7]

Compare this, from *The Two Paths*, sections 33–34: "These statues [of the west porch of Chartres] have been long, and justly, considered as representative of the highest skill of the twelfth or earliest part of the thirteenth century in France; and they indeed possess a dignity and delicate charm, which are for the most part wanting in later works. It is owing partly to real nobleness of feature, but chiefly to the grace, mingled with severity, of the falling lines of excessively *thin* drapery; as well as to a most studied finish in composition, every part of the ornamentation tenderly harmonizing with the rest. So far as their power over certain tones of religious mind is owing to a palpable degree of non-naturalism in them, I do not praise it—the exaggerated thinness of body and stiffness of attitude are faults; but they are noble faults, and give the statues a strange look of forming part of the very building itself, and sustaining it—not like the Greek caryatid, without effort—nor like the Renaissance caryatid, by painful or impossible effort—but as if all that was silent and stern, and withdrawn apart, and stiffened in chill of heart against the terror of earth, had passed into a shape of eternal marble; and thus the Ghost had given, to bear up the pillars of the church on earth, all the patient and expectant nature that it needed no more in heaven. This is the transcendental view of the meaning of those sculptures. I do not dwell upon it. What I do lean upon is their purely naturalistic and vital power. They are all portraits—unknown, most of them, I believe,—but palpably and unmistakeably portraits, if not taken from the actual person for whom the statue stands, at all events studied from some living person whose features might fairly represent those of the king or saint intended. Several of them I suppose to be authentic: there is one of a queen, who has evidently, while she lived, been notable for her bright black eyes. The sculptor has cut the iris deep into the stone, and her dark eyes are still suggested with her smile." [p. 260n1]

". . . But they could still carve, in the fourteenth century, and the Madonna and her hawthorn-blossom lintel are worth your looking at. . . ." [4:7]

Less delightful than the one at Bourges. Bourges is the cathedral of hawthorn. Compare Ruskin, *The Stones of Venice*: "The architect of Bourges cathedral liked hawthorns; so he has covered his porch with hawthorn,—it is a perfect Niobe of May. Never was such hawthorn; you would gather it forthwith, but for fear of being pricked" (*The Stones of Venice*, I, ii, 13–15). [p. 263n1]

"Above this pedestal comes a minor one, bearing in front of it a tendril of vine which completes the floral symbolism of the whole. The plant which I have called a lily is not the Fleur de Lys, nor the Madonna's. . . ." [4:32]

To distinguish these different species of lilies better, refer to the beautiful passages in *The Queen of the Air* and *Val d'Arno*: "Consider what each of these five tribes has been for the spirit of man. First, in their nobleness; the Lilies gave the Lily of the Annunciation; the Asphodels, the flower of the Elysian fields; the Irids, the fleur de lys of chivalry; and the Amaryllids, Christ's lily of the field: while the rush, trodden always under foot, became the emblem of humility.

Then take each of the tribes, and consider the extent of their lower influence. Perdita's 'The Crown Imperial, lilies of all kinds,' are the first tribe; which, giving the type of perfect purity in the Madonna's lily, have, by their lovely form, influenced the entire decorative design of Italian sacred art; while ornament of war was continually enriched by the curve of the triple petals of the Florentine 'giglio' and the French fleur de lys; so that it is impossible to count their influence for good in the middle ages, partly as a symbol of womanly character, and partly of the utmost brightness and refinement in the city which was the flower of cities." (*The Queen of the Air,* II, § 82).

In *Val d'Arno,* in the lecture entitled "Fleur de Lys," one should note (§ 251) the recollection of Cora and Triptolemus concerning the Florentine fleur de lys and Hera's crown, which typifies the form of the purple iris, or the flower mentioned by Pindar when he describes the birth of Ianus, and which is also found near Oxford. The note Ruskin gives on page 211 of *Val d'Arno* points out that Florentine artists generally place the true white lily in the hands of the Angel of the Annunciation, but that on the façade of Orvieto, it is the "fleur de lys" that is given him by Giovanni Pisano, etc., etc. The lecture ends with the beautiful sentence on lilies which I quoted in the preface. [p. 285*n*1]

"The words, 'Except ye eat the flesh of the Son of Man and drink His blood, ye have no life in you' [John 6:53], remain in their mystery, to be understood only by those who have learned the sacredness of food, in all times and places, and the laws of life and spirit, dependent on its acceptance, refusal, and distribution." [4:41, 7A]

In this passage, it was for me, not the words of Christ, but the words of Ruskin that for many years "remained in their mystery." I always thought, however, that what was meant here was the sacred character of *food* in its most general and material sense, that in speaking of the laws of life and of the spirit as linked to its acceptance and to its refusal, Ruskin meant to signify the indispensable and constant sustenance that food gives to thought and life, any partial refusal of food translating itself by a modification of the state of mind, as for instance in asceticism. As to the distribution of food, it seems to me that the laws of the spirit and of life are also linked to it in that they depend, if one takes the subjective viewpoint of he who gives (that is to say, the moral viewpoint), upon the charity of the heart and, if one takes the viewpoint of those who receive, and even of those who give (considered objectively, from the political viewpoint), upon strong social order. But I had no certainty, for I did not find in any of Ruskin's books the same ideas or the same expressions I had in mind. And the works of a great writer are the only dictionary where one might verify with certainty the meaning of the words he uses. However, this same idea, being Ruskin's, had to be found again in Ruskin. We do not think of an idea once only. We like an idea for a while, we come back to it several times, even if it is only to abandon it forever. If you have met in the company of some person a man who is very fickle, I do not say in his friendships, but in his acquaintances, no doubt during the year that follows this meeting you would, if you were the man's doorkeeper, see entering his house the friend or a letter from the friend you met or, were you his own memory, you would see, passing by, the image of his ephemeral friend. So with an intellect, should one wish to see again one of its ideas, even if it were only a passing idea and favored only for a while, one must do as fishermen do: Cast an attentive net, move it from one place to another (from one time period to another) according to its catch, even if this must be constantly repeated. If the mesh of the net is tight and fine enough, it would be surprising if you did not stop in passing one of those beautiful creatures we call Ideas, which delight in the waters of thought, born there by what seems to be spontaneous generation, and where those who love to stroll on the edges of thought are sure to see them one day, if only they have a little patience and a little love. The other day, while reading in *Verona and Other Lectures* the chapter entitled "The Story of Arachne" and having come to a passage (§§ 25–26) on cookery, a key science and the basis of the happiness of states, I was struck by the final sentence. "Now you are likely to laugh when I say this; and I'm very glad that you should laugh, provided only you distinctly understand that I'm not laughing, but in most absolute and accurate seriousness, stating to you what I believe to be necessary for the prosperity of this and every other nation; namely, first, diligent purification and *kindly distribution of food,* so that we should be able, not only on Sundays, but after the daily labour, which, if it is rightly understood, is a constantly recurrent and daily divine service,—that we should be able, I say, then to eat the fat, and drink the sweet, and send portions to them for whom nothing is prepared." [*The Story of Arachne, CW* 20:377] (This last sentence is from Nehemiah 3:10.) Some day I shall perhaps find a precise commentary on the words "acceptance" and "refusal." But I believe that for "food" and "distribution" this passage verifies absolutely my hypothesis. [pp. 299–301*n*4]

"CHARITY, bearing shield with woolly ram, and giving a mantle to a naked beggar. The old wool manufacture of Amiens having this notion of its purpose—namely, to clothe the poor first, the rich afterwards. No nonsense talked in those days about the evil consequences of indiscriminate charity." [4:41, 9A]

Speaking of the realistic and practical character of Christianity in the North, Ruskin again evokes this figure of the Charity of Amiens in *Pleasures of England*: "While the ideal charity of Giotto at Padua presents her heart in her hand to God, and tramples at the same instant on bags of gold, the treasures of the world, and gives only corn and flowers; that on the west porch at Amiens is content to clothe a beggar with a piece of the staple manufacture of the town" (*Pleasures of England,* IV).

The same comparison (certainly a fortuitous encounter) has also occurred to Mr. Mâle, and he has expressed it particularly well: "The Charity which presents God with its passionate heart is of the country of Saint Francis of Assisi. The Charity which gives its coat to the poor is of the country of Saint Vincent de Paul."

Ruskin again compares different interpretations of Charity in *The Stones of Venice*. [p. 302*n*2. Proust's note continues with a passage from *The Stones of Venice, CW* 10:389.]

"For the sake of comparing the pollution, and reversal of its once glorious religion, in the modern French mind, it is worth the reader's while to ask at M. Goyer's (Place St. Denis) for the 'Journal de St. Nicholas' for 1880, and look at the 'Phénix,' as drawn on p. 610. The story is meant to be moral, and the Phœnix there represents Avarice, but the entire destruction of all sacred and poetic tradition in a child's mind by such a picture is an immorality which would neutralize a year's preaching." [4:41, footnote to 10A, "CHASTITY, shield with the Phoenix"]

Mr. Mâle is not far from believing that the artist who represented Chastity at Notre-Dame de Paris (Rose Window) intended to portray on its shield a salamander, symbol of chastity because it lives in flames, even has the ability to extinguish them, and is sexless. But the artist having erred and transformed the salamander into a bird, his error was copied at Amiens and Chartres. [p. 304*n*1]

"WISDOM: shield with, I think, an eatable root; meaning temperance, as the beginning of wisdom." [4:41, 11A]

"Its shield bears a serpent which, at times, coils around a stick. No shield is nobler, since Jesus himself gave it to Prudence. 'Be prudent,' he said, 'like the serpent'" (Mâle).

Giotto gives Prudence the double face of Janus and a mirror (*The Stones of Venice,* I, v, § lxxxiii). [p. 304*n*3]

"All these quatrefoils are rather symbolic than representative; and, since their purpose was answered enough if their sign was understood, they have been entrusted to a more inferior workman than the one who carved the now sequent series under the Prophets. Most of these subjects represent an historical fact, or a scene spoken of by the prophet as a real vision; and they have in general been executed by the ablest hands at the architect's command.

With the interpretation of these, I have given again the name of the prophet whose life or prophecy they illustrate." [4:42]

Usually these prophecies are written on pennants rather than given on bas-reliefs, as at Amiens. To complete with Ruskinian images the tableau that Ruskin provides here, we shall stop quoting only Mr. Mâle and compare the prophecies given at Amiens to those inscribed on the baptistry of Saint Mark's. Readers know that these mosaics are described in *Saint Mark's Rest,* in the chapter "Sanctus, Sanctus, Sanctus." And the baptistry of Saint Mark's, whose dazzling freshness is so sweet during Venice's burning afternoons, is in its way a kind of Ruskinian Holy of Holies. Mr. Collingwood, Ruskin's favorite disciple, to whom we owe, in short, the finest book ever written about him, has said that *Saint Mark's Rest* was to *The Stones of Venice* what *The Bible of Amiens* was to *The Seven Lamps of Architecture.* I think he means that both subjects were chosen by Ruskin as historical examples, intended to illustrate the laws set forth in his theoretical works. This is the moment when, as Alphonse Daudet would say, "the teacher goes to the blackboard." And, indeed, in many respects nothing is closer to *The Bible of Amiens* than this *Gospel of Venice.* But *Saint Mark's Rest* is Ruskin no longer at his best. In the chapter quoted above entitled "Requiem," he himself says very movingly: "Pass on now into the farther chapel under the darker dome. Darker, and very dark;—to my old eyes, scarcely decipherable; to yours, if young and bright, it should be beautiful, for it is indeed the origin of all those golden-domed backgrounds of Bellini, and Cima, and Carpaccio." (*Saint Mark's Rest,* VII, 95 [*CW* 24:283]). But after all it was to try to see what those "old eyes" had seen that we went every day to shut ourselves up in that dark and dazzling baptistry. And we can say of them what he said of Turner's eyes: "Through those eyes, now filled with dust, generations yet unborn will learn to behold the light of nature" (*Lectures on Architecture,* III, 101 [*CW* 12:128]). [p. 306*n* 1]

"The other saints in this porch are all in like manner provincial, and, as it were, personal friends of the Amienois; and under them, the quatrefoils represent the pleasant order of the guarded and hallowed year—the zodiacal signs above, and labours of the months below; little differing from the constant representations of them—except in the May: see below. The Libra also is a little unusual in the female figure holding the scales; the lion especially good-tempered—and the 'reaping' one of the most beautiful figures in the whole series of sculptures; several of the others peculiarly refined and far-wrought." [4:47]

The study of the labors of the month represented in our different cathedrals constitutes one of the finest sections of Mr. Mâle's book. "These are really," he says of these sculpted calendars, "The Works and the Days." After showing their Byzantine and Romanesque origins, he says of them: "In these little panels, in these beautiful French georgics, man repeats his age-long labors." Then he shows in spite of this the very realistic and local side of these works: "Just outside the walls of the small medieval town begins the true countryside . . . the beautiful rhythm of Virgilian labors. The two steeples of Chartres rise above the harvests of the Beauce and the cathedral of Rheims dominates the vineyards of Champagne. In Paris, from the apse of Notre-Dame one could see meadows and woods; sculptors imagining scenes of rustic life could draw on immediate reality." And farther on: "This is all so simple, so sober, so close to humanity. There is nothing of the somewhat insipid Graces of ancient frescoes, no Cupid as grape-gatherer, no winged genius in the role of harvester. Neither are there Botticelli's charming goddesses dancing at the festival of Primavera. It is man alone in his conflict with nature; and so full of life that, after five centuries, it has lost none of its power to move." One sees why after reading this Mr. Séailles, speaking of Mr. Mâle's book, could say he knew no finer book of art criticism. [p. 320*n*1]

"Under Herod—
   A. Massacre of Innocents.
   B. Herod orders the ship of the Kings to be burned."
[4:51, no. 38]

On the façade of Amiens a nude figure whom two servants are placing in a bath is seen under the statue of Herod with the three Magi-Kings. This is Herod who when old tried to postpone death by taking baths of oil. 'Herod when he was seventy years old fell into a grievous malady, for a strong fever took him within and without, his feet swelled and he suffered continual torments, a racking cough, and a pestilential odor from the vermine devouring him. On the advice of doctors he was put into oil from which he was taken half dead' (*Golden Legend*). Herod lived long enough to learn that his son Antipater had not disguised his joy when he heard the story of his father's agony. Divine anger is manifested in Herod's death. . . . The sculptor of Amiens showed his ingenuity in foretelling the future and heralding the coming retribution of God when he placed Herod aged and broken beneath the feet of Herod triumphant" (Mâle, 283).

I have adopted Mr. Mâle's milder version, not wishing to reproduce the crudeness of the original. The reader may refer to Mr. Théodor de Wyzewa's fine translation of the *Golden Legend*, but he does not give the passage about the burning of the Kings' ships.

"As Herod was ordering the deaths of the Holy Innocents, he . . . learned in passing at Tarsus that the three Kings had set sail from that port, and in his anger ordered the burning of all the ships, according to the prophecy of David: "He will burn the ships of Tarsus in his anger" (Jacobus Voragine, *Golden Legend,* Day of the Holy Innocents, December 28). The Magi returning in a boat are visible, says Mr. Mâle, on a section of the rose window at Soissons and on a window relating Christ's childhood that adorns the apsidal chapel at Tours. [p. 328*nn*1, 2]

"All human creatures, in all ages and places of the world, who have had warm affections, common sense and self-command, have been, and are, Naturally Moral. Human nature in its fulness is necessarily Moral,—without Love, it is inhuman,—and without sense, inhuman,—without discipline, inhuman.

In the exact proportion in which men are bred capable of these things, and are educated to love, to think, and to endure, they become noble,—live happily—die calmly: are remembered with perpetual honour by their race, and for the perpetual good of it. All wise men know and have known these things, since the form of man was separated from the dust. The knowledge and enforcement of them have nothing to do with religion." [4:59]

Any reader with some metaphysical flair will find a certain relation between the idea expressed here (beginning with "All human creatures") and the theory of divine inspiration in chapter III [section 48]: "He is not gifted with higher ability, nor called into new offices, but enabled to use his granted natural powers, he becomes inspired . . . according to the capacities of his nature," and this remark: "The form which the monastic spirit took in later times depended far more . . . than on any change brought about by Christianity in the ideal of human virtue and happiness." [3:26] Ruskin often insisted on this last idea, saying that the worship offered by a heathen to Jupiter was not very different from the one a Christian offered, etc. . . . Moreover, in this same chapter III [section 26] of *The Bible of Amiens,* the College of Augurs and the institution of the Vestal Virgins are compared to the Christian monastic orders. Though this idea may seem to be, by the connection one sees, close to those that precede it and allied to them, it is nevertheless a new idea. In direct line it gives to Ruskin the idea of the faith of Horace and, in a general way, all similar developments. But above all it is closely related to an idea quite different from those we mentioned at the beginning of this note, the idea (analyzed in the note on pp. 242–46) of the permanence of an aesthetic feeling, which Christianity does not interrupt. And now that, from link to link, we have arrived at an idea so different from our starting point (though it is not new to us), we must ask ourselves whether it is not the idea of continuity of Greek art, for example, from the metopes of the Parthenon to the mosaics of Saint Mark's and the labyrinth of Amiens (an idea he probably believed to be true only because he found it beautiful), that led Ruskin, extending this primarily aesthetic view to religion and history, likewise to conceive of the College of Augurs as assimilable to the Benedictine Institution, the devotion of Hercules as equivalent to the devotion of Saint Jerome, etc., etc.

But since the Christian religion differed little from the Greek religion (the idea: "rather than on any change brought about by Christianity in the ideal of human virtue and happiness"), Ruskin did not need, from a logical point of view, to separate religion and ethics so strongly. Also, there is in this new idea, even if it is the first that led Ruskin to it, something more. And it is one of those views, rather particular to Ruskin, which properly speaking are not philosophical and not related to any system, and which in the eyes of purely logical reasoning may seem false, but which immediately strike anyone able, by the particular coloration of an idea, to guess its depth, as a fisherman would water's. Of these, I shall mention among the ideas of Ruskin which may seem out of date to ordinary minds, incapable of understanding their true meaning and of feeling their truth, that idea which holds freedom as fatal for the artist, and obedience and respect as essential, the idea that makes memory the most useful intellectual organ to the artist, etc., etc.

If one wanted to try to find the hidden links, the common root of ideas so far apart from each other in the work of Ruskin, and perhaps as little connected in his mind, I need not say that the idea noted at the foot of pages 212–14 on "I am alone, to my belief, in maintaining Herodotus' statement" is merely a different form of "Horace was pious in the manner of Milton," an idea which itself is but a counterpart of the aesthetic ideas analyzed in the note on pages 244–46. "This dome is only a Greek vase, this Salomé a canephora, this cherub a Harpy," etc. [pp. 338–39*n*1]

Amiens. Jour des Trépassés, 1880

The cathedral of Amiens

The south transept and flèche

Notre-Dame, Nourrice. South porch

The north porch before restoration, 1856

The choir stalls

The three west porches

The central pedestal

Virtues (Courage, Patience, and Gentillesse) and vices (Cowardice, Anger, and Churlishness)

Virtues (Love, Obedience, and Perseverance) and vices (Discord, Rebellion, and Atheism)

Virtues (Charity, Hope, and Faith) and vices (Avarice, Despair, and Idolatry)

Virtues (Humility, Wisdom, and Chastity) and vices (Pride, Folly, and Lust)

Subjects from Isaiah, Jeremiah, and Micah

Subjects from Nahum, Daniel, and Ezekiel

Subjects from Amos, Joel, and Hosea

Subjects from Micah, Jonah, and Obadiah

Subjects from Zephaniah, Habukkuk, and Nahum

Signs of the zodiac and labors of the months (December, January,
February, and March)

Signs of the zodiac, labors of the months (April and May), and
subjects from Zephaniah

Subjects from Haggai, signs of the zodiac, and labors of the months
(June and July)

Signs of the zodiac and labors of the months (August, September, October, and November)

Marcel Proust

Preface to John Ruskin's
Sesame and Lilies

Translated and Edited by
Jean Autret and William Burford

On Reading [1]

Tany here are perhaps no days of our childhood we lived so fully as those we believe we left without having lived them, those we spent with a favorite book. Everything that filled them for others, so it seemed, and that we dismissed as a vulgar obstacle to a divine pleasure: the game for which a friend would come to fetch us at the most interesting passage; the troublesome bee or sun ray that forced us to lift our eyes from the page or to change position; the provisions for the afternoon snack that we had been made to take along and that we left beside us on the bench without touching, while above our head the sun was diminishing in force in the blue sky; the dinner we had to return home for, and during which we thought only of going up immediately afterward to finish the interrupted chapter, all those things which reading should have kept us from feeling anything but annoyance at, it has on the contrary engraved in us so sweet a memory of (so much more precious to our present judgment than what we read then with such love), that if we still happen today to leaf through those books of another time, it is for no other reason than that they are the only calendars we have kept of days that have vanished, and we hope to see reflected on their pages the dwellings and the ponds which no longer exist.

Who does not remember, as I do, those [bits of] reading done during vacation time, which one would go and do in secret, one after another, in those hours of the day that were peaceful enough and inviolable enough to be able to give them refuge. In the morning, coming back from the park, when everybody had gone "to take a walk," I would slip into the dining room, where, until the yet distant lunch hour, nobody but relatively silent old Félicie would enter, and where I would have as companions, very respectful of reading, only the painted plates hung on the wall, the calendar whose sheet of the previous day had been freshly pulled, the clock and the fire which speak without asking you to answer them, and whose peaceful talk devoid of meaning does not come, like the words of men, to substitute a different sense from that of the words you are reading. I settled on a chair near the little wood fire about which, during breakfast, the uncle, early riser and gardener, would say: "That doesn't feel bad! We can certainly stand a little heat. I assure you it was pretty cold in the vegetable garden at six o'clock. And to think that in eight days it will be Easter!" Before lunch, which, alas!, would put an end to reading, one still had two long hours. From time to time you would hear the noise of the pump from which water was going to trickle, making you lift up your eyes toward it and look at it through the closed window, there, very near, on the only walk in the small garden, which edged the beds of pansies with bricks and half-moon–shaped tiles: pansies gathered, it seemed, in those skies too beautiful, those skies varicolored and as if reflected from the stained-glass windows of the church seen at times between the roofs of the village, sad skies which appeared before the storms, or afterward, too late, as the day was about to end. Unfortunately, the cook used to come long in advance to set the table; if only she had done it without speaking! But she thought she had to say: "You're not comfortable like that; what if I brought you a table?" And just to answer: "No, thank you," you had to stop short and bring back from afar your voice which from within your lips was repeating noiselessly, hurriedly, all the words your eyes had read; you had to stop it, make it be heard, and, in order to say properly: "No, thank you," give it an appearance of ordinary life, the intonation of an answer, which it had lost. The hour went by; often, long before lunch, those who were tired and had shortened their walk, had "gone by Méséglise,"* or those who had not gone out that morning, "having to write," began to arrive in the dining room. They would all say: "I don't want to disturb you," but began at once to come near the fire, to look at the time, to declare that lunch would not be unwelcome. He or she who had "stayed to write" was the object of a particular deference and was told: "You have attended to your little correspondence," with a smile in which there was respect, mystery, prurience, and discretion, as if this "little correspondence" had been at the same time a state secret, a prerogative, a piece of good fortune, and an ailment. Some, without waiting any longer, would sit ahead of time at the table, at their places. That was real desolation, for it would be a bad incentive to the others as they arrived to make believe that it was already noon, and for my parents to pronounce too soon the fatal words: "Come, shut your book, we're going to have lunch." Everything was ready, the lunch was all set on the tablecloth where only that which was brought at the end of the meal was missing, the glass apparatus in which the horticulturist-and-cook uncle made the coffee himself at the table, a tubular apparatus, elaborate like an instrument of physics that might have smelled good, and in which it was so pleasant to see climbing in the glass bell the sudden ebullition which afterward left on the misty walls a fragrant, brown ash; and also the cream and the strawberries which the same uncle mixed in always identical proportions, stopping, with the experience of a colorist and the divination of a gourmand, just at the required pink color. How long lunch seemed to last for me! My great-aunt would taste the dishes only to give her opinion with a sweetness that

---

*Ed. note: This should be "Méréglise," an interesting lapse on Proust's part where he confuses a real place name with an early appearance of a different fictional one.

tolerated but did not admit contradiction. For a novel, for verses, things of which she was a good judge, she would always, with the humility of a woman, defer to the opinion of more competent people. She thought that this was the wavering domain of fancy, where the taste of a single person cannot settle the truth. But on things whose rules and principles had been taught to her by her mother, on the way to prepare certain dishes, to play the Beethoven sonatas, and to entertain graciously, she was sure to have a precise idea of perfection and to discern whether others approximated it more or less. For those three things, moreover, perfection was almost the same: it was a kind of simplicity in the means, a kind of sobriety and charm. She rejected with horror the idea that one would put spices in dishes that did not absolutely require them, that one would play the pedals with affectation and excess, that "when receiving" one would depart from perfect naturalness and speak of oneself with exaggeration. At the first mouthful, at the first notes, on receiving a simple message, she would claim to know whether she had to do with a good cook, a true musician, a well-bred woman. "She may have quicker fingers than I have, but she lacks taste, playing with so much emphasis this andante that is so simple." "She may be brilliant and full of qualities, but it is a lack of tact to speak of oneself in that way." "It may be that she is a very learned cook, but she cannot fix a beefsteak with potatoes." Beefsteak with potatoes! Ideal competition piece, difficult in its very simplicity, a kind of "*Sonate pathétique*" of cookery, gastronomical equivalent of what in social life is the visit of a lady who comes to ask you for information about a servant and who in so simple an act can so markedly show proof of, or lack, tact and good manners. My grandfather had so much self-respect that he would have liked all dishes to be a success, and he knew too little about cookery ever to know when they were a failure. He was willing to admit that sometimes, if very rarely, they were, but only by pure chance. My great-aunt's criticisms, always justified, implying on the contrary that the cook had not known how to prepare a given dish, could not fail to appear particularly intolerable to my grandfather. Often, to avoid arguments with him, my great-aunt, after having tasted gingerly, did not give her opinion, which would let us know immediately that it was unfavorable. She would say nothing, but we could read in her gentle eyes a firm and deliberate disapproval which had a way of infuriating my grandfather. He would ironically beg her to give her opinion, become impatient at her silence, press her with questions, lose his temper, but one felt she would have been led to martyrdom rather than confess to the belief of my grandfather's: that the sweet dish did not have too much sugar.

After lunch, my reading resumed immediately; particularly, if the day was rather warm, one went up "to retire to one's room," which permitted me, by the little staircase with steps close together, to reach mine immediately, on the only story so low from the straddled windows one would have had to make only a child's jump to find oneself in the street. I went and closed my window, without being able to avoid the greeting of the gunsmith across the street, who, under pretext of lowering his awnings, used to come every day after lunch to smoke his pipe in front of his door and say good afternoon to passersby, who, sometimes, stopped to talk. William Morris's theories, which have been so constantly applied by Maple and the English decorators, decree that a room is beautiful only on condition that it contain solely those things which may be useful to us and that any useful thing, even a simple nail, be not hidden but visible. Above the bed with copper curtain-rods and entirely uncovered, on the naked walls of those hygienic rooms, [only] a few reproductions of masterpieces. To judge it by the principles of this aesthetics, my room was not beautiful at all, for it was full of things that could not be of any use and that modestly hid, to the point of making their use extremely difficult, those which might serve some use. But it was precisely through these things which were not there for my convenience, but seemed to have come there for their own pleasure, that my room acquired for me its beauty. Those high white curtains which hid from sight the bed placed as if in the rear of a sanctuary; the scattering of light silk quilts, of counterpanes with flowers, of embroidered bedspreads, of linen pillowcases, under which it disappeared in the daytime, like an altar in the month of Mary under festoons and flowers, and which, in the evening, in order to go to bed, I would place with care on an armchair where they consented to spend the night; by the bed, the trinity of the glass with blue patterns, the matching sugar bowl, and the decanter (always empty since the day after my arrival by order of my aunt who was afraid to see me "spill" it), these cult instruments, as it were— almost as sacred as the precious orange-blossom liqueur placed near them in a glass phial—which I would no more have thought of profaning nor even of possibly using for myself than if they had been consecrated ciboria, but which I would examine a long time before undressing, for fear of upsetting them by a false motion; those little crocheted openwork stoles which threw on the backs of the arm- chairs a mantle of white roses that must not have been without thorns, since every time I had finished reading and wanted to get up I noticed I remained caught in them; that glass bell under which, isolated from vulgar contacts, the clock murmured intimately to shells come from far away and to an old sentimental flower, but which was so heavy to lift that, when the clock stopped, nobody but the clock-maker would have been foolhardy enough to undertake to wind it up; that very white guipure tablecloth which, thrown as an altar runner across the chest of drawers adorned with two vases, a picture of the Savior, and a twig of blessed boxwood made it resemble the Lord's Table (of which a prie-dieu, placed there every day when they had "done the room," put the finishing touch), but whose frayings always catching in the chinks of the drawers stopped their movement so completely that I could never take out a hand- kerchief without at once knocking down the picture of the Savior, the sacred vases, the twig of blessed boxwood, and without stum- bling and catching hold of the prie-dieu; finally, that triple layer of little bolting-cloth curtains, of large muslin curtains, and of larger dimity curtains, always smiling in their often sunny hawthorn whiteness, but in reality very irritating in their awkwardness and stubbornness in playing around their parallel wooden bars and entangling themselves and getting all in the window as soon as I wanted to open or close it, a second one being always ready, if I succeeded in extricating the first, to come to take its place immediately in the cracks as perfectly plugged by them as they would have been by a real hawthorn bush or by nests of swallows that might have had the fancy to settle there, so that this operation, in appearance so simple, of opening or closing my window, I never succeeded in doing without the help of someone in the house; all those things which not only could not answer any of my needs, but were even an impediment, however slight, to their satisfaction, which evidently had never been placed there for someone's use, peopled my room with thoughts somehow personal, with that air of predilection, of having chosen to live there and delighting in it, which often the trees in a clearing and the flowers on the roadsides or on old walls have. They filled it with a silent and multifarious life, with a mystery in which my person found itself lost and charmed at the same time; they made of this room a kind of chapel where the sun— when it penetrated the little red windowpanes my uncle had inserted in the upper part of the windows—stitched on the walls, after having turned the hawthorn of the curtains rosy, gleams as strange as if the little chapel had been enclosed in a larger stained-glass nave; and where the noise of the bells came so resoundingly because of the proximity of our house and the church to which, besides, during great feasts, outdoor altars linked us by a road carpeted with flowers, so that I could imagine that the bells were being rung on our roof, right above the window from where I greeted the parish priest holding his breviary, my aunt returning from vespers, or the chorister boy bringing us blessed bread. As for the photograph by Brown of Botticelli's *Spring* or the cast of the *Unknown Woman* of the Lille Museum, which on the walls and on the mantlepiece of the rooms of Maple are the part conceded by William Morris to useless beauty, I must confess they were replaced in my room by a sort of engraving representing Prince Eugene, terrible and beautiful in his dolman, and which I was very astonished to see one night, in the midst of a great din of locomotives and hail, still terrible and beautiful, at the door of a railway-station buffet, where it was used as an advertisement for a brand of crackers. Today I suspect that my grandfather had once received it as a gift, thanks to the munificence of a manufacturer, before setting it up forever in my room. But at the time I did not care about its origin, which to me seemed historical and mysterious, and I did not imagine that there might have been several copies of what I thought of as a person, as a permanent inhabitant of the room I simply shared with him and where I found him every year always the same. I have not seen him for a long time now, and I suppose I shall never see him again. But should I have such luck, I believe he would have many more things to tell me than Botticelli's *Spring*. I leave it to people of taste to decorate their homes with the reproductions of masterpieces they admire and to relieve their memories from the care of preserving for them a precious image by entrusting it to a sculptured wooden frame. I leave it to people of taste to make of their rooms the very image of their taste and to fill them only with things of which they can approve. As for me, I feel myself living and thinking only in a room where everything is the creation and the language of lives profoundly different from mine, of a taste opposite to mine, where I find nothing of my conscious thought, where my imagination is excited to feel itself plunged into the womb of the non-ego; I feel happy only when setting foot—on the Avenue de la Gare, on the Port, or on the Place de l'Eglise—in one of those provincial hotels with cold, long corridors where the wind from outside contends successfully with the efforts of the heating system, where the detailed geographic map of the district is still the sole ornament on the walls, where each noise helps only to make the silence appear by displacing it, where the rooms keep a musty perfume which the open air comes to wash, but does not eliminate, and which the nostrils inhale a hundred times in order to bring it to the imagination, which is enchanted with it, which makes it pose like a model to try to recreate it for itself with all the thoughts and remembrances that it contains; where in the evening, when one opens the door of one's room, one has the feeling of violating all the life that has remained scattered there, of taking it boldly by the hand when, once the door is closed, one enters farther, up to the table or to the window; to sit with it in a kind of free promiscuousness on the sofa designed by the upholsterer of the local county in what he believed to be the style of Paris; to touch everywhere the nakedness of that life with the intention of being troubled by one's own familiarity, by putting here and there one's things, by pretending to be the master of that room full to the brim with the soul of others and which keeps even in the shape of its andirons and the pattern of its curtains the imprint of their dreams, by walking barefoot on its unknown carpet; one has then the feeling of shutting in with oneself this secret life when one goes, all trembling, to bolt the door; of pushing it in front of one into the bed and finally lying down with it under the large white sheets which come up over one's face, while close by the church rings for the whole town the hours of insomnia of the dying and of lovers.

I had not been reading a long time in my room before we had to go to the park, a kilometer from the village.[2] But after the compulsory playtime, I cut short the afternoon snack brought in baskets and distributed to the children at the river's edge, on the grass where the book had been put down with instructions not to pick it up again. A little farther, in certain rather wild and mysterious depths of the park, the river ceased to be a straight and artificial line, covered with swans and bordered with walks where statues were smiling, and, suddenly leaping with carp, rushed forward, went at a rapid pace beyond the enclosure of the park, became a river in the geographic sense of the word—a river which must have had a name—and did not take long to spread itself (was it really the same as the one between the statues and beneath the swans?) amid the pastures where oxen were sleeping and where it drowned the buttercups, kinds of meadows it made rather swampy, and which, connecting on one side with the village through shapeless towers, remnants, it was said, of the Middle Ages, joined the other side through climbing roads of sweetbriar and hawthorn, that "nature" which spread infinitely, to villages with other names, to the unknown. I would let the others finish eating at the lower end of the park, beside the swans, and I would run up the labyrinth as far as some hedge where I would sit, not to be found, leaning against the trimmed hazels, discovering the asparagus bed, the strawberry edgings, the pond where on certain days the horses hitched to a wheel would bring up water, the white door which was the "end of the park" above, and beyond, the fields of cornflowers and poppies. In this hedge, silence was profound, the risk of being discovered almost nil, safety made sweeter by the distant cries which, from below, called me in vain, sometimes even came nearer, climbed the first banks, searching everywhere, then returned, having found nothing; then no more noise; only from time to time the golden sound of the bells which in the distance, beyond the plains, seeming to toll behind the blue sky, could have warned me of the passing hour; but, surprised by its sweetness and disturbed by the profounder silence, emptied of the last sounds, which followed it, I was never sure of the number of strokes. It was not the thundering bells that one heard upon return- ing to the village—as one approached the church which nearby had again taken on its high and stiff shape, rearing against the blue of the evening its slated roof punctuated with crows—making the sound fly in bursts over the square "for the good of the earth." Their sound reached but feebly and sweetly to the end of the park, and not addressing me but the whole countryside, all the villages, the peasants isolated in their fields, they did not make me raise my head at all, they went by near me, carrying the hour to distant lands, without seeing me, without being aware of me, and without dis- turbing me.

And sometimes at home, in my bed, long after dinner, the last hours of the evening also sheltered my reading, but then only on the days when I had reached the last chapters of a book, where there was not much more to read to arrive at the end. Then, at the risk of being punished if I were discovered and of the insomnia which, once the book was finished, would perhaps be prolonged throughout the whole night, as soon as my parents had gone to bed I would light my candle again; while in the street nearby, between the gunsmith's house and the post office, bathed in silence, the dark and yet blue sky was full of stars, and while to the left, on the raised path where, curving, its elevated ascent began, one felt watching, monstrous and black, the apse of the church whose sculptures did not sleep at night, the provincial and yet historical church, magic abode of the *Bon Dieu,* of the blessed bread, of the multicolored saints and the ladies of the neighboring castles who on feast days, as they crossed the market, made the hens squall and the gossiping women stare, who came to mass "in their carriages," not without buying, on their way back, at the pastry cook's on the square, just after having left the shade of the porch where the congregation pushing the revolving door strewed the wandering rubies of the nave, some of those cakes in the shape of towers, protected from the sun by a shade— *"manqués," "Saint-Honorés,"* and *"gênoises"*—whose lazy and sugary fragrance has remained mingled for me with the tolling of the bells for high mass and the gaiety of Sundays.

Then the last page was read, the book was finished. I had to stop the headlong rush of my eyes and of my voice which followed noiselessly, stopping only to regain my breath in a deep sigh. Then, in order to give the tumult, too long unleashed within me to be able to calm itself, other movements to govern, I would get up, I would start walking alongside my bed, my eyes still fixed on some point one would in vain have looked for in the room or outside, for it was situated at a soul's distance only, one of those distances which are not measured in meters and leagues like the others, and which, is, besides, impossible to confuse with them when one looks at the "distant" eyes of those who are thinking "about something else." Then, what? This book, was it nothing but that? Those beings to whom one had given more of one's attention and tenderness than to people in real life, not always daring to admit how much one loved them, even when our parents found us reading and appeared to smile at our emotion, so that we closed the book with affected indifference or feigned ennui; those people for whom one had panted and sobbed, one would never see again, one would no longer know anything about them. Already, for several pages, the author, in the cruel "Epilogue," had taken care to "space" them with an unbelievable indifference for one who knew the interest with which he had followed them step by step until then. The occupation of each hour of their lives had been narrated for us. Then suddenly: "Twenty years after these events one could meet on the streets of Fougères[3] an elderly man still erect, etc." And the marriage, to which two volumes had been devoted to make us foresee the delicious possibility, frightening us, then delighting us with each obstacle erected, then removed, it is through an incidental sentence of a secondary character that we learned it had been celebrated, we did not know just when, in this astonishing epilogue written, it seemed, from high up in the sky by a person indifferent to our earthly passions, who had substituted himself for the author. One would have wanted so much for the book to continue, and, if that were impossible, to have other information on all those characters, to learn now something about their lives, to devote ours to things that might not be entirely foreign to the love they had inspired in us[4] and whose object we were suddenly missing, would have wanted not to have loved in vain, for an hour, beings who tomorrow would be but names on a forgotten page, in a book having no connection with life, and about the value of which we were much mistaken since its fate in this world, we understood now, and our parents informed us in case we needed a scornful phrase, was not at all, as we had believed, to contain the universe and destiny, but to occupy a very narrow place in the library of the notary public, between the undistinguished annals of the *Illustrated Magazine of Fashion* and the *Geography of the Eure-et-Loir. . . .*

Before trying to show at the very beginning of "Of Kings' Treasuries" why in my opinion Reading should not play the preponderant role in life that Ruskin assigns to it in this little work, I had to leave out of consideration the charming childhood reading whose memory must remain a benediction for each one of us. No doubt I have proved only too well by the length and character of the preceding development what I had suggested about it to begin with: that what it leaves in us above all is the image of the places and the days when we did this reading. I have not escaped its spell: wishing to speak about it, I have talked about everything but books, because it is not about them that this reading has spoken to me. But perhaps the memories which one after the other it has brought back to me will themselves have awakened some in the reader and will little by little have led him, all the while lingering in those flowery and out-of-the-way roads, to recreate in his mind the original psychological act called *Reading* with enough force for him to be able to follow now, as if within himself, the few reflections I still have to offer.

We know that "Of Kings' Treasuries" is a lecture on reading delivered by Ruskin at the Rusholme Town Hall, near Manchester, on December 6, 1864, to promote the establishment of a library at the Rusholme Institute. On December 14 he delivered a second lecture, "Of Queens' Gardens," on the role of women, to promote the founding of schools at Ancoats. "All through that year, 1864," says Mr. Collingwood in his admirable work *The Life and Works of Ruskin,* "he remained at home, except for frequent visits to Carlyle. And when in December he gave the lectures at Manchester which afterwards, under the name of *Sesame and Lilies,* became his most popular work,[5] we can trace his better health of mind and body in the brighter tone of his thought. We can recognize the echo of his conversations with Carlyle in the heroic, aristocratic, stoic ideals he proposes and in the insistence with which he goes back to the value of books and public libraries, Carlyle being the founder of the London Library. . . ."

As for us, who want only to discuss Ruskin's thesis in itself, without concerning ourselves with its historical origins, we can sum it up fairly exactly with these words of Descartes, that "the reading of all good books is like a conversation with the most cultivated men of past centuries who have been their authors." Perhaps Ruskin did not know this rather dry thought of the French philosopher, but it is in fact the one which is found everywhere in his lecture, only enveloped in an Apollonian gold in which English mists blend, similar to the one whose glory illuminates the landscapes of his favorite painter [Turner]. "But," he says, "granting we had the will and sense to choose our friends well, how few of us have the power, how limited is the sphere of our choice. We cannot know whom we would. . . . We may by good fortune obtain a glimpse of a great poet and hear the sound of his voice, or put a question to a man of science who will answer us good-humouredly. We may snatch ten minutes of conversation in a minister's office, once in our life have the privilege of arresting the glance of a queen. And yet we covet these momentary chances; we spend our years, our passions, and powers in pursuit of little more than these, while, meantime, there is a society continually open to us, of people who will talk to us as long as we like, whatever our rank. And this society, because it is so various and so gentle and we can keep it waiting round us all day long—kings and statesmen waiting patiently, not to grant audience, but to gain it—we never fetch that society from the plainly furnished and narrow ante-rooms that are our bookcase shelves, we never listen to a word they might say to us."[6] [1:6; *CW* 18:58–59] "You may tell me," adds Ruskin, "that if you like better to talk with living people, it is because you see their faces, etc.," and refuting this first objection, then a second one, he shows that reading is, to be exact, a conversation with men much wiser and more interesting than those around us we may have the opportunity to know. I have tried to show in the notes accompanying this book that reading could therefore not be made comparable to a conversation, were it with the wisest of men; that the essential difference between a book and a friend is not their degree of greatness of wisdom, but the manner in which we communicate with them, reading, contrary to conversation, consisting for each of us in receiving the communication of another thought, but while we remain all alone, that is to say, while continuing to enjoy the intellectual power we have in solitude, and which conversation dissipates immediately, while continuing to be inspired, to maintain the mind's full, fruitful work on itself. Had Ruskin drawn the consequences of other truths he enunciated a few pages farther, it is probable that he would have come to a conclusion analogous to mine. But evidently he did not seek to go to the very heart of the idea of *reading*. To teach us the value of reading he simply wished to tell us a beautiful Platonic myth, with that simplicity of the Greeks who have shown us almost all the true ideas and have left our modern misgivings the task of fathoming them. But if I believe that reading, in its original essence, in that fruitful miracle of a communication in the midst of solitude, is something more, something other than what Ruskin has said, I do not believe, in spite of this, that one may grant it in our spiritual life the preponderant role he seems to assign to it.

The limits of its role derive from the nature of its virtues. And, again, it is of our childhood reading that I am going to ask in what these virtues consist. That book which a while ago you saw me reading by the fireside in the dining room, and in my bedroom, sunk in the armchair with a crocheted headrest, and during the beautiful hours of the afternoon under the hazels and hawthorns of the park, where all the exhalations of the endless fields came from far away to play silently near me, without a word offering to my inattentive nostrils the smell of the clover and the sainfoin on which I would at times lift my tired eyes, that book which your eyes, leaning toward, would not be able at twenty years' distance to decipher the title of, my memory, whose sight is more appropriate to this kind of perception, is going to tell you was *le Capitaine Fracasse,* by Théophile Gautier. In it I liked above all two or three sentences which seemed to me the most original and beautiful in the book. I did not imagine that another author might ever have written any comparable to them. But I had the feeling that their beauty corresponded to a reality of which Théophile Gautier would let us catch but a glimpse, once or twice in a book. And since I thought he assuredly knew it in its entirety, I would have liked to read other books by him where all the sentences would be as beautiful as those and would be about things on which I would have wished to have his opinion. "Laughing is not cruel by nature; it distinguishes man from beast, and it is, as it appears in the Odyssey of Homer, poet of Greek fire, the property of the immortal and happy gods, who laugh Olympianly to their heart's content in the leisure of eternity."[7] This sentence truly intoxicated me. I thought I perceived a marvelous antiquity through those Middle Ages which only Gautier could reveal to me. But I would have wished that instead of saying this furtively after the tedious description of a castle which too many terms I did not know prevented me from imagining at all, he might have written throughout the book sentences of this kind and spoken to me of things which, once I had finished his book, I could have continued to know and to love. I would have wanted him, the only wise holder of the truth, to tell me exactly what I was to think of Shakespeare, Saintine, Sophocles, Euripides, Silvio Pellico, whom I had read during a very cold month of March, walking, stamping my feet, running on the roads each time I had just closed the book in the exaltation of the finished reading, of the forces accumulated in immobility, and of the bracing wind which blew in the streets of the village. Above all, I would have wanted him to tell me whether I had more chance of arriving at the truth by repeating or not my first year at the lycée and later being a diplomat or a lawyer at the Court of Appeals. But as soon as the beautiful sentence was ended he started describing a table covered with "such a layer of dust that a finger could have traced letters on it," a thing too insignificant in my eyes for me to pay it any attention; and I was reduced to asking myself what other books Gautier had written that would better satisfy my aspiration and would finally let me fully know his thought.

And there, indeed, is one of the great and marvelous features of beautiful books (and one which will make us understand the role, at once essential and limited, that reading can play in our spiritual life) which for the author could be called "Conclusions" and for the reader "Incitements." We feel quite truly that our wisdom begins where that of the author ends, and we would like to have him give us answers, when all he can do is give us desires. And these desires he can arouse in us only by making us contemplate the supreme beauty which the last effort of his art has permitted him to reach. But by a singular and, moreover, providential law of mental optics (a law which perhaps signifies that we can receive the truth from nobody, and that we must create it ourselves), that which is the end of their wisdom appears to us as but the beginning of ours, so that it is at the moment when they have told us all they could tell us that they create in us the feeling that they have told us nothing yet. Besides, if we put to them questions they cannot answer, we also ask from them answers that would not instruct us. For it is an effect of the love which poets awake in us to make us attach a literal importance to things which for them are significant only of personal emotions. In each picture they show us, they seem to give us but a light glimpse of a marvelous site, different from the rest of the world, and to whose heart we wish they would make us penetrate. "Take us," we would like to be able to say to Maeterlinck, to Madame de Noailles, "to the garden of Zealand where the 'out-of-fashion flowers grow,' on the road perfumed 'with clover and Saint John's wort,' and all the places on earth about which you have not spoken to us in your books, but which you deem as beautiful as those." We would like to go and see that field which Millet (for painters teach us the way poets do) shows us in his *Spring,* we would like Claude Monet to take us to Giverny, on the banks of the Seine, to that bend of the river which he hardly lets us distinguish through the morning mist. But, in reality, it is mere chance acquaintance or family ties, which, giving them the opportunity to travel or reside near them, have made Madame de Noailles, Maeterlinck, Millet, Claude Monet choose to paint that road, that garden, that field, that river bend, rather than others. What makes them appear different to us and more beautiful than the rest of the world is that they bear on them like an intangible reflection the impression they have given to genius, and which we would see, just as singular and just as despotic, moving over the indifferent and submissive face of all the countries they might have painted. This appearance with which they charm and deceive us, and beyond which we would like to go, is the very essence of that thing without thickness, so to speak—mirage fixed on a canvas—that a vision is. And that mist which our eager eyes would like to pierce is the last word of the painter's art. The supreme effort of the writer as of the painter succeeds only in partially raising for us the veil of ugliness and insignificance which leaves us indifferent before the universe. Then he tells us: "Look, look

Perfumed with clover and St. John's wort,
Hugging their swift narrow brooks
The countries of Aisne and Oise

[Editors' trans.]

"Look at the house in Zealand, pink and shiny like a sea shell. Look! Learn how to see!" And at that moment he disappears. Such is the price of reading and such also is its insufficiency. To make a discipline of it is to give too great a role to what is but an incitement. Reading is at the threshold of spiritual life; it can introduce us to it; it does not constitute it.

There are, however, certain cases, certain pathological cases, so to speak, of spiritual depression in which reading can become a sort of curative discipline and assume the task, through repeated stimulation, of continuously reintroducing a lazy mind into the life of the spirit. Books then play for it a role similar to that of psychotherapists for certain neurasthenics.

It is known that in certain diseases of the nervous system the patient, without any one of his organs being affected, is engulfed in a kind of impossibility of willing, as if he were in a deep rut out of which he cannot pull himself on his own, and in which he would finally waste away if a powerful and helpful hand were not extended to him. His brain, his legs, his lungs, his stomach are unaffected. He has no real inability to work, to walk, to expose himself to cold, to eat. But these various actions, which he could quite capably perform, he is incapable of willing. And an organic decay that would end by becoming the equivalent of diseases he does not have would be the irremediable consequence of the inertia of his will, if the impulse he cannot find in himself did not come to him from outside, from a doctor who wills for him, until the day when little by little his various organic wills have been reeducated. Now, there are certain minds which one could compare to these invalids and which a kind of laziness[8] or frivolity prevents from descending spontaneously into the deep regions of the self where the true life of the mind begins. It is not that once they have been led there they are not able to discover and exploit its true riches, but that, without this foreign intervention, they live on the surface in a perpetual forgetfulness of themselves, in a kind of passivity which makes them the toy of all pleasures, diminishes them to the size of those who surround and agitate them, and, like that nobleman who, sharing since his childhood the life of highway robbers, no longer remembered his name, having for too long ceased to bear it, they would finally extinguish in themselves all feeling and all remembrance of their spiritual nobility if an impulse from outside did not come to reintroduce them in some forceful way into the life of the spirit, where they suddenly find again the power to think for themselves and to create. Now, it is clear that this impulse which the slothful mind cannot find within itself and which must come to it from others must be received in the midst of solitude, outside of which, as we have seen, that creative activity which is precisely in need of being revived in it cannot be produced. The indolent mind can obtain nothing from pure solitide since it is incapable of setting its creative activity in motion. But the loftiest conversation, the most pressing advice, would be of absolutely no use to it, since they cannot produce directly this original activity. What is necessary, then, is an intervention which, while coming from another, takes place in our own innermost selves, which is indeed the impetus of another mind, but received in the midst of solitude. Now we have seen that this was precisely the definition of reading, and that it fitted only reading. The sole discipline that can exert a favorable influence on such minds, then, is reading: *which was to be demonstrated,* as the geometricians say. But, here again, reading acts only in the manner of a stimulus which can never be substituted for our personal activity; it contents itself with giving us the use of itself, as, in the nervous ailments to which we alluded a while ago, the psychotherapist does not do anything but restore to the patient the will to use his stomach, his legs, his brains, which have remained undamaged. Besides, either because all minds share more or less in this laziness, in this stagnation, at their low levels, or because, without being necessary to it, the exaltation that follows on reading certain books has a propitious influence on personal work, one can cite more than one writer who liked to read a beautiful page before starting to work. Emerson would rarely begin to write without rereading some pages of Plato. And Dante is not the only poet whom Virgil led to the threshold of paradise.

So long as reading is for us the inciter whose magic keys open to our innermost selves the doors of abodes into which we would not have known how to penetrate, its role in our life is salutary. But, on the other hand, reading becomes dangerous when instead of waking us to the personal life of the spirit, it tends to substitute itself for it, when truth no longer appears to us as an ideal we can realize only through the intimate progress of our thought and the effort of our heart, but as a material thing, deposited between the leaves of books like honey ready-made by others and which we have only to take the trouble of reaching for on the shelves of libraries and then savoring passively in perfect repose of body and mind. At times even, in certain somewhat exceptional, and in other respects, as we shall see, less dangerous, cases, the truth, still conceived of as exterior, is far off, hidden in a place difficult of access. Then it is some secret document, some unpublished correspondence, memoirs which may cast an unexpected light on certain personalities, and about which it is difficult to obtain information. What happiness, what repose for a mind tired of seeking the truth within to tell itself that it is located outside, in the leaves of a folio jealously preserved in a convent in Holland, and that if to reach it one has to go to some trouble, this trouble will be entirely material, will be for one's mind but a relaxation full of charm. No doubt we shall have to make a long trip, to cross in a canal boat the moaning, windy plains, while on the banks the reeds in turn bend and rise again in an endless undulation; we shall have to stop at Dordrecht, whose ivy-covered church is reflected in the still waters of the interlacing channels and in the trembling and golden Meuse where, in the evening, boats gliding along disarrange the reflected lines of the red roofs and the blue sky; and finally, having arrived at the end of the journey, we shall not yet be certain of receiving information about the truth. For that, we shall have to set powerful influences in motion, become acquainted with the venerable archbishop of Utrecht, who has the beautiful square face of an old Jansenist, with the pious keeper of the Amersfoort archives. In these cases, the conquest of truth is conceived of as the success of a kind of diplomatic mission during which neither the difficulties of travel nor the hazards of negotiation are lacking. But what does it matter? All those members of the tiny old church of Utrecht, on whose good will depends whether or not we enter into possession of the truth, are charming people whose seventeenth-century faces change for us the faces we are accustomed to and whom it will be amusing to keep up with, at least by correspondence. The esteem which they will continue from time to time to send us testimony of will enhance us in our own eyes, and we shall keep their letters as a certificate and a curiosity. And one day we shall not fail to dedicate one of our books to them, which is indeed the least we can do for those who made us a gift . . . of the truth. And as for the few inquiries, the brief labors we shall be obliged to undertake in the library of the convent and which will be the indispensible preliminaries to the act of taking possession of the truth—of the truth which for greater prudence, and so that we do not risk its escaping us, we shall jot down—we would be ungracious to complain of the troubles these labors may give us: the calm and coolness of the old convent are so exquisite, where the nuns still wear the tall headdress with the white wings that they have in the Roger van der Weyden in the parlor; and, while we work, the seventeenth-century chimes startle so tenderly the naïve water of the canal which a little pale sunshine is enough to dazzle between the double row of trees, stripped since summer's end, that brush the mirrors fixed to the gabled houses on both banks.[9]

This conception of a truth deaf to the appeals of reflection and docile to the play of influences, of a truth that is obtained by letters of introduction, that is delivered into our hands by one who retained it materially without perhaps even knowing it, of a truth that lets itself be copied in a notebook, this conception of the truth is yet far from being the most dangerous of all. For very often with the historian, as with the scholar, this truth that they go seeking far away in a book is, properly speaking, less the truth itself than its sign or proof, leaving room consequently for another truth which it announces or verifies and which is at least an individual creation of their mind. It is not so for the literary man. He reads for reading's sake, to retain what he has read. For him, the book is not the angel that flies away as soon as he has opened the doors of the celestial garden, but a motionless idol, which he adores for itself, which, instead of receiving a true dignity from the thoughts it awakens, communicates an artificial dignity to everything that surrounds it. Smiling, the literary man invokes in honor of a certain name the fact that it is found in Villehardouin or in Boccaccio, [10] in favor of a given custom that it is described in Virgil. His mind, lacking original quickness, does not know how to separate from books the substance that might make it stronger; he encumbers himself with their pure form, which, instead of being an assimilable element for him, a source of life, is but a foreign substance, a source of death. Need it be said that if I call this taste, this kind of fetishistic respect for books, unhealthy, it is relative to what would be the ideal habits of a mind without defects, which does not exist, and as the physiologists do who describe a functioning of normal organs such as are hardly found in living beings. On the contrary, in reality, where there are no more perfect minds than entirely healthy bodies, those we call great minds suffer like the others from this "literary disease." More than the others, one could say. It seems that the taste for books grows with intelligence, a little below it but on the same stem, as every passion is accompanied by a predilection for that which surrounds its object, which has an affinity for it, which in its absence still speaks of it. So, the great writers, during those hours when they are not in direct communication with their thought, delight in the society of books. Besides, is it not chiefly for them that they have been written; do they not disclose to them a thousand beauties, which remain hidden to the masses? To tell the truth, the fact that some superior minds are what is called bookish does not at all prove that this is a defect. Because mediocre men are often hardworking and intelligent ones often lazy, one cannot conclude that work is not a better discipline for the mind than laziness. In spite of this, finding one of our defects in a great man always inclines us to wonder whether it was not really an unrecognized quality, and it is not without pleasure that we learn that Hugo knew Quintus Curtius, Tacitus, Justin, by heart, that if the legitimacy of a term was disputed before him,[11] he was quite prepared to establish its derivation, even to its origins, by means of quotations which proved a real erudition. (Elsewhere I have shown how this erudition nourished his genius instead of stifling it, as a bundle of faggots which extinguishes a small fire increases a large one.) Maeterlinck, who is for us the opposite of a literary man, whose mind is perpetually open to the thousand nameless emotions communicated by the hive, the flower bed, or the meadow, greatly reassures us on the dangers of erudition, almost of bibliophilism, when as an amateur he describes for us the engravings which adorn an old edition of Jacob Cats or of the abbé Sanderus. Since these dangers, moreover, when they exist, threaten intelligence far less than sensibility, the capacity for profitable reading, if one may say so, is far greater with the thinkers than with the great imaginative writers. Schopenhauer, for instance, offers us the image of a mind whose vitality bears lightly the most enormous reading, each new idea being immediately reduced to its share of reality, to the living portion it contains.

Schopenhauer never advances an opinion without immediately supporting it with several quotations, but one feels that the texts quoted are only examples for him, unconscious and anticipated allusions where he likes to find again some traits of his own thought, but which have not at all inspired it. I remember a page of *The World as Will and Representation* where there are perhaps twenty quotations one after another. It is about pessimism (I abbreviate the quotations, of course): "Voltaire, in *Candide,* wages war on optimism in a witty manner; Byron has done the same, in his tragic way, in *Cain.*

Herodotus recounts how the Thracians greeted the newborn child with lamentations and rejoiced at each death. This is what the splendid verses that Plutarch quotes for us express: 'Lugere genitum, tanta qui intravit mala, etc.' It is to this that must be attributed the custom of the Mexicans in wishing, etc. And Swift obeyed the same sentiment when from early youth (to believe Sir Walter Scott's biography) he was accustomed to celebrate his birthday as a day of sorrow. Everyone knows this passage from the Apology of Socrates, where Plato says that death is a wonderful good. A maxim of Heraclitus ran likewise: 'Vitae nomen quidem est vita, opus autem mors.' The fine lines of Theognis are well known: 'optima sors [natum] homini non esse, etc.' Sophocles in *Oedipus at Colonus* (l. 1224) gives the following abbreviation of them: 'Natum non esse sortes vincit alias omnes.' Euripides says: 'Omnis hominum vita est plena dolore' (*Hippolytus*, 189), and Homer had already said: 'Non enim quidquam alicubi est calamitosius homine omnium, quotquot super terram spirant, etc.' Moreover, Pliny said it also: 'Nullum melius esse tempestiva morte.' Shakespeare puts these words in the mouth of the old king Henry IV: 'O, if this were seen— The happiest youth,—Would shut the book and sit him down and die.' Finally Byron: 'Tis something better not to be.' Balthazar Gracian paints existence in the blackest colors in his *Criticón*, etc." [12] Had I not already been carried too far by Schopenhauer, I would have taken pleasure in completing this little demonstration with the help of *Aphorisms on Wisdom in Life*, which is perhaps of all the works I know the one which implies in an author, along with the most reading, the most originality, so that at the head of that book, each page of which contains several quotations, Schopenhauer was able to write quite seriously: "To compile is not my business."

No doubt friendship, friendship for individuals, is a frivolous thing, and reading is a friendship. But at least it is a sincere friendship, and the fact that it is directed to one who is dead, who is absent, gives it something disinterested, almost moving. It is, moreover, a friendship unencumbered with all that makes up the ugliness of other kinds. Since we are all, we the living, only the dead who have not yet assumed our roles, all these compliments, all these greetings in the hall which we call deference, gratitude, devotion, and in which we mingle so many lies, are sterile and tiresome. Furthermore—from our first relations of sympathy, of admiration, of gratitude—the first words we speak, the first letters we write, weave around us the initial threads of a web of habits, of a veritable manner of being, from which we can no longer extricate ourselves in ensuing friendships, without reckoning that during that time the excessive words we have spoken remain like debts which we have to pay, or which we will pay still more dearly all our life with the remorse of having let ourselves refuse them. In reading, friendship is suddenly brought back to its first purity. With books, no amiability. These friends, if we spend an evening with them, it is truly because we desire them. In their case, at least, we often leave only with regret. And with none of those thoughts, when we have left, that spoil friendship: What did they think of us? Didn't we lack tact? Did we please?—and the fear of being forgotten for some other. All these agitations of friendship come to an end at the threshold of that pure and calm friendship that reading is. No more deference; we laugh at what Molière says only to the exact degree that we find him funny; when he bores us, we are not afraid to appear bored, and when we decidedly have had enough of being with him, we put him back in his place as bluntly as if he had neither genius nor fame. The atmosphere of that pure friendship is silence, purer than speech. For we speak for others, but we keep silent for ourselves. Also, silence does not bear, like speech, the trace of our defects, of our grimaces. It is pure, it is truly an atmosphere. Between the author's thought and ours it does not interpose those irreducible elements of our different egotisms which refuse to submit to thought. The very language of the book is pure (if the book deserves that name), made transparent by the author's thought which has removed everything from it that was not itself, to the point of giving it back its faithful image; each sentence, in essence, resembling the others, for all are spoken with the unique inflection of a personality; hence a kind of continuity, which relationships in life and the foreign elements they involve our thinking in exclude and which very quickly allows us to follow the very line of the author's thought, the traits of his character reflected in this calm mirror. We are able to take pleasure by turns in the traits of each writer without requiring them to be marvelous, for it is a great delight for the mind to distinguish these consummate pictures and to love with an unselfish friendship, without stock phrases, as within oneself. A Gautier, straightforward good fellow full of taste (it amuses us to think they have been able to consider him the representative of perfection in art), pleases us that way. We do not exaggerate to ourselves his spiritual power, and in his *Voyage en Espagne,* where each sentence, without his suspecting it, accentuates and follows the features of his personality, full of grace and gaiety (the words arranging themselves of their own accord in order to sketch it, because it is his personality that has chosen them and disposed them in their order), we cannot help finding, far removed from true art, this obligation to which he believes he must submit, not to leave behind a single shape without describing it entirely, accompanying it with a comparison which, not being born from any pleasing and strong impression, does not charm us at all. We can only reproach the pitiful dryness of his imagination when he compares the countryside with its various farms "to those tailors' cardboards on which samples of trousers and vests are pasted" and when he says that from Paris to Angoulême there is nothing to admire. And we smile at this fervent Gothic who did not even take the trouble at Chartres to go visit the cathedral. [13]

But what good humor, what taste! How willingly we follow him in his adventures, this companion full of spirit; he is so likable that everything around him becomes so for us. And after the few days he spent with Captain Lebarbier de Tinan, kept by the storm aboard his beautiful ship "shining like gold," we are sad when he tells us not a word more about this amiable sailor and makes us leave him forever without telling us what becomes of him. [14] We feel rightly that his ostentatious gaiety and also his melancholy moods are the rather loose habits of the journalist in him. But we allow him all this, we go along with him, we are amused when he returns soaked to the bones, dying of hunger and sleeplessness, and we grow sad when he recapitulates with the gloom of a writer of serial stories the names of men of his generation who died before their time. We were saying apropos of him that his sentences sketched his character, but without his suspecting it; for if words are chosen, not by our thought according to its essential affinities, but by our desire to depict ourselves, this desire is represented and we are not. Fromentin, Musset, in spite of their gifts, because they wanted to leave their portrait to posterity, painted it very poorly; yet, even so, they interest us immensely, for their failure is instructive. So when a book is not the mirror of a powerful individuality, it is still the mirror of curious defects of the mind. Bent over a book by Fromentin or a book by Musset, we perceive at the core of the first what is limited and silly in a certain "distinction," at the core of the second, to what degree the eloquence is empty.

If the taste for books increases with intelligence, its dangers, we have seen, decrease with it. An intelligent mind knows how to subordinate reading to its personal activity. Reading is for it but the noblest of distractions, the most ennobling one of all, for only reading and knowledge produce the "good manners" of the mind. We can develop the power of our sensibility and our intelligence only within ourselves, in the depths of our spiritual life. But it is in this contact with other minds, which reading is, that the education of the "manners" of the mind is obtained. In spite of everything, literary men are still like the aristocracy of the intelligence, and not to know a certain book, a certain particularity of literary science, will always remain, even in a man of genius, a mark of intellectual commonness. Distinction and nobility consist, in the order of thought also, in a kind of freemasonry of customs, and in an inheritance of traditions.[15]

In this taste for and this entertainment in reading, very quickly the preference of great writers is for the classics. Even those writers who to their contemporaries appeared to be the most "romantic" read scarcely anything but the classics. In Victor Hugo's conversation, when he speaks of his reading, it is the names of Molière, Horace, Ovid, Regnard that come up most often. Alphonse Daudet, the least bookish of writers, who in his work, full of modernity and life, seems to have rejected any classical heritage, constantly read, quoted, and commented on Pascal, Montaigne, Diderot, Tacitus.[16] One might almost go so far as to say, renewing perhaps by this interpretation, entirely partial though it be, the old distinction between the classicists and the romantics, that it is the public (the intelligent public, of course) that is romantic, while the masters (even the masters who are called "romantic," the masters preferred by the romantic public) are classicists. (A remark that could be extended to all the arts. The public goes to listen to the music of Vincent d'Indy, Vincent d'Indy studies Monsigny's.[17] The public goes to the expositions of Vuillard and Maurice Denis, while these men go to the Louvre.) That is doubtless because contemporary thought, which original writers and artists make accessible and desirable to the public, is to a certain extent so much a part of themselves that a different type of thought entertains them more. It requires, in order for them to proceed to it, more effort, and also gives them more pleasure; we always like to escape a bit from ourselves, to travel, when reading.

But there is another cause to which I prefer, in concluding, to attribute this predilection of great minds for the works of antiquity.[18] It is that they do not have for us, as contemporary works do, only the beauty which the mind that created them knew how to put there. They harbor another still more moving beauty, from the fact that their very matter, I mean the language in which they were written, is like a mirror of life. A little of the happiness one experiences while taking a walk in a city like Beaune, which keeps intact its fifteenth-century hospital, with its well, its wash-house, its vault of paneled and painted timber, its roof with high gables pierced by skylights crowned with graceful spikes of hammered lead (all those things which a vanishing period seems to have forgotten there, all those things that belonged to it only, since none of the periods that followed saw any similar things appear) one still experiences a little of that happiness when wandering in the midst of a tragedy by Racine or a book by Saint-Simon. For they contain all the beautiful outdated forms of language which preserve the memory of usages and ways of feeling that no longer exist, persistent traces of the past which nothing in the present resembles, and of which time alone, passing over them, has still been able to embellish the coloring.

A tragedy by Racine, a book of memoirs by Saint-Simon, resemble beautiful things that are no longer made. The language in which they have been sculpted by great artists with a freedom that makes their sweetness shine and their native force stand out, moves us like the sight of certain marbles, unused today, which the workers of the past used. No doubt in those old buildings the stone has faithfully kept the thought of the sculpture, but also, thanks to the sculptor, the stone, of a kind unknown today, has been preserved for us, adorned with all the colors he knew how to obtain from it, to bring out, to harmonize. It is indeed the living syntax of the France of the seventeenth century—and in it customs and a manner of thought now vanished—that we like to find in the verses of Racine. It is the very forms of that syntax, laid bare, revered, embellished by his chisel so frank and so delicate, which move us in those turns of phrase familiar to the point of singularity and audacity, [19] and whose abrupt pattern we see, in the sweetest and most touching passages, fading like a swift arrow or coming back again in beautiful broken lines. It is those completed forms, true to the very life of the past, that we go to visit in the work of Racine as in an ancient city which has remained intact. In their presence we experience the same emotion as in the presence of those forms of architecture, also discarded, which we can admire only in the rare and magnificent examples which the past that fashioned them has left to us; such as the old walls of cities, the dungeons and the towers, the church baptistries; such as, near the cloister or under the charnel house of the Atrium, the little cemetery which in the sun, under its butterflies and its flowers, forgets the funerary Fountain and the Lantern of the Dead.

Furthermore, it is not only the sentences which trace for our eyes the forms of the ancient soul. Between the sentences—and I am thinking of very ancient books which were first recited—in the interval separating them, there still remains today as in an inviolate burial chamber, filling the interstices, a silence centuries old. Often in the Gospel of St. Luke, coming to a colon that halts it before each of those passages almost in the form of canticles with which it is sown,[20] I have heard the silence of the worshiper who has just stopped reading aloud in order to intone the succeeding verses[21] like a psalm which reminded him of the most ancient psalms of the Bible. This silence was still filling the pause in the sentence which, having divided to enclose it, had kept its form; and more than once, while I was reading, it brought me the perfume of a rose which the breeze entering through the open window had spread in the upper room where the Congregation was gathered and which had not evaporated for seventeen centuries.

How many times, in *The Divine Comedy,* in Shakespeare, have I known that impression of having before me, inserted into the present actual hour, a little of the past, that dreamlike impression which one experiences in Venice on the Piazzetta, before its two columns of gray and pink granite that support on their Greek capitals, one the Lion of Saint Mark, the other Saint Theodore trampling the crocodile under his feet—beautiful strangers come from the Orient over the sea at which they gaze in the distance and which comes to die at their feet, and who both, without understanding the conversations going on around them in a language which is not that of their country, on this public square where their heedless smile still shines, keep on prolonging in our midst their days of the twelfth century, which they interpose in our today. Yes, in the middle of the public square, in the midst of today whose empire it interrupts at this place, a little of the twelfth century, of the twelfth century long since vanished, springs up in a double, light thrust of pink granite. All around, the actual days, the days we are living, circulate, rush buzzing around the columns, but suddenly stop there, flee like repelled bees; for those high and slender enclaves of the past are not in the present, but in another time where the present is forbidden to penetrate. Around the pink columns, surging up toward their wide capitals, the days of the present crowd and buzz. But, interposed between them, the columns push them aside, reserving with all their slender impenetrability the inviolate place of the Past: of the Past familiarly risen in the midst of the present, with that rather unreal complexion of things which a kind of illusion makes us see a few steps ahead, and which are actually situated back many centuries; appealing in its whole aspect a little too positively to the mind, overexciting it a little, as should not be surprising on the part of a ghost from a buried past; yet there, in our midst, approached, pressed against, touched, motionless, in the sun.

Proust's Notes to
the Preface

1. In this preface I have tried only to reflect in my turn on the same subject that Ruskin had treated in "Of Kings' Treasuries": the utility of Reading. In the process these pages, which are hardly about Ruskin, constitute nevertheless a sort of indirect criticism, if you will, of his doctrine. By making known my ideas, I find myself involuntarily opposing them to his in advance. As a direct commentary, my footnotes at almost every page of Ruskin's text sufficed. I would therefore have nothing to add here were I not anxious to express again my gratitude to my friend Miss Marie Nordlinger who, so much better occupied by those beautiful works of carving in which she shows so much originality and mastery, has nevertheless consented to go over this translation, often making it less imperfect. For all the valuable information he sent me, I also want to thank Mr. Charles Newton Scott, the poet and scholar to whom we owe *The Church and Compassion for Animals* and *The Epoch of Marie Antoinette*, two fascinating books, full of knowledge, feeling, and talent, which should be better known in France.

P.S.—This translation was already at the printer's when there appeared in the magnificent English edition (Library Edition) of

Ruskin's works being published by Allen and edited by Messrs.
E. T. Cook and Alexander Wedderburn the volume containing
Sesame and Lilies (July 1905). I hastened to recall my manuscript,
hoping to complete some of my notes with the help of those of
Messrs. Cook and Wedderburn. Unfortunately, though this edition
interested me very much, it has not been able to help me with my
book as much as I would have wished. Of course, most references
were already indicated in my notes. The Library Edition, however,
provided me with some new ones. These are followed by the words
"the Library Edition tells us," for I have never utilized information
without immediately indicating where I got it. As for the comparisons with the rest of the works of Ruskin, the reader will notice
that the Library Edition refers to texts about which I have not
spoken, and that I refer to texts it does not mention. Those readers of
mine who do not know my preface to *The Bible of Amiens* will perhaps
find that, coming second here, I should have taken advantage of the
Ruskinian references given by Messrs. Cook and Wedderburn. The
others, understanding what my intentions are in these editions, will
not be surprised that I did not do so. These comparisons as I conceive
of them are essentially individual. They are but a flash of memory, a
gleam of feeling which suddenly throw light on different passages at
the same time. And these gleams are not as accidental as they may
seem. Adding artificial ones that would not have leapt forth from my
innermost self would warp the view that, by means of them, I am
trying to give of Ruskin. The Library Edition also gives considerable
historical and biographical information, often of great interest. The
reader will see that I acknowledged this when I could, however
rarely. First, it did not absolutely answer to the aim I had proposed
to myself. Also, the Library Edition, a purely scholarly edition,
refrains from any commentary on Ruskin's text, and thus has ample
room for all those new documents, previously unpublished, whose
bringing to light is its real raison d'être. On the contrary, I have
followed Ruskin's text with a continuous commentary which gives
this volume proportions already so considerable that adding the
reproduction of unpublished documents, different readings, etc.,

would have deplorably overburdened it. (I had to leave out the Prefaces to *Sesame* and the third lecture Ruskin added later to the two original ones.) All this having been said, I apologize for not having taken advantage of the notes of Messrs. Cook and Wedderburn, and also express my admiration for this truly definitive edition of Ruskin, which will be of such great interest to all Ruskinians.

2. What we called a village, I do not know why, was a county seat which according to the Guide Joanne had nearly three thousand inhabitants.

3. I confess that a certain use of the imperfect indicative—that cruel tense which represents life to us as something ephemeral and passive at the same time, which at the very moment it retraces our actions stamps them with illusion, annihilating them in the past without leaving to us, as the perfect tense does, the consolation of activity—has remained for me an inexhaustible source of mysterious sadness. Even today I can have been thinking calmly for hours about death; it is enough for me to open a volume of Sainte-Beuve's *Lundis* and come across for instance this sentence of Lamartine (about Madame d'Albany): "Nothing *recalled* in her at that time. . . . She *was* a small woman whose figure sinking a little under her weight had lost, etc.," to feel myself immediately invaded by the most profound melancholy. In novels, the intent to cause pain is so apparent with the author that one hardens oneself a little more.

4. One may try it, by a kind of detour, with books which are not of pure imagination and where there is a historical substratum. Balzac, for instance, whose work to some degree is an impure mixture of spirit and reality insufficiently transformed, lends himself singularly at times to this kind of reading. Or at least he has found the most admirable of those "historical readers" in Mr. Albert Sorel, who has written incomparable essays on *Une Ténébreuse Affaire* and on *l'Envers de l'Histoire Contemporaine*. How much, moreover, does reading, that delight at once ardent and calm, seem to be suited to Mr. Sorel, to that searching mind, that body calm and powerful, reading, during which the thousand sensations of poetry and of obscure well-being which take wing joyfully from the depth of good

health come to compose around the reader's reverie a pleasure as sweet and golden as honey. Besides, this art of enclosing in a reading so many original and strong meditations—it is not only in regard to semihistorical works that Mr. Sorel has brought it to perfection. I shall always remember—and with what gratitude—that the translation of *The Bible of Amiens* has been for him the subject of the most powerful pages he may perhaps ever have written. [Ed. note: Albert Sorel (1842–1906), the historian, had had Proust as a student at the Ecole des Sciences Politiques in 1890, and when Proust published his first volume of Ruskin translations, *La Bible d'Amiens,* he did Proust the good turn of writing a long, enthusiastic review of the book in the influential Paris newspaper *Le Temps* on July 11, 1904. Sorel's description of Proust's style is the first and still one of the most accurate.]

5. This work was later enlarged by the addition to the first two lectures of a third one: "The Mystery of Life and Its Arts." The popular editions continued to contain only "Of Kings' Treasuries" and "Of Queens' Gardens." In the present volume, we have translated only these two lectures, and without having them preceded by any of the prefaces which Ruskin wrote for *Sesame and Lilies.* The dimensions of this volume and the abundance of our own commentary have not allowed us to do better. The numerous editions of *Sesame and Lilies,* except four of them (Smith, Elder and Co.), were all published by George Allen, the distinguished publisher of all Ruskin's works, the master of Ruskin House.

6. *Sesame and Lilies,* "Of Kings' Treasuries," p. 6. [Ed. note: As he acknowledges later in this Preface, Proust did not follow to the letter the texts he quoted. Rather, he chose what he wanted from them, sometimes without indicating his omissions. We have, in turn, followed Proust's "quotations" without restoring the omitted portions from the original source. We have quoted here those parts of Ruskin's English text which correspond to Proust's translation of them.]

7. Actually, this sentence is not found, at least in this form, in *le Capitaine Fracasse.* Instead of "as it appears in the Odyssey of

Homer, poet of Greek fire," there is simply "according to Homer." But since the expressions "it appears from Homer," "it appears from the Odyssey," which are found elsewhere in the same book, gave me a pleasure of the same quality, I have taken the liberty, so that the example might be more striking for the reader, of fusing all these beauties into one, now that, strictly speaking, I no longer have a religious respect for them. Elsewhere in *le Capitaine Fracasse* Homer is qualified as a poet of Greek fire, and I have no doubt that this too enchanted me. However, I am no longer able to bring back accurately enough those forgotten joys to be assured I have not exaggerated and gone too far in accumulating so many wonders in one single sentence! Yet I do not believe so. And I think with regret that the exaltation with which I repeated the sentence from *le Capitaine Fracasse* to the irises and periwinkles leaning at the river's edge, while I trampled underfoot the stones of the path, would have been more delicious still had I been able to find in a single sentence by Gautier so many charms which my own artifice gathers together today without, alas, succeeding in giving me any pleasure.

8. I feel it inherently in Fontanes, of whom Saint-Beuve has said: "This epicurean side was strongly marked in him . . . without those rather materialistic habits, Fontanes, with his talent, would have produced much more . . . and also more lasting works." Note that the impotent always pretends that he is not. Fontanes says:

> If they are to be believed, I am wasting my time;
> They alone are the honor of the century
>
> > [Editor's trans.]

and he affirms that he does a great deal of work.

The case of Coleridge is still more pathological. "No man of his time, or perhaps of any time," says Carpenter (quoted by Mr. Ribot in his fine book on the Diseases of the Will) "joined together more than Coleridge the reasoning powers of the philosopher, the imagination of the poet, etc. And yet, there is probably no man who, endowed with such remarkable gifts, has accomplished so little with them; the great defect of his character was the lack of will to turn his natural gifts to account, so that, with numerous gigantic projects constantly floating in his mind, he never seriously tried to execute any one of them. Thus, at the very outset of his career, he found a generous bookseller who promised him thirty guineas for poems he had recited, etc. He preferred to come week after week to beg without supplying a solitary line of that poetry which he would only have had to write down in order to free himself." [Ed. note: Cf. Th. Ribot. We have not corrected, so to speak, Proust's abridgment. The Open Court Publishing Co., 1894), pp. 72–73. Again, Proust has omitted certain portions from this quotation as it appears in Ribot. We have not corrected, so to speak, Proust's abridgement. At the time of writing "*Sur la lecture*" in the early months of 1905, Proust was worried about the condition of his own will and was reading various books on pyschoneurosis, among them the one he mentions here by Théodule Armand Ribot (1839–1916), the French psychologist and pioneer in this field of medicine.]

9. I need not say that it would be useless to look for such a convent near Utrecht and that this bit is purely imaginary. It was, however, suggested to me by the following lines of Léon Séché in his book on Sainte-Beuve: "One day, while in Liège, he (Sainte-Beuve) ventured to strike up a conversation with the little church of Utrecht. It was rather late, but Utrecht was quite far from Paris, and I do not know whether *Volupté* [a novel by Sainte-Beuve] would have sufficed to open for him after two knocks the Amersfoort archives. I have some doubt about it, for even after the first two volumes of his *Port-Royal*, the pious scholar who had charge of those archives, etc. With difficulty, Sainte-Beuve secured from the good Master Karsten permission to half-open certain portfolios. . . . Open the second edition of *Port-Royal* and you will see the gratitude expressed by Sainte-Beuve to Master Karsten" (Léon Séché, *Sainte-Beuve,* vol. I, pp. 229 et seq.). As for the details of the trip, they are all based on true impressions. I do not know whether one passes by Dordrecht to go to Utrecht, but it is indeed just as I have seen it that I have described Dordrecht. It was not in going to Utrecht, but at Vollen-

dam, that I traveled by canal boat, among the reeds. The channel I placed in Utrecht is in Delft. At the hospital of Beaune I saw a Van der Weyden, and nuns of an order from, I think, Flanders, who still wear the same headdress, not as in the Roger Van der Weyden, but as in other paintings seen in Holland.

10. Pure snobbery is more innocent. To delight in the company of someone because he had an ancestor in the Crusades, that is vanity, intelligence has nothing to do with that. But to delight in the company of someone because his grandfather's name is often found in Alfred de Vigny or Chateaubriand, or (a truly irresistible seduction for me, I admit) to have one's family coat-of-arms (the reference is to a woman quite worthy of being admired without that) in the great rose window of Notre-Dame d'Amiens, there is where intellectual sin starts. Besides, I have analyzed it at too great length elsewhere, though I still have much to say about it, to have to insist on it further here. [Ed. note: By "elsewhere" Proust is undoubtedly referring to his analysis of "idolatry," synonymous in his vocabulary with "snobbery," in the fourth and last section of his Preface to his translation of Ruskin's *The Bible of Amiens*. See pp. 49 *seq.* above.]

11. Paul Stapfer, *Souvenirs sur Victor Hugo,* published in the *Revue de Paris*.

12. Schopenhauer, *The World as Will and Representation* (chapter on the Vanity and Suffering of Life). [Ed. note: The full text of this passage from Schopenhauer, in the English translation by E. F. J. Payne which we have used here, can be found in vol. II, pp. 585–586, of The Falcon's Wing Press edition, 1958. Proust indicates his abbreviations, in his usual manner, by an *etc.* We have added only one word, which he must have dropped inadvertently, from the line by Theognis.]

13. "I regret having passed through Chartres without having been able to visit the cathedral" (*Voyage en Espagne,* p. 2).

14. He became, I am told, the famous Admiral de Tinan, father of Madame Pochet de Tinan, whose name has remained dear to artists, and the grandfather of the brilliant cavalry officer. It is he

also, I think, who before Gaeta assured for some time the supplies and communications of Francis II and the Queen of Naples. See Pierre de la Gorce, *Histoire du second Empire.*

15. True distinction, besides, always pretends to address itself only to distinguished persons who know the same customs, and does not "explain." A book by Anatole France implies a multitude of erudite ideas, contains perpetual allusions which common people do not notice, and which, aside from its other beauties, account for its incomparable nobility.

16. That is doubtless why often when a great writer engages in literary criticism, he speaks a great deal about the editions of classics being published, and very little about contemporary books. For example, Sainte-Beuve's *Lundis* and Anatole France's *Vie littéraire.* But while Anatole France judges his contemporaries admirably well, one may say that Sainte-Beuve did not appreciate any of the great writers of his time. And let it not be objected that he was blinded by personal hatreds. Having incredibly depreciated the novelist in Stendhal, he praised, by way of compensation, the modesty, the delicate technique of the man, as if there were nothing else favorable to say about him! This blindness of Sainte-Beuve, in regard to his time, contrasts singularly with his pretensions to insight, to foreknowledge. "Everyone is able," he says in *Chateaubriand et son groupe littéraire,* "to pronounce on Racine and Bossuet. . . . But the sagacity of the judge, the perspicacity of the critic, is proved mostly with new works, not yet tested by the public. To judge at first sight, to divine, to anticipate, that is the gift of the critic. How few have it."

17. And, conversely, the classicists have no better commentators than the "romantics." In fact, the romantics alone know how to read classical works, because they read them as they have been written, romantically, because in order to read a poet or a prose writer well, one has oneself to be, not a scholar, but a poet or a prose writer. This is true for the least "romantic" works. It is not professors of rhetoric who called the beautiful verses of Boileau to our attention, it is Victor Hugo:

And in four handkerchiefs soiled with her beauty
Sends to the laundryman her roses and her lilies.

[Editor's trans.]

[Ed. note: This is Boileau's piquant observation on the part cosmetics play in feminine beauty. The roses and the lilies, standard symbols of feminine sexual charms in the poetry of the period, are actually rouge and powder. The illusion, meant for the lady's lover, ends up in the hands of the laundryman.] It is Anatole France:

Ignorance and delusion at their newborn comedies
In uniforms of counts, in gowns of countesses.

[Editor's trans.]

The latest issue of the *Renaissance latine* (May 15, 1905) enables me, as I am correcting these proofs, to extend this remark to the fine arts, by a new example. It shows us, in fact, in Rodin (article by Mauclair) the true commentator on Greek statuary.

18. A predilection which they themselves generally believe accidental; they suppose that the most beautiful books happen by chance to have been written by the authors of antiquity; and no doubt this may happen, since the ancient books we read are chosen from the whole past, so vast compared to the contemporary period. But a reason in some way accidental cannot suffice to explain so general an attitude of mind.

19. I believe for example that the fascination one is accustomed to find in these lines from *Andromaque*:

Why did you kill him? What did he do? By what right?
Who told you?

[Editor's trans.]

comes precisely from the fact that the habitual syntactical link is intentionally broken. [Ed. note: *Andromaque,* v, 3. Though to translate these lines by Racine and the ones to follow into English is to interfere somewhat with Proust's particular attention in this note to their unusual French syntax, nevertheless for readers who may not know French, it was felt that a translation would at least save

Proust's note from incoherence.] "By what right?" refers, not to "What did he do?", which immediately precedes, but to "Why did you kill him?" And "Who told you?" refers also to "kill." (Recalling another line from *Andromaque*: "Who told you, sir, that he scorns me?" [*Andromaque*, II, 2] one may suppose that "Who told you?" goes with "Who told you, to kill him?") Zigzags of diction (the recurrent and broken line I am speaking of above) which somewhat obscure the sense, so that I have heard a great actress, more concerned with clarity of meaning than precision of prosody, say flatly: "Why did you kill him? By what right? What did he do?" The most famous lines of Racine are actually so because they thus charm by some familiar audacity of language thrown like a bold bridge between two banks of sweetness. "I loved you faithless, what would I have done faithful?" [*Andromaque*, IV, 5] And what pleasure is produced by the beautiful encounter of those expressions whose almost common simplicity gives the meaning, as to certain faces in Mantegna, so sweet a plentitude, such beautiful colors:

And on a rash infatuation of my youth *set sail*. . . .
[*Phèdre*, I, 1]

Let us reunite three hearts that could not *agree*.
[*Andromaque*, V, 5]
[Editor's trans.]

And that is why one must read the classic writers in complete texts, and not be contented with selected passages. The famous pages of writers are often those where this intimate structure of their language is concealed by the beauty, of an almost universal character, of the fragment. I do not believe that the particular essence of Gluck's music is manifested as much in a certain sublime melody as in the cadence of his recitatives, where harmony is as the very sound of the voice of his genius when it falls back on an involuntary intonation where all its simple gravity and its distinctions are evident every time one hears him recover his breath, so to speak. Anyone who has seen photographs of Saint Mark's in Venice may believe (and I do not speak only of the exterior of the monument) that he has an idea of that church with cupolas, when it is only by approaching, till one can touch them with the hand, the varicolored curtain of those smiling columns, it is only when seeing the strange and grave power which coils leaves or perches birds in those capitals that one can distinguish only when near, it is only by having on the very same square the impression of that low monument, the whole length of façade, with its flowery masts and festive decoration, its aspect of the "exhibition palace," that one feels its true and complex individuality manifest itself in these significant but accessory traits, and which no photograph retains.

20. "And Mary said: 'My soul doth magnify the Lord, and my spirit has rejoiced in God my Savior, etc. . . .'" "And his father Zacharias was filled with the Holy Spirit and prophesied, saying: 'Blessed be the Lord, the God of Israel; For he hath wrought redemption for his people, etc. . . .'" "He received him into his arms, and blessed God, and said: 'Now lettest thou thy servant depart, Lord, in peace. . . .'" [Cf. Luke 1:67–68; 2:28–29]

21. To tell the truth, no positive evidence permits me to affirm that in those readings the speaker might sing the kind of psalms Saint Luke introduced in his gospel. But it seems to me that this sufficiently stands out in the comparison of various passages by Renan, and mainly in *Saint Paul,* pp. 257 et seq.; the *Apostles,* pp. 99–100; *Marcus Aurelius,* pp. 502–503, etc. [Ed. note: Proust is referring to volumes of Ernest Renan's work, *Origines du Christianisme,* published between 1863 and 1881.]

The Notes to the Preface were edited and translated by William Burford.

Selected Notes of Proust to His Translation of *Sésame et les Lys*

Each note given here is preceded by the passage from *Sesame and Lilies* (*CW* 18) to which it refers; the citation following each passage is to chapter and section number. The page and note number given with the note itself is a citation to *Sésame et les Lys*, septième édition (see p. x above). These selected notes have been translated and edited by William Burford.

"You shall each have a cake of sesame,—and ten pound.
Lucian: *The Fisherman*." [1: Epigraph]*

This epigraph, which did not appear in the first editions of *Sesame and Lilies*, projects like a supplementary ray of light that reaches not only the last sentence of the lecture (see page 125), but illuminates retrospectively all that preceded. Having given his lecture the

---

*Ed. note: Ten pounds sterling. Ruskin's aim in "Of Kings' Treasuries" was not only to recommend the spiritual "treasures" to be found in the reading of good books but at the same time to insist on an economic change of heart in the society of his time that would alleviate the numbing poverty which destroyed any possibility for the poor of partaking of such a "treasure" as reading. See the newspaper story he cites later about the death of a cobbler who "applied to the parish for aid. The

symbolic title of Sesame (Sesame of *The Thousand and One Nights*—the magic word that opens the door of the thieves' cave—being the allegory of reading which opens for us the door of those treasuries where men's most precious wisdom is enclosed: books), Ruskin amused himself by taking up again the word *Sesame* in itself and, without concerning himself further with the two meanings it has here (Sesame in Ali Baba, and reading), by insisting on its original meaning (the grain of sesame) and embellishing it with a quotation from Lucian which in a way makes of it a play on words by bringing out sharply, under the conventional meaning of the word in the oriental storyteller and in Ruskin, its primordial meaning. Actually, Ruskin thus raises by one degree the symbolic meaning of his title since the quotation from Lucian reminds us that Sesame had already been diverted from its meaning in *The Thousand and One Nights* and that thus the meaning it has as the title of Ruskin's lecture is an allegory of allegory. This quotation states clearly at the outset the three meanings of the word *Sesame,* reading which opens the doors of wisdom, Ali Baba's magic word, and the enchanted grain. From the beginning Ruskin thus reveals his three themes and at the end of his lecture he will inextricably combine them in the last sentence where the tonality of the beginning (sesame the grain) will be recalled in the final chord, a sentence that will borrow an extraordinary richness and plenitude from these three themes (or rather five, the two others being those from "Of Kings' Treasuries" taken in the symbolic sense of books, then referring to the Kings and to their various kinds of treasuries, a new theme introduced toward

---

relieving officer gave him a 4 lb. loaf, and told him if he came again he should 'get the stones.' " Therefore Ruskin in this opening epigraph announces that all men in need should get not merely the usual charitable dole but rather a special sesame bread and ten pounds in money, which would give them the possibility of enjoying the pleasures of civilized humanity. The aesthetics of Ruskin, as of Marx who was also appalled at the ugliness in which the poor lived in London, is based on a revolutionary economic ethics—though Ruskin admitted in one of his prefaces to *Sesame and Lilies* that his audience was the upper middle class. We should remember, nevertheless, that by the end of his life Ruskin had given away all of his large fortune.

the end of the lecture). On the quotation from Lucian itself the Library Edition gives a commentary that would seem exact to me only if this quotation were used as an epigraph to "Of Queens' Gardens" and not to "Of Kings' Treasuries." In return it points out (and this is very interesting) Ruskin's admiration (the proof of which is in a notation in pencil on a copy of the book) for a passage from Aristophanes's *The Birds* where the Lark describing the simple life of the birds says that they have no need of money and feed on sesame. I simply believe that Ruskin, a little because of that idolatry of which I have often spoken, thus delighted in worshiping a word in all the beautiful passages of the great writers where it appears. Our contemporary idolator,* to whom I have often compared Ruskin, thus at times places as many as five epigraphs at the beginning of a similar piece. Indeed, Ruskin placed as many as five in succession at the beginning of *Sesame* and if he at last chose the one from Lucian, it is no doubt because, being more removed than the others from the sentiment of his lecture, it was thus newer, more decorative, and, by reviving the meaning of the word *Sesame,* threw a better light on its various symbols. No doubt, besides, it led him to compare the treasuries of wisdom to the charm of a frugal life and to give his counsels of individual wisdom the scope of maxims for social happiness. This latter intention becomes more exact toward the middle of the lecture. But it is precisely the charm of Ruskin's works that between the ideas of one book and among various books there may be links he does not show, which he hardly lets appear for an instant and which he has perhaps woven as an afterthought, but never artificially, however, since they are always taken from the substance, always identical with itself, of his thought. The multiple but constant preoccupations of this thought, that is what assures these books of a unity more real than the unity of composition, generally absent, it must be said.

I see that, in the note placed at the end of the lecture, I thought I

---

*Ed. note: Undoubtedly Robert de Montesquiou, the model for Charlus in *A la recherche du temps perdu*.

could find up to seven themes in the last sentence. In reality Ruskin arranges side by side, mingles, maneuvers, and makes shine together all the main ideas—or images—which appeared with some disorder in the course of his lecture. This is his method. He goes from one idea to another without apparent order. But in reality the fancy that leads him follows his profound affinities which in spite of himself impose on him a superior logic. So that in the end he happens to have obeyed a kind of secret plan which, unveiled at the end, imposes retrospectively on the whole a sort of order and makes it appear magnificently arranged up to this final apotheosis. Besides, if the disorder is the same in all his books, the same gesture of bringing the reins together at the end and of feigning to have constrained and guided his steeds, does not occur in all of them. Here as well should we not see more than a game. [pp. 61–63*n*1]

"But granting that we had both the will and the sense to choose our friends well, how few of us have the power! or, at least how limited, for most, is the sphere of choice! [1:6]

This idea seems very striking to us, in fact, because we feel the spiritual usefulness it is going to have for Ruskin and because the "friends" here are only tokens, and because in these friends we cannot choose, we feel already about to appear the friends we can choose, those who are the main character of this lecture: the books, which, like a famous actress, the star who does not appear in the first act, have not yet made their entrance. And in this specious and yet true reasoning, we can still recognize, led so naturally by the disciple and brother of Plato that Ruskin was, something like a Platonic reasoning. "But again, Critias, you cannot choose your friends as you would like, etc." But here, as very often with the Greeks who said all the true things but did not search out the true, more-hidden paths that lead there, the comparison is not conclusive. For one *may* have the kind of position in life that allows one *to choose the friends one wants* (a position in life to which of course intelligence and charm must be joined, without which even the persons we would be able to choose we could not have as *friends* in the exact sense of the word). But these things *may* in the end happen to come together; I do not say that they do frequently, but it is enough that I can find several examples near me. But, even for these privileged beings, the friends they will be able to choose as they please will in no way take the place of books (which proves that books are not merely friends one may choose, however wise one wishes them) because in reality the essential difference between a book and a person is not the greater or lesser degree of wisdom in the one or the other, but the manner in which we communicate with them. Our mode of communication with people implies a diminution of the active powers of the soul which, on the contrary, are concentrated and exalted by this wonderful miracle of reading, which is communication in the midst of solitude. When we read, we receive another's thought, and yet we are alone, we are in fully thinking work, in full aspiration, in full personal activity: we receive the ideas of another person in spirit, that is to say, in truth, we can therefore unite with them, we are that other person and yet all the time we are developing our own I with more variety than if we thought alone, we are driven by another on our own ways. In conversation, even leaving aside the moral, social influences, etc., created by the presence of the interlocutor, communication takes place through the intermediary of sounds, the spiritual shock is weakened, inspiration, profound thinking, is impossible. Much more, thought by becoming spoken thought is falsified, as is proved by the inferiority as writers of those who enjoy and excel too much in conversation. (In spite of illustrious exceptions one may mention, in spite of the testimony of an Emerson himself, who attributes a truly inspiring virtue to conversation, it can be said that in general conversation sets us on the road to brilliant expressions or pure reasonings, almost never to a deep impression.) Therefore the gratuitous reason given by Ruskin (the impossibility of choosing one's friends, the possibility of choosing one's books) is not the true one. It is only a contingent reason, the true reason is an essential difference between the two modes of communication. Once again, the sphere where one's friends are chosen may not be limited. It is true that in these cases it is, however, limited to the living. But if all the dead were living they could talk with us only in the same way that the living do. And a conversation with Plato would still be a conversation, that is to say, an exercise infinitely more superficial than reading, the value of the things heard or read being of less importance than the spiritual state they can create in us and which can be profound only in solitude or in that peopled solitude that reading is. [pp. 70–71*n*1]

"A book is essentially not a talking thing, but a written thing." [1:9]

This distinction results of course from the theory we were outlining just now. A man can inspire us only if we hear him in solitude, that is to say, if we read him, but he himself must have been inspired too. Only solitude allows us to put ourselves in the state in which he himself was, a state which could not be produced if the book were a spoken book; one can no more read than write while speaking. Reading again this sentence of Ruskin's: "A book is not a talking thing, but a written thing," I feel that I have contradicted him less than I thought. But it remains in any case to say that if a book is not a talking thing, but a written, it is also a thing read and not listened to in conversation, and that consequently it cannot be likened to a friend. If Ruskin has not said this, it is because one of the original aspects of his genius is to bring together, with the delving insistence of a Carlyle, the serene and hidden simplicity (not agitated and expounded), the smile, the "aesthetic" side of the Greeks. He has not tried to analyze the original state of soul of the "reader." [p. 75*n*1]

"But a book is written, not to multiply the voice merely, not to carry it merely, but to perpetuate it." [1:9]

To perpetuate is there for contrast. But, in reality, it is no longer the same voice that is to be perpetuated. If it were simply the same kind of voice—nothing but "spoken" words—to perpetuate them would be as frivolous as to transmit or multiply them. [p. 75*n*2]

"In the sum of his [the author's] life he finds this to be the thing, or group of things, manifest to him;—this, the piece of true knowledge, or sight, which his share of sunshine and earth has permitted him to seize. He would fain set it down for ever. . . ." [1:9]

I did not know this passage from "Of Kings' Treasuries" when I wrote in the preface of *The Bible of Amiens*: "Ruskin was one of those men . . . warned of the presence near them of an eternal reality, intuitively perceived by inspiration, . . . to which they dedicate their ephemeral life in order to give it some value. Such men, attentive to and eager about the universe to be explored, are made aware of *the parts of reality* which their special gifts provide them with a particular understanding of, by a kind of demon that guides them, etc. Ruskin's special gift, etc. The poet being for Ruskin . . . a sort of scribe writing at nature's dictation a more or less important part of its secret, the artist's first duty is to add nothing of his own to the sublime message." Now this passage from "Of Kings' Treasuries" confirms more or less what I was saying at that time about Ruskin; since in order to contemplate his thought (one can only see with something similar to what is looked at; if the light were not in the eye, Goethe said, the eye would not see the light; in order to be understood by the scholar, the world has to have the substance of thought) I had happened to take an idea so similar to one of his ideas, a glass so pure that his light would easily penetrate; since between my contemplation and his thought I had introduced so little alien, opaque, and refractory matter. [p. 76*n*1]

"Will you go and gossip with your housemaid, or your stable-boy, when you may talk with queens and kings. . . ." [1:11]

[. . . .] But in reality, and if this were not a metaphor, Ruskin would not at all find it better to talk with a king than with a servant. (a) Thus the word *kings, nobility,* to cite only those that refer exactly to the passage in question, are used by writers who know the nothingness of these things, to give more grandeur to an idea (a grandeur these things cannot give, however, since in reality they do not possess it). I find in Maeterlinck ("L'Evolution du Mystère," in *Le Temple Enseveli*) a remark of the same kind as mine (with greater depth and beauty, it goes without saying): "Let us ask ourselves," he says, "if the hour has not come to make a serious revision of the beauties, the images, the symbols, the sentiments, which we still use to glorify the spectacle of the world. It is certain that the greatest part of them have no more than precarious connections with the thoughts of our actual existence, and if they still hold us it is rather by virtue of being innocent and gracious souvenirs of a more cred-ulous past, nearer to the childhood of man. But to live in the midst of false images is not unimportant, even if we know they are false. In the end, misleading images take the place of the true ideas they represent," etc. [. . . .] Maeterlinck does not deserve in this respect the same reproaches as Ruskin. For his metaphors seek rather to characterize a certain beauty than to furnish it with titles which impose on our imagination. When Ruskin says of the Lily that it is "the very flower of the Annunciation" he has said nothing that might make us better perceive the beauty of the Lily, he only wants to make us revere it. When Maeterlinck says: "Meanwhile, in a blaze of light, the great white Lily, old lord of gardens, the only authentic prince among all the commoners issuing from the kitchen gar-den, . . . unvarying chalice with six petals of silver, whose nobility

(a) Ruskin less than any other man. "The biographers of Ruskin," says the man who has best spoken of Ruskin and has made him known in France, Robert de la Sizeranne, in the preface he wrote for Mme. P. Crémieux's beautiful translation of *The Stones of Venice,* "the biographers of Ruskin know that it is not in drawing rooms that we must seek personal recollections of him, but among . . . masons, carpen-ters, second-hand book dealers, and gondoliers. Ugo Ojetti has found and pub-lished the letters of Ruskin to his gondolier.

dates back to that of the Gods themselves, the immemorial Lily raises his ancient scepter, inviolate, august, which creates around it a zone of chastity, of silence, of light," [. . .] no doubt the nobility of the Lily is portrayed here (as in our mind when we see it elsewhere, historic, mystic, heraldic, in the midst of the garden), but "in a blaze of light" in the midst of the other flowers, in full reality. And the most noble images, that of the scepter, for example, are drawn from what is most characteristic in its form. Yet (for we could follow endlessly these two minds in their coincidences, their diversions, their crisscrossings) the name of Maeterlinck necessarily arose here and it is finally on his name that the sermon inspired by these pages from Ruskin should be preached. [. . .] What is most beautiful in the life of the bees: perhaps a certain "azure" color of the beautiful summer hours. Again in "La Vie des Abeilles," in *Le Temple Enseveli,* what remains most precious are such pictures as those where the Wise Man appears who makes the author like the bees and the old-fashioned flowers, or the worker who contemplates the sun from the top of the ramparts, and which accentuate for us the affinity of the Virgil of Flanders with his Mantuan ancestor. Maeterlinck has added an admirable philosopher to the wonderful writer he was. But, and even if, as I believe, this writer has become still greater, his friend the philosopher has contributed nothing to it. We feel quite justly that it is not because the thinker has developed that the writer has grown. Conclusion: beauty of style is in essence irrational. Therefore we picked an unjust quarrel with Ruskin, but not a vain one, since it has let us discover why he was essentially right. [p. 79n1]

". . . the motives with which you strive to take high place in the society of the living [will be] measured, as to all the truth and sincerity that are in them, by the place you desire to take in this company of the Dead." [1:11]

Actually the place we wish to occupy in the society of the dead in no way gives us the right to desire to occupy one in the society of the living. The virtue of the first ought to detach us from the second. And if reading and admiration do not detach us from ambition (I speak of course only of ambition in the commonplace sense, that which Ruskin calls "the desire to have a good position in the world and in life"), it is a sophism to say that we have acquired through the first the right to renounce the second. A man is not more entitled to be "received in good society," or at least to wish to be, because he is more intelligent and cultivated. This is one of those sophisms that the vanity of intelligent people picks up in the arsenal of their intelligence to justify their basest inclinations. In other words, having become more intelligent creates some rights to be less. Very simply, diverse personalities are to be found in the breast of each of us, and often the life of more than one superior man is nothing but the coexistence of a philosopher and a snob. Actually, there are very few philosophers and artists who are absolutely detached from ambition and respect for power, from "people of position." And among those who are more delicate or more sated, snobism replaces ambition and respect for power in the same way superstition arises on the ruins of religious beliefs. Morality gains nothing there. Between a worldly philosopher and a philosopher intimidated by a minister of state, the second is still the more innocent. [pp. 82–83*n*2]

"Not that he [the author] does not say what he means, and in strong words too; but he cannot say it all; and what is more strange, *will* not, but in a hidden way and in parables, in order that he may be sure you want it." [1:13]

But this sort of obscurity which envelops the splendor of beautiful books like that of beautiful mornings, is a natural obscurity, the breath in some way of genius, that it gives forth without knowing it, and not an artificial veil with which he willfully surrounded his work in order to hide it from the common public. When Ruskin says: "He wants to know if you are worthy of it", he is speaking plainly. Because to give his thinking a brilliant form, more accessible and more seductive to the public, diminishes it, and makes for the facile writer, the writer of the second class. But to envelop his thought so that it can be grasped only by those who might take the trouble to lift the veil, makes for the difficult writer who is also a writer of the second class. The first-class writer is he who uses the very words dictated to him by an internal necessity, by the shape of his thought of which he can change nothing—and without asking himself if these words will please the common public or "turn them away". Sometimes the great writer feels that instead of those sentences in whose depths an uncertain gleam trembles which so many eyes will not perceive, he could manage (merely by putting together and displaying the appealing precious metals that he mercilessly melts and gets rid of in order to create that dark enamel), to make himself recognized as a great man by the crowd, and, what is a more diabolic temptation, by those of his friends who deny his genius, even more by his mistress. Then he will write a second-rate book with everything that is kept silent in a good book and that composes its noble atmosphere of silence, that marvelous varnish which shines with the sacrifice of all that has not been said. Instead of writing *l'Education sentimentale* he will write *Fort comme la Mort* [Guy de Maupassant]. And it is not the desire rather to write *l'Education sentimentale* which should make him renounce all those vain beauties, it is not any motive foreign to his work, any reasoning in which he says: "*je.*" He is only the place where those thoughts take shape that choose themselves at every moment, construct and retouch the necessary and unique form in which they are going to embody themselves. [p. 85*n*1]

"I cannot quite see the reason of this [obliqueness of authors], nor analyse that cruel reticence in the breasts of wise men which makes them always hide their deeper thought." [1:13]

We would be wrong to see here a whim of the thinker's, which on the contrary would take away from the depth of his thought: but this fact, that to understand is, in some way, as we have said, to be equal to, then to understand a profound thought is to have, at the moment one understands it, a profound thought oneself; and this demands some effort, a genuine descent to the heart of oneself, leaving far behind one, after having passed through them, any clouds of transitory thought through which we are ordinarily content to look at things. Only desire and love give us the strength to make this effort. The only books that we truly absorb are those we read with real appetite, after having worked hard to get them, so great had been our need of them. [p. 86*n*1]

"A well-educated gentleman . . . is learned in the *peerage* of words; knows the words of true descent and ancient blood, at a glance, from words of modern canaille; remembers all their ancestry, their intermarriages, distant relationships, and the extent to which they were admitted, and offices they held, among the national noblesse of words. . . ." [1:15]

Here again the metaphor gives dignity to the idea precisely with the aid of things whose dignity Ruskin certainly does not recognize. He was probably indifferent to the armorial, and the kind of persons who know exactly whether such and such a person is *received* or not received—"Madame de Beauséant received her, it seems to me. . . ."—"At her receptions!" the vicomtesse replied (Balzac: *Gobseck*)—who know the illustriousness of each person's ancestry and intermarriages, must not have possessed in his eyes a very enviable science. Whether a person is of good blood or of obscure blood, that is something that has little importance in the eyes of a thinker. But it is to the idea that it has on the contrary great value that Ruskin's image appeals: "he knows the words of true descent and ancient blood", etc., so that the pleasure such images give to the reader (and first to the author) is in reality based on intellectual insincerity. [p. 89*n*1]

"So, again, consider what effect has been produced on the English vulgar mind by the use of the sonorous Latin form 'damno,' in translating the Greek κατακρίνω, when people charitably wish to make it forcible; and the substitution of the temperate 'condemn' for it, when they choose to keep it gentle; and what notable sermons have been preached by illiterate clergymen on—'He that believeth not shall be damned'; though they would shrink with horror from translating Heb. xi. 7, 'The saving of his house, by which he damned the world,' or John viii. 10–11, 'Woman, hath no man damned thee?' " * [1:18]

Ruskin, who has so effectively and so often shown that the artist, in what he writes or in what he paints, infallibly reveals his weaknesses, his affectations, his faults (and in effect isn't the work of art through the hidden rhythm of our soul—so much more alive than we perceive it ourselves—similar to those sphygmographic traces in which automatically the pulsations of our blood are registered?) Ruskin would have had to see that if the writer in his choice of words obeys a concern for erudition (which will soon give way to a vulgar show of erudition and to the most banal and unbearable affectation, as happens with our more mediocre historians who, in the slightest tale, think they have to show they know that in the XVIIth century the word *astonished* had great force and that *moved* meant *shaken*), it will be this concern for erudition—interesting as it may be, but never more than interesting—which will be reflected, which will inscribe itself in his book. A curious writer ceases because of this very fact to be a great writer. With a Sainte-Beuve the perpetual shifting of his style, which leaves at every moment the direct route and current usage, is charming, but immediately betrays the limits of a talent—wide as it is—that in spite of everything is of the second rank. But what can we say of the simple renewal of a word by taking it back to its ancient meaning? This is learned so easily that it quickly becomes a mechanical procedure and the entertainment of

*Ed. note: In both these latter passages from the New Testament the King James version reads "condemned" rather than "damned." The first quotation from Hebrews refers to Noah's building of the ark. Ruskin is mocking the preachers of his day who did not know the essential meaning of the words that came out of their mouths.

all those who do not know how to write. Certain "distinctions" of this kind are as ridiculous, having so little personality, as certain vulgarities. To use such a word in its ancient sense becomes, in a serious style, the mark of a mind without inventiveness and without taste, just as it is in a humorous style to follow a slang expression with the words: "as the Bishop of Hulst says." All this is mechanical, that is to say the opposite of art [. . .]. This does not mean of course that a great writer, and here Ruskin is indeed right, ought not to know his dictionary by heart, and be able to follow a word through the ages in all the great writers who have used it [. . .] a great writer knows his dictionary and his great writers before writing. But while writing he no longer thinks of them, but of what he wants to express, and chooses the words which say it best, with the most power, color, and harmony. He chooses them from an excellent vocabulary, because it is the one which, in his memory, is at his disposition, his studies having firmly established the particular virtue of each term. But he does not think of this when he writes. His erudition gives way to his genius [. . .].

His language, as learned and as rich as it may be, is only the keyboard on which he improvises. And as he does not think of the rarity of a word while he is writing, his work bears no trace, no blemish, of an affectation [. . .]. [pp. 93–95*n*1]

" '*Blind mouths—*'*

"I pause again, for this is a strange expression; a broken metaphor, one might think, careless and unscholarly.

"Not so: its very audacity and pithiness are intended to make us look close at the phrase and remember it. Those two monosyllables express the precisely accurate contraries of right character, in the two great offices of the Church—those of bishop and pastor.

"A 'Bishop' means 'a person who sees.'

"A 'Pastor' means 'a person who feeds.' " [1:22]

*Ed. note: From Milton's *Lycidas*.

When two triangles have an equal angle formed by two equal sides, the two other angles and the third side also coincide. In the same way when we have been able to make certain generative points in two minds coincide, other coincidences will spring from these: we will be able to observe them not only afterward, but they are contained in the initial truth. When after that we make the circuit of two minds we perceive coincidences which were there before us and had already arranged themselves in the place we had assigned them. (Thus an astronomer sees for the first time, when he has a powerful enough telescope, a star whose existence and place he had previously demonstrated by simple calculation.) More modestly(!), in the Preface to *The Bible of Amiens,* I had compared to Ruskin a modern idolater whose talent and mind I value immensely, and I had noticed between them several points of coincidence, quite easy to see. Here now Ruskin presents me with fresh examples, which verify what I say, and in showing me that they pass through the same points, confirms that they follow (a little, and not for long, minds are not so geometric) the same line. Yes, "a Bishop means a person who sees," here is a sentence that all those of my friends who know the poet and the idolatrous essayist of whom I wish to speak,* will say almost involuntarily in a loud voice, with an accent which underlines and hammers home, which with him is so original: "A Bishop is a person who *sees.*" We hear him say it, for, like Ruskin (*trahit sua quemque voluptas*) he is elated to find in the depths of each word its hidden sense, ancient and full of savor. A word is for him the flask full of memory, of which Baudelaire speaks.** Apart even from the beauty of the sentence where it is placed (and here is where danger could commence), he reveres it. And if we do not recognize its content (in using it falsely) he cries sacrilege (and in that he is right). He is amazed at the secret virtue there is in a word, he marvels at it; pronouncing this word in the most informal conversation, he points it out, draws attention to it, repeats it, exclaims in admiration.

*Ed. note: Again, Robert de Montesquiou.
**Ed. note: Baudelaire's poem, "Le Flacon."

Thus he gives the simplest things a dignity, a grace, an interest, a life, the result being that those who have approached him prefer his conversation to almost all others. But from the viewpoint of art one sees what the danger would be for a writer less gifted than he; words are in fact beautiful in themselves, but we are not for nothing in their beauty. For a musician there is no more merit in using a mi than a sol; but when we write we have to consider the words at the same time as works of art whose profound meaning we should understand and whose glorious past we should respect, and as simple notes which will have value (in respect to us) only by the place we will give them and by the relations of reason or of feeling we will establish between them. [pp. 102–03*n*1]

"Take up your Latin and Greek dictionaries, and find out the meaning of 'Spirit.' It is only a contraction of the Latin word 'breath,' and an indistinct translation of the Greek word for 'wind.' The same word is used in writing, 'The wind bloweth where it listeth'; and in writing, 'So is every one that is born of the Spirit. . . .' " [1:23]

[. . . .] And now contemporary medicine seems on the point of telling us, it too (though a proponent of a viewpoint so different, so foreign, so opposed), that we are "born of the spirit" and that it continues to regulate our respiration (see the work of Brugelmann on asthma), our digestion (see Dubois, de Berne, *The Nervous Disorders* and his other works), the coordination of our movements (see *Loneliness and Psychotherapy* by Drs. Camus and Pagniez, preface by Professor Déjerine). "When in dissecting a dead body you can show me its soul, I will believe in it," physicians easily said twenty years ago. Now, not in cadavers (which in Ezekiel's wise speculation are only truly cadavers because they no longer have soul, Ezekiel, XXXVII, 1–12), but in the living body, in every step, in every malfunction, they sense the presence, the action of the soul, and in order to cure the body, it is to the soul that they direct themselves. Not long ago medical doctors said (and literary men behind the times still repeat it) that a pessimist is a man who has a bad stomach. Today Dr. Dubois in unmistakable print states that a man who has a bad stomach is a pessimist. And it is no longer his stomach that must be cured if we wish to change his philosophy, it is his philosophy that must be changed if we wish to cure his stomach. It is understood that we are leaving aside here metaphysical questions of origin and essence. Absolute materialism and pure idealism are equally obliged to distinguish the soul from the body. For idealism the body is an inferior spirit, still made of spirit, but obscured. For materialism the soul is still composed of matter, but more complex, subtler. The distinction exists in any case for the convenience of language, even if the one and the other philosophy are obliged, in order to explain the reciprocal action of the soul and the body, to identify their nature. [p. 106*n*2]

". . . your sectarians of every species, small and great, Catholic or Protestant, of high church or low, in so far as they think themselves exclusively in the right and others wrong; and, pre-eminently, in every sect, those who hold that men can be saved by thinking rightly instead of doing rightly, by word instead of act. . . ."

But acts are nevertheless not enough [. . .]. The text of *Sesame* and that of *The Bible of Amiens* do not, moreover, appear to me incompatible. What should be good, is the human being itself. Now a desire for goodness, followed by a bad act, cannot be sufficient to establish the goodness of the human being, for then the bad act is caused by something bad that is in us. So much for *Sesame*. And for *The Bible of Amiens*: But the good act should not be different from our deep self, it should not be good in a purely formal manner. It should express the goodness of our being. [p. 107*n*3]

"And also, outside of your own business, there are one or two subjects on which you are bound to have but one opinion.

> That roguery and lying are objectionable, and are instantly to
> be flogged out of the way whenever discovered. . . ." [1:25]

Such passages appear to small minds the work of a small mind;
great minds on the contrary recognize that this is, morally, the
conclusion to which all great minds come. They might regret (for
the others) only that Ruskin explains himself as little as he does and
gives this rather bourgeois and rather brief form to truths that could
have been presented less prosaically. Cf. (for this manner of laying
bare a truth by willfully abbreviating it, by giving it an offensive appearance of the old-fashioned commonplace) *The Bible of Amiens*, IV,
59: "All human creatures who have had warm affections, common
sense and self-command have been, and are, Naturally Moral . . . a
good and wise man differs from a bad and idiotic one, simply as a
good dog differs from a cur." Ruskin, when he writes, never bears in
mind Mme. Bovary, who can read him. Or rather he loves to offend
her and to appear mediocre to her. [p. 111*n*1]

> ". . . and if you heard that all the fine pictures in Europe
> were made into sand-bags to-morrow on the Austrian forts, it
> would not trouble you so much as the chance of a brace or two
> of game less in your own bags, in a day's shooting." [1:34]

The first four editions printed: "All the Titians"; after 1871 these
words are replaced by "all the fine pictures." The Library Edition,
which points out this variant, concludes from it rather delicately and
a bit speciously that Ruskin's admiration for Titian had somewhat
diminished. In fact, we have more precise evidence than that which
the Library Edition gives of the revolution which took place in
Ruskin's taste and which overturned the hierarchy of his admira-
tions. Unfortunately we do not have the space here to give any
indication of this aesthetic crisis which unloosed the religious crisis
in Ruskin and allayed his gravest doubts by showing him that the
painters who had faith like Giotto were superior to the unbelieving
painters like Titian. [p. 132*n*1]

"When men are rightly occupied, their amusement grows out of their work as the colour-petals out of a fruitful flower. . . ."

And from the lowest steps of the ladder of work. From the humblest work a pleasure is born, humble no doubt like the stem, which supported it, without variegated colors and which nevertheless manages to charm the life that it embellishes. This pleasure is satisfaction in oneself, pleasure at being with others, optimism { . . . }. [p. 146*n*1]

"Mighty of heart, mighty of mind—"magnanimous"—to be this, is indeed to be great in life; to become this increasingly, is, indeed, to "advance in life"—in life itself—not in the trappings of it."

Unquestionably, and yet if we consider the life of so many great writers, so many artists, we recognize that very few have entirely disregarded the other "advancement in life, in the trappings of it." How few, to take only this example, have scorned election to the Académie française or some other form of power, of prestige. Such and such a poet, plunged in life itself so long as he is writing, immediately the heat of inspiration has fallen, has already returned to the "advancement in life," in the "trappings of life," and with his hand still trembling from having wanted to follow in its flight the swiftness of his thought, he inscribes on the first page of the poem which soars so high above all contingencies and above his own life, the name of the benevolent Queen to whom he dedicates it, in order to make known the social rank he occupies, how far he has "advanced in life." He is anxious that humble mortals should know him and other queens also, that men respect him and that queens seek him out, and that all of them thus complete his "advancement in life." Perhaps this poet will tell you that if he dines with this Queen and then dedicates his book to her, it is because being conscious of the eminent dignity of "the man of letters" he wants to give him the place in society that he should have, equal to that of Kings. For a short while, to believe him, he devotes himself, he sacrifices his tastes, his talent, to his duties as citizen of the Republic of letters. However, if you say to him that such a one of his colleagues would be glad to burden himself with this role and that from now on he will be able in inelegance and obscurity to work without troubling himself over Queens, perhaps he would realize then that in reality it was rather to his own grandeur than to that of the man of letters that he devoted himself and that the conquests of his colleague would in no way take the place for him of his own. Besides, the man of letters loaded with honors, is he greater than another, even in the frivolous eyes of posterity? It is very doubtful, and a man of letters scornful of all influence, of all honors, of all worldly position, like Flaubert, does he not appear to us greater than the academician, his friend, Maxime du Camp? Certainly the desire "to advance in life," the snobism, is the greatest sterilizer of inspiration, the greatest deadener of originality, the greatest destroyer of talent. I have pointed out elsewhere that because of this it is the gravest vice for a man of letters, the one that his instinctive morality, that is to say, the instinct of conservation of his talent, depicts to him as the most sinful, for which he has the most remorse, much more than debauchery, for example, which is far less fatal to him, the order and the scale of vices being to a certain extent reversed for the man of letters. And yet the genius makes sport even of this artistic morality. How many snobs of genius have continued like Balzac to write masterpieces. How many impotent ascetics have not been able to draw from an admirable and solitary life ten original pages. [p. 150n1]

"But what teachers do you give your girls, and what reverence do you show to the teachers you have chosen? Is a girl likely to think her own conduct, or her own intellect, of much importance, when you trust the entire formation of her character, moral and intellectual, to a person whom you let your servants treat with less respect than they do your housekeeper (as if the soul of your child were a less charge than jams and groceries), and whom you yourself think you confer an honor upon by letting her sometimes sit in the drawing-room in the evening?"

"We agreed with the marquise that, whenever I was not wanted in the salon, she would say to me: 'I think the clock is slow.' " (Letter of Mlle. de Saint-Geneix, in the marquis de Villemer, quoted from memory.) But the marquise de Villemer was intelligent and good. On the other hand I know people who think themselves very elegant and of refined culture, who asked their daughter's French professor, a quite remarkable person, to leave by the backstairs in the afternoon "in order not to meet visitors." [p. 204*n*1]

"It is now long since the women of England arrogated, universally, a title which once belonged to nobility only; and, having once been in the habit of accepting the simple title of gentlewoman as correspondent to that of gentleman, insisted on the privilege of assuming the title of 'Lady,' which properly corresponds only to the title of 'Lord.'

I do not blame them for this; but only for their narrow motive in this. I would have them desire and claim the title of Lady, provided they claim, not merely the title, but the office and duty signified by it." [2:88]

In the course of *Sesame and Lilies* (and we could not make note of it each time) we often see Ruskin thus seeming to grant something to the wrong, to give way to human weaknesses. Far from scorning the feelings, he finds rather that we do not have enough of them (§ 27), that the forms of joy are more important still than those of duty (§ 36). On the preceding page he extolled the thirst for power. And now he is going to say that never will a woman wish enough to be a great lady and never will she have enough retainers. But as soon as he explains himself, the privilege is withdrawn: it was only necessary for us to agree on the sense of the words. From the moment that "the passions" mean the love of truth, and "worldly ambition" charity, the severest physician of our soul can allow us their usage. In reality, what is forbidden by one morality is forbidden by all the others, because what is forbidden is what is harmful and because it does not depend on the physician of the soul to change its constitution. Only appearances are made new and the rules, at most, "aromatized" with the perfume of forbidden things. An ethics of pleasure is at bottom an ethics of duty. The name alone is allowed us. (I am not speaking here with regard to Ruskin, of course, and do not mean to ignore the vast diversity of moral philosophies, in spite of the identity of rules they prescribe for us, and which they each keep differently and owe to their origin, utilitarian, mystical, etc.) But we can ask if the best way of accustoming a sick man to take some milk is to mix in it a little cognac, and not rather to teach him right away to like the taste of the milk. This concept of social duty "flattering to our self-esteem" in reality misses its mark. When a woman desires to be a lady, she does not concern herself with the etymology of the word, but with the worldly privileges that are attached to it. And if she was a lady in the sense that Ruskin says, that is to say, if she wished only to be a good woman, she would not wish (or, in her, it would not be the same person who would wish it) to be called "lady." (I am not speaking of those who, always, have been ladies. With those, the will to be called "lady" corresponds to something absolutely natural and legitimate, and as foreign to snobbery as the will of a general to be called "my general.") To give her this little enticement of the title of lady to help her to do good, is to cultivate her self-esteem in order to increase her benevolence, that is to say, something contradictory, as we have already seen Ruskin authorize us to be ambitious provided we are first philosophers. A philosophy or a charity to which snobbery is the introduction or the conclusion, is a philosophy and a charity which are not conceived very clearly. Doubtless I am straining, and rather roughly, Ruskin's thought here. And doubtless the word *lady* does not have here its strict meaning. But finally in spite of all it keeps something of that meaning (it is a little like one of those "masked" words* against which Ruskins puts us on guard and does not put himself enough on guard) introducing into the reader's thinking those gracious confusions in which also certain French writers take pleasure when they mix—in speaking as of things analogous—the "nobility" of talent, "the nobility" of "birth" and of character. Nobility of birth, that means to be a duke, etc. And to be sure, in the order of the grandeurs of the flesh and as a social factor, and for all the sentiments that it sets in motion . . . in others, it is important. But it is a pure pun to compare this to "nobility" in the spiritual sense; it is very useful to recognize the sense of the words, not to mix everything, and, from so many confused ideas, not to derive a pretended aristocracy of the intelligence which borrows from the aristocracy of birth its system of descent by blood, not by spirit, in order to apply it to the nobility of the spirit, and finally makes a "noble" (in all the senses of the word which in reality then no longer has any) of the nephew of Michelet.** (Needless to say I don't know if a nephew of Michelet exists and I chose this great name at random.) [p. 212*n*2]

---

*Ed. note: See section 16 of "Of Kings' Treasuries": "Yes, and words, if they are not watched, will do deadly work sometimes. There are masked words droning and skulking about us in Europe just now . . . there are masked words abroad, I say, which nobody understands, but which everybody uses. . . ."

**Ed. note: The French historian, 1798–1874.

Bibliographical Note

by Richard Macksey

As the continuing labors of the textual scholars working in the Proust archives remind us, his life's work was literally as well as allegorically a vast palimpsest; revisions, hesitations, and transpositions mark every stage of Proust's creative development. Like all of his writings, the studies that Proust dedicated to Ruskin during the first years of this century constitute a complicated fabric of redactions, partial publications, and internal quotations. Even the titles of these critical pieces are unstable, undergoing transformations as they pass from journal to preface to *mélanges,* and all too often misleading even initiated Proustians. The following biblio-archaeology, which details the publication history and major revisions, may be of some utility to any readers interested in following the evolution of Proust's apprenticeship to Ruskin. (A selected bibliography of secondary studies is appended.)

The following abbreviations have been used in the description of Proust's Ruskinian texts and their evolution:

BA   *La Bible d'Amiens,* traduction, notes et préface par Marcel Proust. Paris: Mercure de France, 1904. 347 pp.

CSB   *Contre Sainte-Beuve, précédé de "Pastiches et mélanges" et suivi de "Essais et articles,"* ed. Pierre Clarac avec Yves Sandre. Paris: Bibliothèque de la Pléiade, 1971. 1022 pp. [Invaluable biblio-graphic and diplomatic information.]

PM   *Pastiches et mélanges*. Paris: Gallimard, 1919. 272 pp.
SL   *Sésame et les lys*, "Des Trésors des rois," "Des Jardins des reines,"
      traduction, notes et préface de Marcel Proust. Paris: Mercure de
      France, 1906. 224 pp.

PROUST'S RUSKINIANA

Translations (with Introductions and Commentary)

The Bible of Amiens

a.   Prepublication of the Preface and parts of the translation:

"Ruskin à Notre-Dame d'Amiens":
Mercure de France, April 1900, pp. 50–88.
BA, translator's Preface, pp. 15–47: "Notre-Dame d'Amiens selon
Ruskin"; many stylistic corrections of the *Mercure* version; Proust adds
some notes to the text, but also suppresses at least as many marginal
passages from Ruskin.
PM, pp. 100–47: "En mémoire des églises assassinées: II. Journées de
pèlerinage: Ruskin à Notre-Dame d'Amiens, à Rouen, etc."; Proust
reprints here the text of *BA* but with longer citations from Ruskin (pp.
108–10) and has also added copious notes.
CSB, pp. 69–105.

"John Ruskin—I" ("Sur Ruskin"):
Gazette des beaux-arts, April 1900, pp. 310–18.
BA, translator's Preface, pp. 48–61, continuing *BA* above; the text of
the *Gazette des beaux-arts* article concludes with the paragraph ending
" . . . une autre vie" (p. 61); light stylistic corrections and some
supplementary notes.
PM, pp. 148–61: "John Ruskin"; Proust reprints the text of the
Gazette article with a few corrections; he suppresses, however, some of
the marginal Ruskin citations (p. 158, *BA*, p. 58).
CSB, pp. 105–15.

"John Ruskin—II" ("Sur Ruskin"):
Gazette des beaux-arts, August 1900, pp. 135–46.
BA, translator's Preface, pp. 61–77, continuing *BA* above; light
stylistic corrections and some supplementary notes.
PM, pp. 161–80, continuing "John Ruskin" above; again Proust
suppresses certain passages cited from Ruskin (p. 161, *BA*, p. 62; p.
179, *BA* p. 76; pp. 179–80, *BA* p. 77), but adds an important four-
page note (pp. 164–67).
CSB, pp. 115–29.

Excerpts from the Proust translation:
La Renaissance latine, 15 February 1903, pp. 314–45: "La Bible d'Amiens. I. Arrivée à Amiens: Saint-Martin [excerpt from the first chapter: "By the River of Waters"]; II. Sainte-Geneviève [excerpt from the second chapter: "Under the Drachenfels"]; III. Saint-Jérôme [excerpt from the third chapter: "The Lion Tamer"]."

BA, pp. 105–08, 109–10, 126–37; pp. 148–50, 151–52, 189–91; pp. 210–24, 225–28, 229–48; Proust adds substantial notes.

Excerpts from the Proust translation:
La Renaissance latine, 15 March 1903, pp. 620–43: "La Bible d'Amiens. IV. La Cathédrale [excerpt from the fourth chapter: "Interpretations"]."

BA, pp. 249–68, 280–89, 290–91, 295, 297–98, 317, 319–20, 322–24, 329–40; Proust adds substantial notes.

b. *La Bible d'Amiens* (publication in book form):
John Ruskin, *La Bible d'Amiens,* traduction, notes et préface par Marcel Proust. Paris: Mercure de France, 1904. 347 pp. In the Preface Proust reprints the texts analyzed above, completing it with an "Avant-propos," pp. 9–14, and a "Post-Scriptum," pp. 78–95.

PM, pp. 180–97, for "Post-Scriptum."

CSB, pp. 129–41 ("Sous quelles formes . . ."), for "Post-Scriptum."

Sesame and Lilies

a. Prepublication of parts of the translation and the Preface:

Excerpts from the Proust translation:
Les Arts de la vie, 15 March 1905, pp. 171–86: "Les Trésors des rois. I."

SL, pp. 61–91, 115–22; paragraphs numbered 17–26 inclusively (pp. 91–115 here) had been replaced in the *Arts de la vie* prepublication by a summary; Proust makes a few minor corrections but adds numerous and important notes.

Excerpts from the Proust translation:
Les Arts de la vie, 15 April 1905, pp. 248–56: "Les Trésors des rois. II."

SL, pp. 122–41; a few minor corrections but numerous and important notes added.

Excerpts from the Proust translation:
Les Arts de la vie, 15 May 1905, pp. 312–410: "Les Trésors des rois. III."

SL, pp. 148–61, 163–65; a few minor corrections but numerous and important notes added.

"Sur la Lecture," translator's Preface ("Journées de lecture"):
La Renaissance latine, 15 June 1905, pp. 379–410.
SL, pp. 7–58: "Préface du traducteur sur la lecture"; many stylistic corrections and additional notes.
PM, pp. 225–72: "Journées de lecture" (not to be confused with the 1907 review of the same title published in *Le Figaro* and reprinted in *Chroniques*); reprint with minor alterations to the text and notes of the Preface to *SL;* one important difference: the last two paragraphs of the Preface are summarized here in a single paragraph.

b. *Sésame et les lys* (publication in book form):
John Ruskin, *Sésame et les lys,* "Des Trésors des rois," "Des Jardins des reines," traduction, notes et préface par Marcel Proust. Paris: Mercure de France, 1906. 224 pp.

Obituary Notices

"Nécrologie: John Ruskin"
La Chronique des arts et de la curiosité, no. 4, 27 January 1900, pp. 25–36, signed "M. P."
CSB, pp. 439–41.

"Pèlerinages ruskiniens en France"
Le Figaro, 13 February 1900, p. 5.
Chroniques, pp. 145–49.
CSB, pp. 441–44.

Reviews

John Ruskin, sein Leben und sein Wirken, von Marie von Bunsen. Leipzig: Hermann Seeman, 1903. 123 pp.
La Chronique des Arts et de la Curiosité, no. 10, 7 March 1903, pp. 78–79.
CSB, pp. 455–56.

Charlotte Broicher: *John Ruskin und sein Werk: Puritaner, Künstler, Kritiker.* I. Reihe: *Essays.* Leipzig: Diedrichs, 1902. 298 pp.
John Ruskin: *Moderne Maler* (vol. I et II). Im Auszug übersetzt und zusammengefasst von Charlotte Broicher. Leipzig: Diedrichs, 1902. 312 pp.
La Chronique des arts et de la curiosité, no. 1, 2 January 1904, pp. 6–7, signed "M. P."
CSB, pp. 478–81.

"Un Professeur de beauté" (essay-review on Robert de Montesquiou and Ruskin)

Les Arts de la vie, 15 August 1905, pp. 69–79; the immediate occasion of the piece was a review of Montesquiou's *Professionelles beautés*.
Montesquiou reprinted the text but not the notes in the appendix to his *Altesses sérénissimes* (Paris: Juven, 1907), pp. 387–99.
CSB, pp. 506–20, containing some important corrections by the editor.

John Ruskin: *Les Pierres de Venise*, traduction par Mme. Mathilde P. Crémieux, préface de M. Robert de la Sizeranne. Paris: Laurens, n.d. 322 pp.
  La Chronique des arts et de la curiosité, 5 May 1906, pp. 146–47. (Also published in *Revue générale de critique et de bibliographie*, IV, 37 [25 July 1906], pp. 282–85.)
  CSB, pp. 520–23.

John Ruskin: *Pages choisies*. Paris: Hachette, 1908.
John Ruskin: *Le Repos de Saint-Marc* . . . Paris: Hachette, 1908.
  La Chronique des arts et de la curiosité, 26 December 1908, p. 416. Unsigned [Proust?]; reprinted in *Textes retrouvés*, ed. Ph. Kolb, 1971.

Pastiche of Ruskin

"*La Bénédiction du Sanglier*. Etudes des Fresques de Giotto représentant l'affaire Lemoine à l'Usage des jeunes Etudiants et Etudiantes du Corpus Christi qui se soucient encore d'Elles, by John Ruskin" [*inédit* written in late summer 1908]:
  NNRF, 1 October 1953, pp. 762–67; introduction by Bernard de Fallois.
  CSB, pp. 201–05.

STUDIES OF PROUST AND RUSKIN

Autret, Jean. *L'Influence de Ruskin sur la vie, les idées et l'oeuvre de Marcel Proust*. Genève: Droz, 1955.
Bisson, L. A.. "Proust and Ruskin: Reconsidered in the Light of *Lettres à une amie*," *Modern Language Review*, 39 (January 1944): 28–37.
Chabannes, Jacques. "Du côté de chez Ruskin," *Bulletin Marcel Proust*, 1 (October 1930): 25–35.
Chantal, René de. *Marcel Proust: Critique littéraire*. 2 vols. Montréal: Presses de l'Université de Montréal, 1967, pp. 263–68, 537–48.
Cocking, John. "Proust and Painting," in *French 19th Century Painting and Literature*, ed. Ulrich Finke. Manchester: Manchester University Press, 1972.

Fontainas, A.. "Ruskin, Proust et la lecture," *Le Figaro* (2 September 1933): 3.

Gaubert, Serge. "Marcel Proust: Le Viel Homme et la peinture," in *Mélanges offerts à Georges Couton,* ed. Jean Jehasse et al. Lyon: Presse Universitaire de Lyon, 1981.

Guillierm, Jean-Pierre. "La Ruskinisme en France ou la célébration du fou," *Revue des sciences humaines* 1 [189] (1983): 89–110.

Guyot, Charly. "Ruskin et Proust," *Lettres,* V (1944), 55–70.

———. "Sur Ruskin et Proust," *Revue de littérature comparée,* 21 (January–March 1947): 54–68.

Hahn, Reynaldo. "Proust et Ruskin," *Le Figaro* (21 April 1945): 1.

Harlow, Barbara. "Sur la lecture," *MLN,* 90 (1975): 849–71.

Johnson, J. Theodore J., Jr.. "Proust and Giotto: Foundations for an Allegorical Interpretation of *A la recherche du temps perdu,*" in *Marcel Proust: A Critical Panorama,* ed. Larkin B. Price. Urbana: University of Illinois Press, 1973.

Kasell, Walter. *Marcel Proust and the Strategy of Reading.* Amsterdam: John Benjamins B. V., 1980, ch. 1.

Kolb, Philip. "Proust et Ruskin: nouvelles perspectives," *Cahiers de l'Association internationale des études françaises,* 12 (June 1960): 259–73.

Lemaître, Henri. *Proust et Ruskin.* Toulouse: Privat-Didier, 1944.

———. "De *Jean Santeuil* à *La Recherche du temps perdu:* la médiation ruskinienne," *Bulletin Marcel Proust,* 3 (1953): 58–71.

Macksey, Richard. "Proust on the Margins of Ruskin," in *The Ruskin Polygon,* ed. J. D. Hunt and F. M. Holland. Manchester: Manchester University Press, 1981.

———. "'Conclusions' et 'Incitations': Proust à la recherche de Ruskin," *MLN* 96 (1981): 1113–19.

Maurois, André. "Proust et Ruskin," in *Essays and Studies by Members of the English Association.* Oxford: Clarendon Press, 1932.

Mein, Margaret. *A Foretaste of Proust: A Study of His Precursors.* New York: Atheneum, 1974.

Maledon, Will L., "Ruskin, Morris et la première esthétique de Marcel Proust," *Le Bayou,* 70 (1957): 402–14.

Monnin-Hornung, Juliette. *Proust et la peinture.* Genève: Droz, 1951, pp. 26–34, 64–72.

Murray, Jessie. "Marcel Proust et John Ruskin," *Mercure de France,* 189 (1 July 1926): 100–12.

———. "Marcel Proust as a Critic and Disciple of Ruskin," *Nineteenth Century,* 101 (1927): 614–20.

———. "The Influence of Ruskin on Marcel Proust," *Proceedings of the Leeds Philosophical and Literary Society,* II, 8 (May 1932): 465–515.

Nordlinger-Riefstahl, Marie. "Proust et le génie de Ruskin," *Les Arts* (October 1955): 7.

———. "Proust as I Knew Him," *London Magazine* (August 1954): 51–61.

———. *Marcel Proust: Lettres à une amie.* Manchester: Ed. du Calame, 1942.

Painter, George, *Marcel Proust: The Early Years.* Boston: Little, Brown, 1959, ch. 14.

Roche, A. J.. "Proust as a Translator of Ruskin," *PMLA,* 45 (December 1930): 1214–17.

Souza, Sybil de. *L'Influence de Ruskin sur Proust.* Monpellier: Manufacture de la Charité, 1932.

Strauss, Walter. *Proust and Literature: The Novelist as Critic.* Cambridge: Harvard University Press, 1957, pp. 177–86.

Wihl, Gary. *Ruskin and the Rhetoric of Infallibility.* New Haven and London: Yale University Press, 1985, ch. 4.